Middle-Aged Spread

Middle-Aged Spread

Moving to the Country at 50

Sonia Day

KEY PORTER BOOKS

Library and Archives Canada Cataloguing in Publication

Day, Sonia
    Middle-aged spread : moving to the country at 50 / Sonia Day.

ISBN 978-1-55470-193-3

    1. Day, Sonia. 2. Country life—Ontario—Humor. 3. Urban-rural migration—Ontario—Humor. 4. Women authors—Ontario—Biography. 5. Middle-aged women—Ontario—Biography. I. Title.

S522.C3D39 2009   C818'.603   C2009-901317-7

THE CANADA COUNCIL | LE CONSEIL DES ARTS
FOR THE ARTS | DU CANADA
SINCE 1957 | DEPUIS 1957

ONTARIO ARTS COUNCIL
CONSEIL DES ARTS DE L'ONTARIO

The publisher gratefully acknowledges the support of the Canada Council for the Arts and the Ontario Arts Council for its publishing program. We acknowledge the support of the Government of Ontario through the Ontario Media Development Corporation's Ontario Book Initiative.

We acknowledge the financial support of the Government of Canada through the Book Publishing Industry Development Program (BPIDP) for our publishing activities.

Key Porter Books Limited
Six Adelaide Street East, Tenth Floor
Toronto, Ontario
Canada M5C 1H6

www.keyporter.com

Illustrations: Artzooks / Havana Street
Text design and electronic formatting: Alison Carr

Printed and bound in Canada

09 10 11 12 13 5 4 3 2 1

For Barrie

Contents

Great Expectations

"A man needs a little madness, or else he never dares cut the rope and be free."
—*Zorba the Greek*
Nikos Kazantzakis

One

"Drive faster."

"I can't! This road is full of potholes."

"It's the wrong road."

"No, it isn't."

"Yes, it is. Gordie said to watch out for a red barn."

"We passed it back there."

"We didn't. We didn't."

It all began with bickering on a bumpy road.

There we were, bouncing through rolling farm country northwest of the city on a Sunday morning. It was the middle of July and unbearably hot. A yellowish haze covered the sky, blotting out every trace of blue. The air felt heavy as a wet dishrag inside the car, making breathing difficult. Although all four windows were wound down as far they would go, I couldn't even detect a whimper of wind coming in.

He drove. My job was to navigate. Yet squinting at the passing farmhouses and fields, map in hand, I had no idea where we were. Nor, apparently, did he. And the heat was only half of it. Anxiety gripped us too because we were running late for an appointment. A very important appointment with a gent called Mr. Gordie McTavish.

So we bickered, in the predictable, pointless way that long-time couples always bicker, snapping like terriers at one another with every bend in the road. Yet this spat, unlike so many others, didn't degenerate into an all-out shouting match because he suddenly defused it by saying in a surprisingly gentle voice: "Relax. We'll get there. Please stop worrying." And then he stroked my bare arm and smiled. And I squirmed on the sticky plastic car seat, smiled back and felt deliriously happy.

Even then we knew. We both sensed it. What we were about to do that humid morning was going to change our lives.

It's a familiar scenario, this galloping off to the countryside on weekends. You can see the same drama played out in countless of thousands of automobiles, east to west, north to south, in countless countries all over the world. From Canada to the United Kingdom, Australia to Argentina, the urge is universal. Especially in summertime. It never stops. We were simply following a long-established pattern. What had impelled us to leap into the car and head out of the city—at an hour when saner souls are pouring their second cup of coffee on the deck and flipping through the arts section of the newspaper—is what impels urbanites everywhere to follow a similar path. Quite simply, real estate. The magic lure of real estate. Ah, the fantasy of a country place, a weekend retreat far from the madding crowds, the dangers, the dirt, the cramped and irritating realities of city living. Get to the fifty mark and those two little words, real estate (and especially country real estate) take on an irresistible ring. They become the most seductive words on the planet. In fact, often as not when you've achieved a certain maturity, at least in years, the prospect of a fling with real estate is like sex. Only better. You get all the same ingredients—the same lustful glances, the same thrill of discovery, the same need to compete with others who have more to offer than you do, the same agonies of rejection, the same orgasmic bliss of fulfillment if you get lucky in the end—yet there's no need to take your clothes off.

And we were no different from anybody else. We, or rather I, wanted it badly. Very badly. And like the best kind of sex, it was spontaneous, spur-of-the-moment, with an enticing undercurrent of danger. It came right out of the blue too, because we hadn't, like many people we knew, spent months or even years dragging ourselves out of the city every weekend, peering at fixer-uppers with leaky roofs and dodgy wiring, then trekking home again discouraged and exhausted to gobble chips in front of the TV. A country place had in fact been the last thing on our minds. The object of my lust simply presented itself one day—by accident.

Some curtains were the trigger for this explosive turn of events. Orange and brown polyester curtains, in a zigzag pattern. Relics of the '60s, ugly and faded. They hung inside a pop-up camper he kept on an airstrip in farm country northwest of the city, because he was a weekend glider pilot. Fanatical about it, too, although I wasn't. Not at all. Gliding is a pastime that tends to be heavily tilted towards the male half of humanity. There are female gliders, to be sure, but you won't find too many of them floating around up there in the heavens. The only time I'd tagged along on a Friday night, sitting around a bonfire until the small hours with a bunch of guys in baseball caps jawing on about thermal lift and convection layers, I felt like a spare wheel on one of their bat-winged flying machines. So, no more, by mutual agreement. On summer weekends, off he went on his motorbike to soar in the sky, while I stayed on *terra firma* at home in the city, reasonably content with my lot. It was certainly urban, i.e., postage-stamp size, but that meant a front and back yard where no weeding was required and where I could be a lazy kind of gardener, potting up containers of petunias one year, *Nicotiana* the next, then the rest of the time sit on the shady deck and paint watercolours all day. And when these gentle midlife pursuits lost their appeal, there was the ever-present possibility of a stroll to our neighbourhood hangout, Bread and Roses, for a cappuccino and chocolate cupcake of larger proportions than I should probably be ingesting at my age. Yet did I care? No. A solitary cappuccino and some kind of calorie-laden confection on summer Sundays (accompanied of course by the weekend papers) can be mighty satisfying to the no longer young. And middle age is surely a time to accept what is, flaws and all, and not deny ourselves the little pleasures that make life worth living.

Thus a weekend routine developed. Me city girl. You country boy. It suited us. Although one neighbour did slyly hint at funny goings-on in the marital department ("You mean he's gone and left you on your own AGAIN this weekend, my dear?") we liked this together-yet-separate-on-Saturdays-and-Sundays arrangement, because it gave us something to talk about when the weekend was over. He came home Sunday nights, related his flying adventures over dinner and a glass of wine on the deck. I related how I'd muddied up yet another water-colour. He encouraged me to try again. The actress Marilyn Lightstone once portrayed this phase of life as "the dreaded expecteds"—a flat, despairing time, devoid of conversation, when long-time couples stare blankly at each other over tables in restaurants because they have nothing whatsoever left to say. It certainly happens, I've seen it. Yet somehow—thanks to this un-orthodox weekend arrangement—we seemed to be avoiding that dismal turn of events.

Then, one Sunday night, he arrived home looking awful, with bags under his eyes.

"I'm so tired. Did a three-hour flight yesterday, but couldn't sleep after," he grumbled. "It's the drapes in the camper. They're really old now, you know. Completely shredded. The sun comes in SO early in the morning."

Poor lamb. And with the cunning that is a characteristic of the cohabiting male, he dumped a big bag of asparagus stalks from a farm near the airstrip on the kitchen counter. An unaccustomed spurt of spousal solicitousness ensued, just as he'd planned, because I adore asparagus—especially the fresh, local kind. New drapes were duly sewn and a couple of weeks later off I drove, out of the city to deliver them. Then, oh fickle finger of fate, the long dirt road leading up his flying club was sealed off with a barricade because a bridge had collapsed. And the infuriating thing about closed-off rural roads is that they never tell you where to go instead. The locals know, they all do, of course. And if you don't—well, tough. The blunt truth is, they're not awfully keen on interlopers from the city nosing around out there anyway. Blundering down dusty lanes straight as bowling alleys with unhelpful names like Sideroad 20 and County Line 4 and without any sense of where the car was heading, I cursed some complacent-looking Holstein cows that were taking refuge from the heat under a maple tree, chewing their cud, then finally, reluctantly, I stopped to consult a map. And with a sideways glance out of the window, there it was.

The house. It was partially hidden among burgeoning spruce trees and some old sugar maples. It had dark grey clapboard and white trim. It looked old and tired. A Victorian lady of modest means, now fallen on hard times but still standing rather proudly on the brow of her gentle hill. Mysterious, yet welcoming. Generations of fascinating stories had been secreted away within her dark walls, I sensed that immediately, but not in a creepy, Stephen King kind of way. Good things, happy things, had clearly happened within the huddle of leafy trees.

One of the windows on the ground floor was open. A Vivaldi concerto played briskly on violins flowed out. Pling, pling. The music sounded shrill and strange in this agricultural region of soybean fields and chicken farms, so far from the decadent canals of Venice. Yet the strings pulled. Pling, pling. *Venite, vedrete.* Come. Take a look. I got out of the car, walked across the road, admired a soaring purple smokebush and a stand of dusty lilacs growing out front, vaguely wondering what they'd looked like in bloom. Then I noticed the red and white "For Sale" sign, half-hidden in a tangle of goutweed—and it hit me. A strange, electric sensation, almost as if a finger were stuck in a light socket yet without any accompanying sense of pain. It was uncanny, unnerving, the strength of this feeling. And when it stopped, as suddenly as it had started, I knew. I was going to live in this house. Of that there could be no doubt. The certainty of such an event occurring was impossible to ignore. This would be—in the not too distant future—my new home.

How to explain it? I couldn't. It was too astonishing. Up at the flying club (which proved to be only a few concession roads away) I breathlessly poured out the story.

"You'll never guess," I said with a giggle, "…I've just seen this old house near here and I had a really funny feeling looking at it and…"

"Yeah?" A marital shrug.

"I somehow think that we're going to wind up buying this house…"

"Yeah?" Another shrug. "Can't this wait? I have to go do the logbooks…"

"Well, I know that, but, well, could I…could I just call the realtor?"

"Yeah, if you want." A sigh now, protracted and annoyed. "But you know, I'm really busy with the logbooks."

He ambled away down the long flying-club hangar in his beige cotton chinos with pockets on the legs—the kind of pants men love, but which always make them look as sexy as a sack of potatoes.

"Is it okay if I use the club's phone?" I called out, my voice echoing through the building.

"Sure. It's over there," he said without turning back. He disappeared into a tiny room at the end of the building and shut the door.

I dithered. I debated. I knew what would happen if I called. An irresistible force made me pick the phone up.

Enter Gordie McTavish. His was the name on the red and white "For Sale" sign. It took a few calls to track him down, back in those calmer quieter days before a cellphone occupied every pocket. Country people aren't slaves to commerce the way city people are, even if they work in the real estate business. Gordie may have earned his living hawking rural properties to eager urbanites just up for the weekend, but his office was closed on Saturdays. A helpful woman at an answering service told me to call his wife at home. Mrs. McTavish, bright and chirrupy as a chickadee, revealed that he was "out rehearsin' at the community centre" but didn't say what for. A male voice at the community centre said to try Buck's Car Wash.

And Gordie wasn't very forthcoming when finally reached at this establishment.

"There's an offer in on the place," he said into the phone.

Oh. So much for my sense of inevitability.

"Yes, sorry about that, dear."

"But ..." he spoke slowly, seeming to enjoy the suspense, "Let me check somethin' here. Um. hang on a minute ..." There was sound of a car door being opened and a riffling through some pages, as mechanical brushes whirred and clunked in the background.

"The offer is goin' to expire at eight tamorrer mornin' and...."

And? I stopped breathing.

"...it's goin' to be too low. I know they're goin' to refuse it."

He ruffled more papers.

"Um ... I could perhaps arrange for you guys to come up tamorrer at about ten to see the place," Gordie went on in a funny falsetto voice that sounded rather girlish. "Wouldja like that?"

"Sure."

"But I'll have to check with the folks who have the house, it being Sunday and all."

"Yes, could you?"

"Aw right, maybe I can. You ARE interested, eh?"

"Yes, definitely."

"Um," Gordie took a deep breath himself. "See, I was thinkin' of taking the wife up to a beach we go to on a lake after church tamorrer. I've just washed the car and she likes the drive and it's kinda hot right now and..."

I pictured Mrs. Gordie McTavish. She was plump and maternal in pink sweatpants and big white running shoes with Velcro fasteners. I willed her to leave one of those fasteners undone, so it tripped her up twisting an ankle. She'd thus be immobilized, unable to go to church or the beach.

"Yes, we are really interested," I said.

"Okay, dear," he said. "I'll see what I can do."

And he hung up.

Two

Ten o'clock, Gordie had said. I glanced my watch. Yikes, it was already after eleven. And dammit, the house was still nowhere in sight along this dusty dirt road that shimmered in a white ribbon towards the horizon. Wonky telephone poles strained towards the colour-drained sky. Interminable ditches of dusty orange day lilies lined the roads, backed by hazy rectangles of crops in green and brilliant yellow. Occasionally, farmhouses and barns popped up too, random pieces on this vast Monopoly-board landscape, yet they all looked bleached white or the characteristic reddish hue of local brick. No house clad in dark clapboard materialized. And no person to ask for directions either.

The minutes galloped by. Eleven twelve. Eleven sixteen. Eleven twenty-three. Eleven thirty-one. Taut as a kite string in a gale, I kept seeing the face of Gordie, who'd sounded so nice and friendly on the phone. The offer had indeed been too low and thus rejected, he'd said earlier that morning. So the house was available and why don't you folks come on up? Yet now, angry and perspiring, he'd be waiting outside, glancing at his watch every few minutes, fidgeting and shrugging about unreliable city slickers. And with a snort, he'd go home to Mrs. McTavish grumbling "Typical. They didn't show. Let's go." Then the house, my precious house, would slip through our fingers, simply because we were too tardy.

And the annoying part was, Logbook Man wanted it too now. Almost as badly as I did—he'd driven by the house on his motorbike, en route back to the city the previous night, and conceded that the place did indeed look "pretty nice." And over dinner, pondering the possibility in the slow, analytical way that men of his age like to ponder things, sipping his beer and looking down into the amber liquid, he'd concluded thoughtfully that yes, it would definitely be a practical proposition, the more he considered it, to have a proper house to sleep in at weekends, with real sheets, instead of that grubby old camper on the flying club airstrip and a damp, moth-eaten sleeping bag to curl up in when fall nights up there turned as crisp as a McIntosh apple. And a bigger garden than in the city, well yes, that might be good too, because I'd be able to potter about with my flowers and things and perhaps we could try growing our own fresh corn and tomatoes as well, and then he could come back after flying all day and we'd eat dinner together. Sit with a glass of wine and soak up the silence. Look at the stars. Veg out. Yes, a weekend place in the country. He rubbed his chin. Wasn't such a bad idea after all.

Except that this wasn't going to be a weekend place. No way. The conviction that we'd quit the city and move lock, stock, and barrel out to the boonies remained, as stubborn as a coffee stain on a white T-shirt. This was pre-ordained, karma, fate, whatever you want to call it. We were going to leave our old life behind and forge a new, very different one. Where, I knew. The extraordinary sensation I'd experienced the day before decreed that inevitability. It was just a matter of when.

But long-term cohabitation counsels caution in matters that involve drastic change—Logbook Man was the kind of guy who didn't even like the sofa being shifted to a different area of the living room—so I bit my lip. Hard.

And as he talked, in increasingly enthusiastic tones, drawing diagrams of vegetable beds and compost heaps on the place mat with a finger, I just sipped my own beer and listened. And I kept picturing that window, where the Vivaldi had played.

Tim and Caron were thirty-something acquaintances of ours in the city—the kind of individuals you mentally file under the category of "Useful People to Know" but who are, underneath the veneer of politeness that cheek-by-jowl urbanites are forced to affect, as likeable as stale beer. They were just too slim, too hip, too immaculate in their black leather jackets and crisply ironed designer jeans, too smug, too arrogant, too bloody everything. And what had made them that way was real estate. They often held court at the local Starbucks, bragging to anyone who cared to listen that they hadn't needed jobs for years because they now bought properties instead—in the city, in the country, in Florida, in Mexico, on the west coast, anywhere they could get a "whammy of a deal" as Tim called it—and then resold them for vast profits. Tim and Caron had been our neighbours once, back when they both toiled for some nondescript technology company. We'd shared a couple of fairly agreeable barbecues on our mutual back deck. But then they'd gone upscale after selling that first house for a tidy pile, because they redid the kitchen cabinets. And now, thanks to succeeding houses, Tim and Caron occupied a three-storey monster in a ritzy area north of our modest part of the city, where they had four decks, a hotel kitchen with stainless steel fridges and granite counter tops (although neither of them could even boil an egg) and parking for four cars. And this latest acquisition, theirs for less than five months, was about to go on the market again.

As loathsome as Tim and Caron were, the embodiment of capitalism gone berserk, their cucumber coolness over the whole rigmarole of real estate was awe-inspiring. They never seemed to bite their fingernails over these transactions and apparently undertook every one of them as casually as other people drop by the local convenience store for chips and pop. So why not pick their acquisitive little brains for a few tips now that we, surprisingly, were about to embark on such a venture ourselves? After Logbook Man subsided with another beer into the living room to watch some PBS yawner on the history of aviation, I punched their number into the phone.

"You really want this place?" Tim sounded amused in a condescending way. He was chewing something. They had, he explained breathlessly, just picked up some take-out sushi from a new Japanese place in the neigh-bourhood.

"You gotta try their sashimi," he said, smacking his lips noisily into the receiver. "Awesome."

"Yes, okay," I said, "but about this house…"

He swallowed. "Make them an unconditional offer."

"You mean…" I swallowed nervously myself "…we can't make our offer dependent on getting financing or having the place inspected?"

"Nope."

"But isn't that awfully risky?"

"Yep."

Tim laughed and choked.

"Whoops, too much wasabi. I seem to be…," he spluttered, "…spitting tuna all over Caron." He made a kissing noise. "Sorry, Car. Listen, kiddo," he continued. "Life's a risk. And when you want something, you gotta go for it. Right?"

"Well, yes, but…."

"See, it's harder, much harder to move country places than city houses and mostly…" more chewing "…mostly with properties out in the sticks, you get offers which involve waiting around for months or even years for your buyer to sell the place he's currently living in."

"Oh. So if the offer has no strings attached, we'll get it?"

"Yep." He swallowed loudly and belched. "If the price is right."

Caron clicked herself into the conversation now.

"Tim's right, you know. Really he is," she said. "Go for it. But Timmy…"

Another kissing noise.

"...Timmy, hon, you're forgetting two things. First, they should write in their offer to purchase that they want a guarantee that the water is potable..."

"Oh yeah," interjected Tim. "Yeah right. Forgot that. Wells are often in terrible shape in the country. Contaminated with E. coli from the farms..."

"...and," Caron continued, "you must insist that they pump the septic tank out."

Then they kept interrupting each other, telling a story about a septic tank that had backed up one night when Caron's mother was visiting them at a cottage they'd just picked up for a song on a lake.

"She was so annoying. Just showed up in her car for Thanksgiving..."

"Yeah, we thought she was going to Caron's sister's place and we'd been planning to go out..."

"...and she brought along some humungous Butterball turkey, even though she knows I've hated turkey since I was six years old..."

"I was kinda annoyed myself, to tell you the truth..."

"and a jellied salad. Bright green, with bits of celery and stuff floating in it. I mean, who eats that kind of thing nowadays..."

"But the septic tank sure got to her, didn't it, Car?"

"Mmm, that tank. Should have had it pumped out. We put her in the back bedroom which had its own toilet a step or two down from the rest of the cottage and..."

"...and she woke up and found a pile of crap floating around her bed..."

"And icky poo, what a lot of it there was..."

They laughed in unison.

"Oh," I said. "Awful." Septic tanks. I hadn't even given them a thought. But what urbanite does, when a country fantasy is gripping the old grey cells?

"Yeah, but the old dragon doesn't come visit us anymore, so every, er, septic system has a silver lining. Ha, ha," Tim added.

"Good luck then," Caron said briskly. "Sorry, but we gotta run. See, there's this fantastic place, an estate sale, only one owner, all original wood-work. Just come on the market a few streets away, so we're going out for a drive-by."

"Sure, thanks," I said.

"Just remember, kiddooo," Tim added in a conspiratorial tone, "make that offer unconditional and you'll get it. And check out that sushi bar, woncha? It's awesome. See ya."

"Fine. We will."

We skipped the sushi. Raw fish makes me gag. And Logbook Man, coming out of the living room, empty beer bottle in hand, shook his head at the prospect of an unconditional offer.

"That Tim," he snorted. "He's so full of it. What did you call them for?"

Yet we took Tim's advice anyway. We shouldn't have.

And in the meantime, we were still searching. The house waited out there somewhere on that memorable morning, yet monarch butterflies migrating to Mexico couldn't have been more elusive. The car kept going round and round in circles. The same bleached telephone poles. The same day lilies. The same fields. The same brick farmhouses. It was getting boring now. We back-tracked, we craned our necks looking out for the bloody red barn, but it had vanished into the haze like a drop of water flicked on to a hot omelette pan.

Nearly a quarter to twelve. Gordie would surely be at his lakeside beach by now, unpacking the folding aluminum chairs, helping the wife carry the cooler down to the sands. And they'd be settling down, looking at the lake, sipping cans of iced tea and talking about the grandkids, perhaps laying out the styrofoam plates for their ham and cheese sandwiches. And they'd have forgotten all about us, those rude folks from the city. In fact, my house had probably already been snapped up by some other eager urbanite on a Sunday outing. Moving there wasn't predestined after all. I wanted to weep.

And then, miracle of miracles, it happened again. A repeat performance. The scenery changed abruptly, becoming more wooded, the road curving beside a long lake. We climbed a hill, over a clattering wooden bridge, past THE big red barn, then a turn to the left, a stand of spruce trees shimmering blue green in the moisture-laden atmosphere. And we were there.

Yes. Yes! Orgasmic scream of happiness. Well, nearly a scream. I took some deep breaths instead. And what relief, the place looked exactly the same as yesterday, nestled in the trees off the road, calmly waiting for me like some obedient dog. No one had slapped a "Sold" sticker over the red and white sign. Nothing had happened at all, except that Vivaldi's violins no longer pling-plinged out of the window. And the lilac bushes

looked dusty and drooping now, slapped into submission by the stifling heat. Yet that faint, insistent tug was still there, pulling me out of the old Toyota, across the road. And I could swear the house was whispering: "What kept you? What kept you? I've been waiting for people like you to come along for SO long...."

Gordie was waiting too, in a big black Chrysler with the engine running. He slid out, on to short chunky legs. He was probably, as I'd surmised from our conversation, in his sixties, with a round red face framed by carrot-coloured hair that looked suspiciously like a wig. He wore, incongruously on such a hot day, a red tartan sports jacket, shiny polyester pants in a 1960s shade of plum, and black lace-up shoes. The shoes were coated in fine white dust from the road, as if they'd been dipped in a bin of flour.

"Howdy," he said, flashing a mouthful of capped teeth. He extended a hand. "You folks have difficulty finding the place?"

"Yes, yes," I said. "I'm sorry, Gordie. Sorry we're so terribly late."

"Not to worry, dear. I didn't mind waiting for ya." His expression changed into the aren't-I-clever look of an eight-year-old. "See, I bin playin' my tapes in the car."

He touched his lapel pocket proudly.

"I'm in a quartet, see. Barbershop. We're singin' at the Legion next month."

"Oh," I said. "Nice."

"Want some tickets?" He reached into the pocket. "Lots in here."

"Yes, we'd love some," I said, as Logbook Man rolled his eyes behind Gordie's carrot head. "That would be fun."

"Mmm." I examined the tickets with an exaggerated show of enthusiasm. "But could we um, you know, see the place first?"

"Oh yeah, sure." He turned slowly towards the house, as if only then struck by the realization of why we were there. The tickets went back in the lapel pocket with a protective pat. Then he drew out a key with a big paper label from another pocket.

"We got lotsa time anyways," he said, checking his watch and shooting a glance down the long straight road, which was empty. "The folks who live here told me they'd be out playin' tennis till 'round two. So have a good look 'round, folks. You take your time now."

We didn't. Surveys show that most people spend less than twenty minutes examining real estate that they're going to spend their entire net worth on. We fit the mould. Gordie led the way in. The entrance hall, which faced north, was gloomy, painted an odd battleship grey, but beyond it lay a long bright room with a high ceiling and big windows, where motes of dust danced in the pale sunlight. The room had birch floors and interesting art hanging on the walls. The part of the house that faced the road, next to this room and clearly much older, probably dating from Victorian times, was badly in need of repairs. Expensive repairs. Walls and windows exhibited the kind of cracks that snake across sidewalks after winter, and paint had completely worn off in places. A funny sour smell permeated everything—an amalgam of dog, damp carpets and a hundred years' worth of cabbage, boiled too long on the stove. Hmm. This was disappointing. Yet the newer part, where the kitchen was, seemed more encouraging, It revealed modern cupboards—nice IKEA ones made of birch to match the floors. Don't women always buy houses because of the cupboards? Score one, then. And the woodstove in the middle of the kitchen, a shiny grey enamel job with a fat black chimney, fuelled fantasies at once. Why, I could sit beside it on cold nights, darning socks like Father McKenzie in the old Beatles song—except that who darns socks nowadays?

A rusting oil furnace the size of a Sherman tank filled the low-ceilinged basement, where thick walls, made of rough stones chinked with dirt, resembled some turn-of-the-century ice house and felt just as chilly, in spite of the searing heat outside. Someone had painted the basement floor an icy blue. More wild colour choices were revealed up in the attic rooms. The first, reached by a narrow, steep staircase, had deep avocado walls. Another was a sickly shade of yellow. Yuck. But back downstairs again, the view compensated—the extraordinary vista that I'd figured would be there, out of the living room window. It framed tumbling fields, woods of poplar and cedar, and a big pond down the hill. And its beauty took my breath away. Wow. Score ten.

"You can swim in the pond, if you like that kinda stuff," Gordie said in his Truman Capote falsetto, nose wrinkled in a moue of distaste as if to indicate he wouldn't dream of doing such a thing himself. "It's real deep. Spring fed. No algae. The folks here like swimmin', so I'm told."

Wow, I liked swimming too. Chalk up another ten for the pond. Out the back door, on a large deck, sat a white plastic chaise lounge with a shocking pink towel draped over one arm—a David Hockney tableau that I ached to insert myself into, garbed in some turquoise robe like one of his California models. Beyond that lay a football field of a lawn, scrubby and pale green in the heat, and creamy powder puffs of Queen Anne's lace, thousands of them, leading down the hill to the pond.

We descended to the pond past clumps of rhubarb, their stiff candelabra spires gone to seed. Bellflowers in purple and white. Lemon-yellow day lilies. Coneflowers tipping out of flowerbeds. Untidy sprawls of oregano, thyme and wild catnip. These folks didn't just play tennis, it seemed. They gardened too. Mmm, wonderful. I bent over and crushed a fresh thyme leaf between my fingers, revelling in the resiny scent. Score ten more. And look at that big redcurrant bush. Ten again. And again.

Beside the pond clung an old wooden jetty. It sagged in the middle like a sponge cake that hasn't risen properly in the oven and at one end, under an ancient apple tree, there was a small, rickety bench of the kind found in school gyms. We all sank heavily down on it, grateful for the shade. The bench creaked. It seemed for a moment ready to collapse and send us all hurtling headfirst into the pond—and part of me wanted this to happen, because the heat and excitement were suffocating and the water was like some monster punchbowl filled with lime-ade. So cool, green, inviting. I wanted to descend into its depths and stay there. A sweet smell of grass and wild flowers, coupled with a faint swampy odour, hung in the air. Little dragonflies, darting dabs of iridescent blue, swooped and collided with one another above the pond, then rose quickly to the white-hot sky. Water boat-men swam in circles just beneath the surface, making dark oval circles of shadows against the sandy bottom. Bees buzzed. A bird chirped somewhere. *To-whee, to-whee.* There were no other sounds. I felt touched by God in this paradise of greenery and insects and a peace so rare in our increasingly crowded, noisy world. The gentleness of the scene sank immediately into my bones. It was how I imagined heaven, if such a place existed, might be.

Gordie sat awkwardly between us, a schoolboy waiting for a meeting with the headmaster, hands splayed out on polyester-clad knees. The plump hands looked soft and pinkish and far too smooth for someone who had spent his life in the country and he was sweating profusely, lobster face almost matching the red tartan jacket. Yet there was an endearing quality to him, a kind of innocence, because he seemed so unlike any realtor I'd met in the city, so unconcerned if we were interested in buying this place or not. It was tempting to turn and hug him and say thank you, thank you, funny little man. Thank you for bringing us here and making my heart soar in a way that it hasn't for years. And now my dear Gordie, why don't you relax a little? Why not take that ridiculous jacket off?

But my nerve failed me—and it doesn't do to get too chummy with realtors, so they say. So I let Gordie sweat and watched a frog instead. A remarkably striking frog, squatting on the shiny mud at the edge of the pond. It had a chest the colour of an emerald and brown spots on its legs. Gobstopper eyes bulged. *Ruhk, ruhk. Ruhk, ruhk*, it croaked. Hello, hello. Welcome to my home. You like, ma'am? Pretty nice here, huh? I responded in kind. *Ruhk, ruhk.* Yes, pretty marvellous place, Mr. Frog. See you again soon, I think. *Ruhk ruhk.*

Gordie smiled politely at this childish exchange and mopped his brow. Logbook Man just stared into the pond, dazed.

That's all I remember now. Memories become as fuzzy with age as the old striped Hudson's Bay blanket that now keeps me snug on winter nights, but what does linger is the lickety-split nature of our encounter with Gordie, and just how speedily we capitulated to our fate. Fifteen minutes, max, that's all we spent, examining this forty-eight-acre property in the middle of nowhere, this great unknown that was to transform our lives in so many ways, not all of them pleasant. We made no demands. We didn't look at the well, the wiring, the insulation, the plumbing, the roof, the eavestroughing or any of those practical things you are supposed to look at before you buy a house. We didn't even, although Gordie urged us to, walk out to the back of the pond, where, fronted by overgrown twirly stemmed dogwoods and wild clematis, the woods waited—those woods, that were to reveal such startling and dangerous secrets. It was far too hot for exploring, and why bother anyway? We'd have all the time in the world to do that in the years to come. We just sat there, drinking everything in. And daydreaming.

And then I turned and nodded at Logbook Man. And he nodded back, a hint of a smile twitching up one side of his mouth. It was the signal, the kind of unspoken code that passes between two people who have lived together for a long time. It said yes. Let's do it. So we heaved ourselves off the shady little bench, panted back up the hill into Gordie's air-conditioned Chrysler, headed into the nearby town of Fernfield, and made an offer. The unconditional offer that Tim had said we should make. Only two clauses— requests for potable water and a pumped-out septic tank—were added.

And we bought two barbershop tickets.

We must have been mad.

Three

"What are we going to do?"

I sat with a girlfriend, Lorraine, in Bread and Roses. My stomach churned. One of the deli's homemade chocolate cupcakes, a confection that normally disappeared from my plate faster than the TGV leaving Paris, sat on the counter untouched. The cappuccino beside it was getting cold.

It was proving impossible to eat or drink anything. Gurgle, gurgle, I sounded like a city drain during a January thaw. And it was all due to fear. Paralyzing fear. And rage.

"What the FUCK are we going to do?"

Lorraine blanched a bit at this repetition and looked pointedly at an ugly poster of a French café on the wall beside us. She never swore. Her idea of an expletive was "fiddlesticks."

"Could you cash in your RSPS?" she asked.

"Don't really have any," I said, sighing. "We can never afford to put more than a few hundred dollars a year in. And," I added sheepishly, "I confess that we hardly ever do that, either."

Indeed, newspaper stories that ran with depressing regularity every February, lecturing everyone to contribute "the maximum" into their RSPS every year or face a tea and toast existence in old age, always had the effect of making me want to drop dead before getting that far. Who had the financial wherewithal to put aside $16,000 every year? I didn't. Nor did Logbook Man.

Lorraine obviously did, however. She looked prim.

"Well, what about asking your mother?"

She fastidiously cut into her crumbly *millefeuilles* with a knife and fork.

Yes, now there was a possibility. Why not Mum? Dear old Mum. Widowed for nearly ten years, Mum occupied an upscale senior citizens' condo on the outskirts of the city and was enjoying a pretty comfortable old age, thanks to a bewildering array of investments with names like long term capital instruments and fixed income debentures. They were administered for her by a sugary-voiced man she called Geoffrey, who sometimes dropped by the condo. In fact, she was always praising Geoffrey to the skies, much to the irritation of Logbook Man who thought Geoffrey was an oily creep. Maybe I'd better talk to Mum. Get the number of this Geoffrey. See if we could find a way to borrow a few of her instruments for a while.

Yet Mum happened to be a frugal Freda. If there had been an award for the most accomplished penny-pincher on the planet, she'd have won it, hands down. My mother was the kind of person who cut up her old underwear to use as dishrags and when presented with a fresh French baguette from our downtown bakery, she'd insist on eating up her sliced plastic-wrapped Wonder Bread first, because she didn't want to waste it. And the last time we'd gone out for lunch at a swanky restaurant, she'd said, "I'll leave the tip, dear," then counted out twenty-five cents in pennies on to the white linen tablecloth.

No, asking Mum was definitely not in the cards. She didn't even know about this terrifying turn of events anyway, because I hadn't told her yet. I didn't dare.

"She wouldn't go for it," I whimpered to Lorraine. "She'd say we were foolish to do such a crazy thing."

Lorraine raised her eyebrows with a look that indicated she shared Mum's sentiments. She took another dainty bite of her *millefeuilles*.

I stared gloomily into my cappuccino.

The problem was the bank. The bloody bank. They wouldn't lend us the money to buy the house. Our offer had been made quickly and unthinkingly thanks to my conviction that the move was destiny but also because of the conversation with Tim and Caron. And it meant paying cash—there was no conditional-on-financing clause. Then Gordie had called the following day with the good news: the owners accepted our terms right away. Well, of course they had. They weren't fools. Who wouldn't accept such a generous offer? In fact, they were probably dancing with delight right then, around that grey woodstove. And I'd done a demented jig around the dining room myself after talking to Gordie. Yes. Yes! The place was going to be ours, just as I'd known it would be. So bring on the rural daydreams....

And then, the following morning, brimming with excitement, I'd called our bank branch—the local financial institution where we'd loyally kept our accounts for nearly fifteen years, paying off loans with religious regularity, never giving the bank a moment of concern. And at the request of one Ms. Oksana Kowalchuk, mortgage loans representative, I'd dropped off three years of tax returns and other paper paraphernalia that the money mavens insist on seeing before they deign to lend hoi-polloi like us any of their precious funds.

And they'd turned us down. Flat.

"We have examined your loan application, Ms. Day," she said into the phone precisely three hours later. Her voice was smooth, low-pitched. It oozed the kind of phony sincerity that Geoffrey's always did when he sat on Mum's sofa, sipping a cup of her cheap teabag tea. She paused. "We have examined your application carefully—very carefully indeed."

And?

"We regret to inform you that your combined income is not sufficient for you to assume such a mortgage."

"WHAT?"

"The income reported on your tax returns is...er... very small," she said delicately. She coughed. "We have a formula on which we base all loan applications and yours, um ..." she paused, "... I understand that you are a writer, is that correct?"

"Yes." And so ...?

"And your husband is a graphic artist?"

"Yes, that's right."

"Well, um...."

The prolonged silence that followed spoke volumes about the high regard in which financial institutions hold the creative professions.

"The fact is," she eventually went on, "the fact is, that in the kind of employment that you and your partner are, er, engaged, your combined income does not fit the guidelines that the bank uses to determine the viability of funding."

"But, but," I spluttered. "I'm a commercial writer, not some penniless novelist. I make good money. I write for corporate newsletters, which pay well, and my husband is in packaging design and ..."

"Yes?"

"So ..." An indignant chuckle. "We aren't exactly your starving artists living in a garret, are we?"

She didn't answer. Ms. Kowalchuk was clearly in no mood for levity. Banalities about striving for continued excellence in customer service poured out of the receiver next. Then this bottle blonde with big calves and a tight leather miniskirt—whom I'd often seen sitting self-importantly in a green and white cubicle at the bank, with a huge poster blaring "Kickstart your dreams now" positioned behind her desk—decided it was time to turn off the charm.

"The only possible financing facility we can offer you at this time is a high ratio mortgage," she snapped. "That means a rate two percentage points higher than the rates we provide for our more creditworthy clients. And even that is in doubt. I am very sorry."

As abruptly as the Ukrainian government shut down the oil pipeline to Europe, she was gone. "Have a nice day," and click, our conversation was terminated.

I put the phone down and nearly collapsed.

Jesus H. Christ!

We were on the hook for hundreds of thousands of dollars, and we had only sixty days to find it.

Unable to reach Logbook Man (who mercifully for him, had gone to lunch), I called Lorraine at work and begged her to meet me at Bread and Roses. And she came right way, took the subway over from her provincial government office in her corporate suit and heels, because that's what close women friends do for each other. And Lord, how grateful I was for her shoulder to whine on. Yet Lorraine, who was contentedly single and had just bought her first house after driving realtors mad for twenty years, wasn't an awful lot of help. She nibbled her layers of pastry and custard and made sympathetic noises, but it was obvious what she was really thinking.

People who are foolish enough to plunge in at the deep end wind up getting washed over Niagara Falls.

And then there was John, the Korean owner of Bread and Roses, to contend with.

"Somesing wrong with ze kopkek?" he asked, looking perplexed at my untouched plate.

"No, no, John," I said. "It's fine. Really. Sorry, but I'm just not hungry today."

Clearly, the best thing was to just go home.

Shoulders hunched, head down in the posture of the defeated, still stunned by the devastating news from the bank, I retraced my steps. And a couple of blocks away, I walked by Starbucks.

"Hey!"

It was Tim. He sat on the narrow pavement patio outside, chair tipped backwards, long spidery legs sprawled out in front of him, oblivious to the pedestrians who had to step over his feet. It was his Real Estate Mogul pose, the one he always adopted when he held court. A tall shiny silver metal mug of coffee sat on the metal table in front of him. For a change, Caron didn't seem to be grafted to his right hip. Yet several of his acolytes, all male and young, were there as usual, gathered around the table, leaning forward on their own chairs, hanging on to his every word.

"Hey!" he called, louder this time.

Teeth clenched, I kept walking.

"Hey, you," he bellowed, standing up, taking off his mirror sunglasses. "HEY YOU, Sandra." He never could get my name straight. "Stop, will ya? Didja getcha HOUSE?"

Yes, Tim. We got it. And now we don't know what to do with it. You asshole. You total jerk-off. Thanks to your stupid advice, we're probably going to lose everything we own.

Grimly, I continued on. He kept on shouting. People stared at him, then at me. I didn't stop. I just walked and walked. And reaching the corner of our street, I hoped—hoped with all my heart—that when he plonked his bony butt down again on that chair, it would tip over backwards and he'd go sprawling, right on to the hot black tarmac of Bloor Street.

And then a great big bus would come along.

Our house in the city wasn't much to look at. None of them in the neighbourhood were. They could best be described as functional, mostly semi-detached and very narrow, built in the 1920s using the brownish-orange bricks that are emblematic of Toronto, churned out by the millions at a now-defunct quarry in the Don Valley. The houses had a boxy shape and little wooden porches and steps out front, which people painted in cream or forest green or pale blue, in an effort to offset the effect of the utilitarian architecture. Tree-lined streets and flowerpots helped too, but no one could ever describe these houses as pretty or exciting. They were what they had been designed to be—homes for the blue collar workers who had toiled at the huge steel factory a couple of kilometres away, down the hill—and they still, whatever improvements had been made, fit that image.

Yet the factory had long gone, all the jobs had moved to China, and exciting or not, these ordinary working-class residences were now worth a pretty penny, because ours was a neighbourhood that had gradually become gentrified. Delis like Bread and Roses and hip furniture stores selling imported teak chaise lounges and uncomfortable-looking metal chairs had moved onto

Bloor, the main drag. The subway stopped three blocks from our house and it took only fifteen minutes to get the heart of downtown. This was, in short, becoming a very hot place to live.

So walking home along our street, soothed by the comforting coolness of maple trees in full leaf, something besides my gurgling stomach nagged.

Why, when we owned a house in a neighbourhood like this, would the bank refuse to fork over the money to buy another house? Didn't we have that highly desirable commodity known as "equity"? Bankers love to salivate over equity, and there was surely at least a saucerful of the stuff overflowing from our balance sheet, because of our little brown brick semi. Modest though it was, we'd lived there for twelve years, fixed up the front and back yards, kept the place in good shape. And we'd paid off the mortgage several years before. We had no debts either. Indeed, the more I thought about it, there was something mighty odd about the point-blank refusal by Ms. Oksana Kowalchuk.

I decided to contact Andy.

Andy was our accountant. We'd been clients of his, albeit minor ones, for years. He was Hungarian, with twinkly eyes and a goatee now speckled with grey. I loved his sexy voice and the way, unlike many of his ilk, Andy seemed to find humour in everything. In fact, we both loved Andy because on our annual visits to his office out in the suburbs, he always managed to convey the delightful news that we didn't owe much income tax.

"That's a legitimate deduction," he would say over and over again, with a dry chuckle, pointing to rows of incomprehensible figures in our financial statement. "Yes, it's in the range."

"In the range" was one of Andy's favourite expressions. That and "legalized thievery" when he talked about measures being undertaken by governments.

Reached by phone, he responded in predictable fashion. He laughed.

"Those banks," he said in his soft seductive drawl. "Where do they get their staff?" I could picture him shaking his head, eyes crinkled up in amusement. "Here's what you should do. Tell your bank to take a hike."

"Really?"

"Yes. They're being absurd. Totally absurd. Tell them that you're going to shop around. Because with that house you own as collateral, and your debt-free situation, they should be falling all over themselves to lend money to you."

He paused.

"And," he added, "call some other banks. Try that new Dutch virtual bank that's just opened up here and is advertising on TV. I hear they're good. My guess is that they'd love to have you on their books."

Reassuringly, he said that "of course" we were in good enough financial shape to buy another house.

Always follow the advice of your accountant, the experts say. So I did. Ms. Oksana Kowalchuk was left a rude message on her voice mail. The Dutch bank came next. Within an hour, I had a verbal agreement for a mortgage from a polite gent who spoke perfect, grammatically correct English and who I suspected was speaking to me from somewhere like Mumbai, not the Netherlands.

Another hour passed. I relaxed. My stomach stopped gurgling. I ate a sandwich. The phone rang again. It was Ms. Kowalchuk.

"Ms. Day?" she said, all sweetness and solicitude now. "I regret that an error has been made. We do apologize. The wrong formula was used in your case. Because you and your husband are self-employed, not salaried employees, we should have put different parameters in place when determining the viability of a loan to you. As a result—" she paused dramatically, as if she was about to present me with the crown jewels—"we can certainly provide you with the mortgage you applied for."

"Really," I said.

"Would you like to drop into my office this afternoon to finalize the paperwork?"

"I don't think so," I said. "No thanks."

"Tomorrow?"

"No."

"When, then?"

"Never, I think."

There was a stunned silence. I could picture her squirming in the leather miniskirt, big white calves pressed against the metal legs of her chair.

"Oh. May I ask why?"

"Because I already have a mortgage."

"You have?"

"Yes. With that new Dutch bank. They seem delighted to be getting us as customers."

"I see." She took a breath.

"Of course," she said, her voice taking on a wheedling tone now, "of course, you're aware that we'd rather you didn't do that, aren't you? You have, after all, been clients of ours for years and I think you will agree, moving forward, that we've provided excellent service during that time, have we not?" Another breath. "Ours has been a mutually satisfactory relationship that has prov...."

I cut her off.

"All right then," I said. "We'll stick with you."

"Good, good. And thank you, Ms. Day. I think you will find that is a very...a VERY prudent decision."

"But wait a minute," I said, unable to resist a little chuckle of triumph. "There IS a catch. I want a percentage point lower than the regular rate on this mortgage."

"Well, now," she said airily. "Ms. Day, we can probably—I think CER-TAINLY—make some adjustment in the rate in your case. But I'm afraid that I'm not sure about a whole per—"

"Okay then, no dice."

Another pause, longer this time.

"Let me get back to you, all right?"

"I'll give you fifteen minutes max."

And true to her word, she did call back. We got our mortgage. And for a bargain price.

The moon was coming up. It rolled over the hill ahead of us, like some enormous cantaloupe melon. Then, climbing into the indigo sky, it got paler and smaller, casting a bluish glow. Necklaces of little diamonds started sparkling around us. The air felt like warm towels on our necks. A truck swooshed along some distant road. We passed the odd light in a farmhouse window but mostly the countryside northwest of Toronto at night was empty and silent. It felt eerie, even a little dangerous, to be out there alone, unprotected, vulnerable, cruising along in the quietness, the wheels of the motorbike thudding against the tarmac. I hugged Logbook Man tightly around the waist, snuggling up against his crackly grey leather jacket, happy to be with him on this journey. And my heart soared as high as the moon.

We were celebrating, heading out to the countryside on his motorbike to see our new house. It was a few hours after we'd signed the mortgage papers at the bank. What we normally did on special occasions was to walk over to Pasta Magnifica two blocks away, and sit down to enormous white plates ornamented with overpriced Italian morsels of this and that. But I'd hungered to see the house again. How thrilling it would be to linger outside and stare, to fantasize, to ponder, to take it all in, the enormity of the fact that this was going to be our new home.

Logbook Man had been dubious. "What if the people we're buying the house from see us outside? They might think we're weirdos or trying to rob them or something. And they'll call the police ..."

I brushed his objections aside.

"Let's go after it gets dark, then. Come on, it will be so exciting. They won't notice us."

And exciting it was. My motorbike helmet, consigned to the back of the downstairs coat closet for years, came out again. I wiped the dust off and put it on, suddenly thirty years younger, off for a wild night ride with my boyfriend, legs astride his big black machine. I felt sexy, full of energy. Raring to go. We purred out of the city as the sun was going down.

The drive took two hours. He cut the engine when we reached the end of the road, OUR road now. Sideroad 15, the signpost said. It was unpaved, narrow, straight, bleached to pale violet in the moonlight. Devoid of people, cars, any sign of humanity. And blissfully quiet after the constant roar of the city. Yet the gravel beneath the bike's wheels made a disconcertingly loud crunch, crunch, crunch as the bike glided along without power and then came to a halt, right in front of the house. Putting our feet on the ground to steady the bike, we sat without speaking, hardly daring to breathe. A twig cracked somewhere. There were shuffling noises. Then a rank, animal smell. A large creature had clearly started rooting around in the underbrush next to the road, close to us. A raccoon perhaps. Or a deer. Or even a bear? Bears did occasionally come down to this area from up north. I snuggled a bit closer to Logbook Man.

Our future home stood only a few metres away, but it was impossible to discern much in the dark. The house loomed up, a vague dark shape with a front door painted turquoise, its white window frames and a long dangling length of drainage pipe luminous in the moonlight. Silhouettes of trees

surrounding the place looked as if they'd been scratched with a piece of char-
coal into the silvery sky behind. Everything was muted, in shadow, except
for one window, THE window. Someone had opened it wide again, and the
orange glow of a light filled the space. Music billowed out into the hot humid
night. Not the baroque jauntiness of Vivaldi this time, but indolent jazz:
Miles Davis's *Sketches of Spain*, surely the best, most evocative music for
sultry summer nights ever written.

I listened, speculating on the people inside. We knew nothing about
them: were they like us? Are certain kinds of people drawn to certain kinds
of houses? Realtors would say so. And what were they doing at that moment?
Sitting on the sofa in the living room reading perhaps, or simply savouring the type of music we liked too? They couldn't be watching TV, not with
Miles blasting away on his trumpet. The possibility of that—music, not TV—
was pleasing. I didn't want a TV up here. I was sick of TV. And had they been
happy in this house? If so, did that mean we were going to be happy here
too? But why were they leaving? Had something gone wrong in their lives to
make them go? Why had they decided to sell? And what peculiar attraction
had drawn me to this place? When you buy a house that has belonged to
somebody else, there are so many unanswerable questions.

A mosquito found its way inside my bike helmet. Nyeee . . . nyee. . . .
nyeeeee. It flew about then fastened itself on to a cheek and struck. OUCH!
I leaped off the bike, scrabbling under the helmet's visor.

"Don't make such a noise!" Logbook Man hissed. "They'll hear you."

They didn't. The music came to an end and a dog suddenly barked
inside the house. It sounded loud and threatening. Yikes, we'd forgotten

about that dog. These folks had a cocker spaniel. Had it caught our scent? We'd seen it tied up in a kennel, mute, well-behaved, on our visit with Gordie.

"Let's go," I whispered, fearful for the first time of being discovered. "Quick. Before the dog comes out."

He started up the motorbike as quietly as he could. I adjusted my helmet. And we sped away like phantoms into the night, dreaming of the day in late September when we'd be back.

To stay.

Fall

"There [has] always been, in life and literature, the exhilaration of getting away from something."

—Shirley Hazzard

Four

Scratch, scratch. I wake with a start. Scratch, scratch, scuffle. An animal sound. Something is moving in the attic directly above my head, and it sounds big.

But I close my eyes again. Dawn has only just started to peep in. The sky is still bluish-black beyond the spruce trees outside the attic window, with not even a faint smudge of vermilion staining the horizon. It's far too early for a transplanted urbanite to think about getting up, especially after a late night of moving furniture and unpacking boxes. I roll over, try to sleep. Whatever this bloody thing is fumbling around up there in the attic, it will undoubtedly go away in a minute.

It doesn't go away. The scuffling continues, louder, more assertive. Scratch, scratch, scuffle. There are thumps now and the sounds of a seemingly heavy body moving across the attic ceiling. The critter lurking unseen up there has clearly decided it's time to get up and face the day even if I haven't, because it's coming down. Towards me.

I sit up erect on the mattress, ears cocked, like some fearful rabbit. Put one ear to the wall. Yikes. Animal feet. Creak, creak, thump, thump. More scratching. The feet seem to meet some obstacle, a wad of fibreglass insulation perhaps, and then after a few seconds move on again, in a downward descent, drawing closer and closer. Now they are almost level with my ear and the only thing separating us is a piece of old particleboard, thin as a communion wafer. Is that breathing I can hear now? Yes. Yes, it is. The creature on the other side has clearly become curious about the human on the other side of the wall. It has decided to come down and take a look.

I run feverishly through the possibilities. A mouse? No, far too large and heavy. A bat. Forget it, bats don't get up at dawn. A raccoon? But how could a raccoon possibly clamber down between the studs of a wall? A rat, then? Yikes, horror of horrors, that's it. Centimetres from where I am sitting lurks some huge, horrible gristly-tailed rat, intent on taking a stand against human intrusion into its territory.

Paralyzed, unable to move, I wait. Close my eyes. Open them again. I can for sure hear the rat breathing now. And yes, suddenly there it is, a snout, pushing through a chewed hole in the particleboard. Then the flash of a beady eye and a bundle of worn grey fur struggling through and....

Except that it doesn't happen. No snout appears. Nothing happens. My imagination has gone into overdrive. After pausing for a second or two, the creature simply continues its downward course, on the other side of the wall, past where the mattress is.

Whew. I breathe again, wonder about getting up. Tea would taste good now. My tongue feels like sandpaper. But then a few seconds later, the nightmare starts all over again—an eruption of more scratching, more scuffling, right up above my head. Louder, heavier this time, accompanied by chittering noises. It sounds as if a tribe of baboons has taken up residence in the attic and they're arguing over who is going to get the first banana of the day. The cacophony starts in one corner of the attic, then moves to the other side. Down below, in this small room under the eaves, it's amazingly loud. In seconds, the entire attic floor is creaking and shaking with scrabbling, squeaking animals, probably dozens of them, as they wake up, jostle each other, bicker and move down through the walls.

And then the realization hits. Of course. How stupid. How utterly stupid. You idiot. It's only squirrels. They're living up there, right above you. And as squirrels are not nocturnal creatures, they've simply woken up and are now making their way outside to gather nuts, or do whatever it is that squirrels do in late September. It's nothing more than that. They're not remotely interested in you, a silly citified human being lying terrified inches away, on the other side of the wall.

I feel foolish now. And angry. I bang on the particleboard. Shut up, you monsters. Like magic, the noise ceases. They all stop in their tracks, and there's total silence, but only for a couple of seconds. Then one of them emits a squeaky all-clear, high-pitched as a children's whistle, and off they go again, bouncing against the particleboard, in a madcap rush to reach an exit hole that's evidently somewhere down at the bottom of the house.

"Hey down there, you awake yet?" I call out, relieved.

A male voice, sour as pickling vinegar, wafts up from the room directly below mine.

"Yes, of course I'm awake."

"Well, can you hear those squirrels?"

"Yes, I SURE CAN HEAR THEM."

Hmm. Sarcasm now. This doesn't bode well. It's our first morning in our new home, this place that I felt compelled to buy. And I'm occupying a mattress upstairs because, after years of sleeping in a city bedroom that faced west, I'd wanted the experience of being woken up by the sun slanting in through the attic window. Yet Logbook Man, too tired last night to clamber up the steep stairs to join me, opted to crash on a mattress in a downstairs room, and he clearly hasn't slept very well.

"I've been awake for hours, HOURS," he calls out, querulous as an old man wanting his breakfast. "We must have wrecked this stupid mattress hauling it in, because there's a spring sticking up in the middle of my back. And now these … these fucking squirrels…."

Chittering to one another, the bushy tails are still scrabbling and shoving themselves downward through the wall. He bangs on it now, making the particleboard shake like Jell-o up in the attic.

"Shut up, you fuckers," he shouts "Shut up! Will you get outta here!"

Then he sighs the kind of loud, impossible-to-ignore sigh that long marrieds become familiar with, the sigh that signals I Am Mighty Pissed Off

About Something And You Are Probably Blame.

"Shall I get up and make tea?" I call out timidly.

"No, I'm going back to sleep. Or at least I'm TRYING to. Good night!"

What time is it? Where's my watch? It got tossed somewhere on the floor when I crawled between damp, crumpled sheets after midnight. I can never get to sleep without removing my watch. And in the dim early light, I can't find it. Finally, the luminous hands show up under a blue sock. They read just before 6 a.m. The September sky outside is still grey. Yet I feel too alert, too anxious to lie down again now. I slip on a bathrobe without making a sound and tiptoe down the steep attic stairs into the kitchen. Cardboard boxes, some empty, others unopened, lie scattered about on the floor, along with scrunched-up piles of newspaper. The debris engendered by a move always makes you wonder why you were foolish enough to do it. One of our cats, a Maine coon tabby called Patrick, is clearly wondering the same thing. He sits crouched on a box, leaning forward instead of lying down, the stance that cats adopt when they're either about to barf up a hairball or are unhappy about something. "What the heck is going on?" his look says.

I pat the cat's head, desperately wanting a cuppa. But where is the box labelled "Breakfast Things"? The paraphernalia to make tea and toast, plus a new pot of expensive strawberry jam, was carefully assembled before the move. Then I watched, feeling smug, as my Boy Scout kit got carried out to the moving truck. Its inclusion meant we'd be able to have breakfast outside on the deck today, easily, quickly, with no hassle, while everything else was still a mess. What fun to sit on the steps in the fall sunshine, laughing, congratulating ourselves, pondering the curious matter of fate as we nibbled toast and jam and made excited plans. Yet now my precious box seems to have gone missing. Yawning, rubbing my eyes, I stumble about in the gloom, scared to turn on the light for fear of waking Logbook Man. I pull boxes open, scrabble through the contents. Kitchen utensils, books, clothes, CDs are impatiently heaved out and tossed on the floor. Dammit, where IS the breakfast stuff? Then the penny drops. Patrick must be sitting on the box, obscuring its label. He is. I push him off. He slopes away to Logbook Man's room, tail swishing.

The morning tea ritual is as comforting as a pair of old slippers. Warm the pot, put in two teaspoonfuls of leaves, pour on boiling water, let it steep. Repeated endlessly in the city for nearly two decades, staring half-awake at a boring wall in our tiny kitchen. And now here I am, doing it for the first time in my new home, with a glorious view as accompaniment. Leaning on the sink, I stare out of the kitchen window. The sky is turning oyster pink behind the pond. Shafts of the sun slipping over the horizon are lighting up the branches of spruce and poplars, transforming them into gold threads and creating great purple fingers of shadows across the lawn.

The sight should be exhilarating. It isn't. My world has suddenly become a hot air balloon that's just returned to earth with a great gaping hole in its side. I feel deflated, worried, filled with a sense of foreboding. Logbook Man is angry about this move, angry about the squirrels, that's obvious. Even the cat feels the same way. The place is undoubtedly infested with the blasted animals. I dread what we are going to discover next. Why, oh why, didn't we get the house inspected? Then we could have dropped the whole insane idea of coming here.

It wasn't fate. It was foolishness. This start to our new life in the country is not turning out in the way I expected.

Logbook Man lies sprawled on the mattress in a downstairs room. His feet are stuck out from under a blanket that's pulled up to his chin, the signal that he feels cold. Indeed, the whole house seems chilly as a fridge and unpleasantly damp. Patrick has pushed Logbook Man's legs wide apart and settled in between them on his back, belly in the air, paws dangling. Both have their eyes shut tight, and the face of my spouse is set in his Do Not Disturb Under Pain of Death expression, lips pressed hard together. I know he's only pretending to be asleep, and in reality he's still seething about this move. So I bend over, leave a mug of tea beside the mattress and slip away.

Warmed by my own tea, I go outside. Clumps of dogwoods down the hill have the smudgy hue of old roses in the rising sun. The long grass in front of them is gold. Powder puffs of Queen Anne's lace, so creamy white in July, now resemble little ornamental urns, their pale brown seeds crammed like sphagnum moss within a cagework of coppery-coloured bars. Gauzy pink clouds of mist rise from the pond like dry ice pumped across the stage of a theatre and behind these clouds, dense poplars, leaves still clinging to their branches, shimmer in a slight breeze with the brightness of a million silver coins tossed down from heaven. What an achingly beautiful sight. My heart lifts a notch.

I walk around the garden, breathing in the crisp fall air, which smells faintly of apples. Tilly, our other tabby, accompanies me. She picks out dainty steps across the wet lawn like a ballet dancer, looking around her with the characteristic caution of all cats, yet unlike Patrick she seems eager to explore her new home. The lawn has been transformed by the rising sun into a magic carpet, sparkling with dewdrops. There are animal footprints, little ones, in the dew, leading from one side of the house to a towering black walnut tree. Nuts lie scattered about in the grass under the tree's drooping branches like green tennis balls. So that's what occasioned the squirrel stampede. Our resident bushytails were all heading out at dawn to collect these nuts. I notice a trail through the dew going to the west side of the house from the walnut. Obviously that's where their entry point is. In the city, we had the odd squirrel get into the attic—but they always jumped onto the roof from a tree branch and then found their way in through the eaves or an air vent. Yet out here, because this is a frame house, they're clearly somehow doing it at ground level. But where are the squirrels now? There's no sign of them. Not one of the sneaky grey critters is chittering in the trees or scampering along the split rail fence down into the woods. And I don't see any of them dashing about in the frantic way that squirrels do in fall, scrabbling in the soil to bury their nuts, then moving on, leaving the job half finished. The whole garden seems empty. Completely empty. Apart from my curious tabby, tentatively investigating some floppy brown foliage in the flowerbeds, I am alone this September morning. And it's so incredibly quiet.

The peacefulness seeps into my soul. But of course. Have I forgotten already? That's why I came. The utter serenity of this place was what bewitched me back in July. After years in the city, a dull roar always there nagging in the background, it felt so restorative, so calming to discover that there are still places left in the world as silent as this. I look up at the stars now. They're fading into the blue-green of morning and I think of monks living in caves on mountaintops in Greece and I realize why they do it, why they cut themselves off from the world, not speaking, not hearing, totally mute. It's the silence that seduces them.

Abruptly I scoop up Tilly in my arms, spinning her around and around on the lawn, until she struggles and jumps away. I'm feeling optimistic again, seduced myself by the power of silence. And optimism is a wonderful thing, yet it's so prone to drip, drip, drip away in middle age like water escaping from a leaky tap. Now, my tank of hope is filling back up, buoyed by the peace and beauty of these new surroundings. I am bursting with happiness, full of energy for this adventure to begin. I mentally start ticking off the benefits of being in the country. Out here, a long way from the city, there will be no karaoke bar two blocks away spewing out drunks and their stomach contents in the early hours. No teenage boys in falling-down pants screaming obscenities at each other up and down the street and tossing their pop cans and McDonald's wrappers into my front flower bed. No mysterious person (I suspect a jealous neighbour) who every spring sneaked in under the cover of night and picked every one of the Apricot Beauty tulips that I planted at the front of the house. And of course no Mrs. Brassiere. A formidable Russ-ian woman who spoke no English, she lived at the back of us, had breasts like beachballs, and all year round hung her hammocky pink satin bras on a washing line above the back fence, blocking out our afternoon sun.

It's bliss to be dodging Mrs. Brassiere. And even better, I've escaped the traffic. Endless, unstoppable, crushing in its constancy, the predominant noise of the city, it used to seep through every crack and crevice into our little house there, even when the windows were closed.

I've left all that behind in Toronto, swapped it for this. This amazing silence. The thought makes me feel incredibly free. So what if the house is a pile of crap, overrun by squirrels? Squirrels are fixable, aren't they? Every-thing is fixable.

Yet silence is rare. And as precious as this golden morning.

Five

Four nights in a row the squirrels kick up a racket. Sleep is impossible for more than a couple of hours. The critters scuffle, scratch and squeak before dawn and then again in the evening, after coming back to the house from their nut gathering exercises. Yet I keep my mattress upstairs, lying right beneath their attic lair. Logbook Man continues to occupy the tortuous box spring below. Neither of us has the energy or the enthusiasm to combine our sleeping arrangements elsewhere in the house. We're both overwhelmed, fed up, not sure what to do.

On the fifth morning, he gets up, makes himself a huge peanut butter and strawberry jam sandwich. Then, big white motorbike helmet tucked under his arm, he announces that he's had enough. He's leaving.

"I'm going over to the club. They need me over there," he says. "I think I might stay the night in Norm's trailer."

"But for heaven's sake, we've just moved in!" I say, furious. And I need you too, I want to add. Yet the words stay frozen on my lips because there's never any point in arguing with Logbook Man. Not when he's made up his mind about something. He's like the Rock of Gibraltar.

"And there's so much to do here."

I stare around the downstairs room in the old Victorian structure, gripped by a Susanna Moodie fit of despair.

It is certainly proving to be a train wreck of a house. Whatever possessed us to buy it? None of the sash windows open or shut properly, the wiring is a disaster, the toilet in the pink sixties bathroom is leaking all over the floor leaving a horrible smell behind on the old patterned linoleum and the roof on the south side of the house has holes. We discovered this the second night, during dinner. A sudden burst of heavy rain appeared out of nowhere, splattering on the roof above the dining area. A few minutes later a drop of dirty water landed right in the middle of Logbook Man's butternut squash soup. More drops followed, spaced at intervals of ten seconds or so. Then as the rain got harder, becoming a steady drumbeat above our heads, the drops turned into a stream, requiring a saucepan on the dining table, positioned directly below the hole. More discouraging discoveries revealed themselves the next day. At baseboard level throughout much of the house, ominous-looking holes in the walls were in evidence. We never even noticed these during our enraptured visit with Gordie. Were they chewed by the squirrels? Mice? Rats? Or God forbid, some bigger critter? Do these critters creep out of the holes at night, when we are in bed? Probably. And that flimsy particleboard panelling…what's the state of the insulation behind it? I dread prying off a panel to look. With so many squirrels trekking constantly back and forth through the walls, hauling their precious provisions—i.e., nuts from the walnut tree outside—the fibreglass insulation (if indeed there is any) has surely been torn to shreds by now. Totally wrecked, flattened. There must be a ton of squirrel crap piled up in there too. Perhaps even some dried-up corpses. What is the life cycle of squirrels? Where do they go to die? I have no idea. Nor does Logbook Man.

What will happen to them, and to us, once winter arrives? My mind races, wondering how we can fix up this dump, install new insulation, make everything warm and safe before the weather gets really cold. It seems perpetually clammy inside the house already—and storms can be ferocious in this part of Canada. The property is located in what's rather ominously called the "snow belt." Perhaps that means a big whomp of white stuff will blow in one night and cover us while we sleep, like the prospectors in the Gold Rush days, hunkered down exhausted in their makeshift log cabins. The possibility doesn't seem too farfetched. I've noticed a couple of cracks under the windows upstairs that are so disconcertingly wide, you can see the sky behind them.

And now this. He wants to fly the coop. I want to scream and hit him with the hammer. I'm sitting on the floor trying to rip out shredded remnants of an ancient beige carpet as he makes this dramatic announcement. The Victorian part of the house still stinks of dog and boiled cabbage and that indefinable musty odour that old houses always have, no matter how often you fling open the windows to air everything out. Convinced the old stained carpet is at least partly to blame, I want it gone, double quick. It's not the first time I've undertaken such a ritual. Removing the existing floor coverings is always satisfying when moving into a new home. This act of cleansing signals new beginnings, a fresh start, a rebirth of sorts for the house and for its new occupants. And after all, who knows how much puke and pee and other unspeakable excretions have soaked into the underpinnings of the former owners' domestic life? I'm keen to imprint some of our own smells on this place, via a rather elegant Persian rug in hues of brown and plum, splurged on before coming up from the city. The rug lies rolled up in the corner, still in its plastic wrapping. Yet completing the task is proving elusive. Rusted staples holding the odoriferous old nylon carpet to the floor were obviously gunned into place by some big beefy guy years ago. Hoicking them out with hammer and pliers feels more strenuous than I'd anticipated. My arm muscles are already aching.

"Yes, I know there's lots to do," Logbook Man says grimly, watching with a critical expression my clumsy efforts with the hammer, but not offering to help. He's poised for flight, black motorbike boots and crackly grey leather jacket on. "Lots and lots to do. And it'll never end, will it, in a place like this?"

"No, I guess not," I say puffing with the effort of pulling at a stubborn staple. I put the hammer down and take a deep breath.

He sighs.

"And it was your idea to buy it."

"What?"

"You wanted this house. You saw it and decided we should move up here."

"Oh come on, that's not fair," I shoot back, yanking angrily at a staple that refuses to budge. "You wanted it too."

"I . . ." he says, maddeningly slowly. "I allowed you to talk me into it. I didn't really want to do this, you know."

"Bullshit."

We glare at each other in silence for a few moments.

"Well, whoever had the mad idea to come here," he sighs again, looking gloomily around the room like an undertaker assessing where to place a coffin for viewing purposes, ". . . the fact remains that I still have to go and do the club's logbooks."

"Why?" The hammer bounces across the floor as I throw it hard at the wall, startling Patrick, who remains crouched in the corner on a cardboard box. Our wimpy cat still refuses to go outside. He's clearly not wild about this new life in the country either. "Why do you have to do the damn books? You haven't been flying for weeks. That's just an excuse to get out of here, so you can avoid your share of"—I begin to sob, tears dripping on my outstretched legs—"jobs like this."

Banging at the floor with the pliers now, I make an ugly dent in the wood. The whole house shakes from the force of the blow.

Logbook Man winces as if I've struck him, not the floor, and backs away.

"It's not an excuse," he says, his face assuming the Oh-God-not-the-waterworks-now look that men always adopt when women start to cry. "And you're wrecking the floor with those pliers you know."

"Oh, shut up, will you? I'll wreck the whole damn place if I want." I'm blubbering now. "It IS an excuse, a pathetic excuse that you're making. Give me one good reason…" Sob, sob. "One good reason why you keep having to do those fucking logbooks for the club."

"Because I said I would."

"Can't someone else take over, at least until we get settled in?" I blow my nose against a sleeve. The snot comes out black, the old carpet has kicked up so much old dirty dust in the room. "What about that guy Jerry?"

Jerry's a retired engineer for an aeronautical company, in his fifties, divorced. He lives in a swanky Airstream camper on the airstrip. A lot of men do. I've started noticing that most of the club's members are like Jerry, i.e., male, going solo, sans wives. It seems hardly surprising.

"Jerry's gone to Florida for the winter in his camper," Logbook Man says. "And there isn't anyone else to do the books. The club is run by volunteers, you should know that." He shoots me a reproachful look. "It's been a busy summer, you know. Lots of people coming up from Toronto for intro flights. The books have to be kept up or else everything goes haywire. And after all, I did volunteer to do it, before this…this house came along."

He turns to go. But he has one more thing to say.

"It's a COMMITMENT … for the whole SEASON." The words are uttered carefully, with sarcastic emphasis on the salient ones, as if I'm short a few grey cells. "The LOGBOOKS. I have to do them. It's my JOB. Don't you understand?"

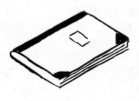And then he's gone, out the back door, swinging the peanut butter and jam sandwich in a big white grocery bag in one hand, and his motorbike helmet in the other.

I retrieve the hammer, wish I'd thrown it at him, dry my eyes, make a cup of coffee, pat the cat, carry on attacking the carpet. What else is there to do? And it's therapeutic, this physical labour. The new Persian rug looks great after I roll it out, the old shredded remnants of the previous carpet removed and stashed in two green garbage bags. A small improvement to physical surroundings can make a world of difference to mental outlook. This transformation cheers me up tremendously. I wash my hands at the sink, stare out at the pond, contemplate going outside for a while to hack at a few burdocks that are spewing their seedheads everywhere. But suddenly there's a disturbing noise. A vehicle of some kind. I can hear it coming slowly on to the property, behind the thick stand of spruce trees. It sounds as if the driver is heading down to the bottom of the driveway. Yikes. I feel ridiculously scared, reluctant to go to the side window in the living room and check who it is. This place is so quiet, so isolated. Hardly any cars ever go by on the dirt road in front of the house and we aren't expecting visitors. Not yet. We've told everyone in the city they can't come up until the place is a bit more organized. So who is this visitor now? A neighbour rolling out the welcome wagon? An axe murderer? Some maniac inspired by that terrifying movie of a few decades ago, called *Deliverance*? I listen, rooted to the spot. The vehicle sounds more like a motorbike than a car. And it IS a motorbike. As the engine stops, I recognize the sound. Logbook Man has come back. His solid frame in the grey leather jacket materializes a minute later in the back doorway. He has a sheepish look on his face.

"Hi," he says nervously, shuffling his feet, cradling the white helmet in his arms like a baby.

"Hi."

"You've um…you've done a good job on the carpet, I see. Got rid of it."

"Yes."

An awkward silence ensues as he hangs the helmet up on a peg by the back door, then bends down and takes his boots off.

"Well, sorry I got mad," he says at length, straightening up again, rubbing his back. "I'm just so tired. But you must be too." And like a magician, he produces something that was hidden behind his back. It's a basket of field tomatoes from the asparagus farm.

"Peace offering," he says, plunking the basket on the kitchen counter.

The tomatoes look good. Big, bulgy, streaked in yellow and red, nothing like the supermarket kind. I heave myself up from the floor, poke a ripe-looking specimen, contemplate lunch.

"That's nice," I say. "Thanks. Offering accepted."

We smile at one another in the tentative manner of all couples who have had a spat and aren't quite sure if the sparring is about to erupt again.

But there's no more sparring. Not now anyway. We're anxious to make up, to put a brave face on things, to cope in a unified way with this mess we've created for ourselves. In another peacemaking gesture, Logbook Man decides to open some wine for lunch and we polish off the whole bottle. Afterwards, we haul our king-sized bed—still propped up against the living room wall—into a room at the end of the house that had once been used as a garage. It feels even damper in this room than other parts of the house because there's no basement underneath, but he reasons that perhaps the squirrels will bother us less there. And there's a lovely view from the room's two small windows of the split rail fence leading down into woods.

"Shall we, you know, try the bed out in here?" he says after we've laid the mattress on top of the box springs. He raises his eyebrows in a questioning way, looking a little pink and inebriated.

"Yes, why not?" I say and giggle. My head is spinning from the wine but there's also relief—so much relief—that he's dropped the idea of sleeping at the club. "Um, I'm rather grubby, you know," I survey my filthy jeans and shirt, "what with ripping up that carpet and everything."

"I don't care," he says. "You look great."

We collapse together on the pale blue shiny mattress and roll over and over, laughing in the crazed way of middle-aged people who have imbibed too much in the middle of the day.

Later, heads aching, sitting up and leaning against the wall of our new bedroom, he sighs—and I sigh too. Loudly. Because there's that unmistakable sound again—a scuffling and scratching coming from somewhere above our heads.

"The little bastards," Logbook Man says, looking up at the ceiling. "They've obviously managed to get everywhere in this house. But hey," he adds in response to my worried look, "don't worry, we're going to fix them."

"What do you mean?"

"I didn't want to mention it before because you were so upset, but I think I've found a solution to the squirrels."

He grins and leaps up naked on the mattress. Jumping about like a kid trying out a new trampoline, he extends one arm above his head and starts banging on the ceiling with a clenched fist.

"Hey you, you little fuckers up there," he yells gleefully. "Listen up." *Bam, bam, bam.* "Boy are we going to fix you. Just wait." *Bam, bam.* "Just you wait till you see the hardware cloth."

Hardware cloth? Brunnhilde and her buddies come to mind. I picture the Valkyries garbing themselves in this fabric before riding off to Valhalla. It's obviously some kind of heavy-duty material, metallic and grey, capable of withstanding repeated washings and pitched battles with the forces of evil. Isn't it?

Logbook Man laughs at my ignorance. Hardware cloth isn't really a cloth at all, he explains patiently. It's a very strong galvanized mesh with a narrow square gauge. And the chief virtue of hardware cloth is that there's hardly an animal on the planet capable of chewing or clawing through it. People in the know, and especially those who live in the country, become intimately familiar with the merits of this tough type of wire fencing, because it's a godsend anywhere that wildlife makes its presence felt. Surround a chicken run with a length of hardware cloth and it will, in most cases, stop a fox getting in to gobble up the hens. Staple it over the edge of eavestroughing, around chimneys and over roof vents, and it will prevent Rocky Raccoon from finding himself a cosy indoor berth up under the eaves for the winter. Farmers everywhere use hardware cloth to keep snakes, gophers and rats out of farm buildings. And although it's hard to work with because the wire is not very pliable, hardware cloth can, Logbook Man has learned, be a highly effective barricade against our persecutors, the squirrels.

"A guy at the club who lives up here told me he had exactly the same problem," he says excitedly. "Squirrels kept getting in at the bottom of his house, tunnelling in around the foundations. And hardware cloth's the answer. If we install a wide length of the stuff all around the house, below ground level, it will keep them out."

He shakes his head. "Great idea. Don't know why I didn't think of it myself."

"But won't that mean ..." I choose my words carefully, not wanting to pour cold water on this project, which clearly has the potential to be extremely arduous, "...won't that mean having to dig up all around the house to install this ... er ... cloth?"

"Sure," he says briskly, leaping off the bed and getting dressed. "It's going to mean a lot of digging. But I don't mind. I'll do it. Has to be done, right?"

He grins.

"Let's go get some."

The weather has turned helpfully mild. We drive the seven kilometres into the nearest town, Fernfield, under a cornflower blue sky. Fields of ripened crops look like rivers of molten gold under the warm, September sun. Trees everywhere are taking on the hues of autumn, splattered here and there with chrome and vermilion, as if an artist had daubed them with some giant paintbrush. But there are no bold sweeps of deep crimson. Not yet. It's too early. Only a few leaves of that hue flutter randomly in the air like butterflies, then twist gently down into the road. Fall still seems unsure of itself, waiting in the wings, wondering when to drift in and transform the landscape—and the farmers we pass, wobbling along concession roads in their tractors and massive green and yellow combines, anxious to get the soybeans and barley gathered in, are doubtless as grateful for this delay in the cycle of seasons as we are. With luck we'll be able to have the hardware cloth installed around the house and the damn squirrels shut out before winter comes.

Fernfield reveals itself at first glance to be a Stephen Leacock kind of town. There's no lake hovering on the outskirts as in his mythical Mariposa, yet a gorge runs through the town centre and at its bottom is a greenish-brown river, reduced to a trickle because it's the end of summer. All around this focal point are the "square streets and trim maple trees" portrayed in *Sunshine Sketches of a Little Town*—in short, it's a neat-as-a-new-pin kind of place. Yet on closer examination, there are differences. Sad differences. Something has gone awry since Leacock wrote his 1930s paean to the virtues of littleness. Like all towns of a similar size scattered across North America, Fernfield is failing at its core, yet thriving on the outskirts.

The main street consists mostly of three-storey buildings made of attractive local grey stone, and these edifices house a variety of small businesses that look as if they are struggling to stay alive. Signs saying "End of season sale" and "Shop early for Xmas" hang in windows of many stores. A long rack of bargain books stands forlornly outside the bookstore, with not one browser in evidence. Only three pedestrians are walking on the entire street. A fat young woman in turquoise sweatpants and a shocking pink windbreaker is pushing a baby carriage and pulling along beside her an equally fat child who seems determined to dawdle. She keeps yanking his arm crossly. On the opposite sidewalk next to the bank, an old thin man wearing a trilby hobbles with a cane into the Busy Bee coffee shop looking as if he just stepped out of Norman Rockwell painting.

We head right through this main thoroughfare to the south end of town because that's where the action is now. At the Fernfield Shopping Mall, naturally. It houses a huge supermarket, a dollar store, a housewares emporium, a Tim Hortons, Gordie's real estate office where we made the offer to purchase the house, and an auto parts shop with a sign outside saying "Save a squirrel. Replace your Shocks and Struts." At its extreme eastern end stands our destination, a boxy building with a flat roof called the LumberMart. It has cream aluminum siding and red trim that looks very new, in sharp contrast to the tired stone buildings in the town centre. Big black pickup trucks pack the parking lot in front. The trucks, ornamented with scarlet and silver stripes, glint in the sun like Roman chariots.

The LumberMart is crowded. A lineup of customers, mostly men in plaid jackets and baseball caps, reaches nearly to the plate glass front doors. Other men are heading outside, arms full of copper tubing, rolls of wire, plumbing supplies and gallon cans of paint. This is clearly the time to fix up houses in Fernfield. The deadline of winter is approaching and everyone knows it. Presiding over this activity is a plump middle-aged woman with a froth of frizzy brown hair and little silver earrings. She's dressed in a tight red T-shirt and stands on a raised dais where the cash desk is. She keeps grinning at everyone. Her name tag says "Brenda. Have a nice day" and she looks as if the sentiment is genuine.

Brenda has, I note, an enormous rear, poured into hipster jeans. A tube of fat bulges over the top of these pants, pressing against the thin fabric of the T-shirt, and her buttocks wobble crazily up and down whenever she hits the buttons on the cash desk. It's fascinating to watch. We stand in the line-up and she keeps slapping her bum and making comments like "Get outta here, Verne. You've gotta be kidding me," as she serves one guy, then—smack—goes on to share a joke with the next one. Brenda takes her sweet time too. She chats and laughs with most of her customers, yet no one seems to mind. It's a revelation. The last time I was in a home renovation store like this, in the city, upscale dudes in Dockers tapped the checkout counter impatiently and kept glancing at their Rolexes if they waited longer than a few seconds. Here I'm immediately struck by how different things are. If this is life in a small town, then count me in. There's a no-hurry atmosphere to this establishment that is endearing. In Fernfield, it seems, everyone knows each other and nobody is in so much of a hurry that they can't stop to exchange a few words on the absurdities of life. And Brenda is evidently one of those rare people who actually enjoys her job.

"What can I do for you folks?" she says in a booming loudspeaker voice when our turn comes.

Logbook Man tells her about the squirrels.

"Squirrels, eh?" she says and shakes her head. "Nasty little rodents, eh? Yeah, the hardware cloth might keep 'em out. But a shotgun would be better."

She mimes a bang-bang gesture, guffaws and gives us an appraising stare.

"You're the folks who bought the Wilkinson place, aren't ya? Up on Queen Elizabeth road?"

We look blank.

"Yes, our house was owned by some people called Wilkinson," I say, "but we're on Sideroad fif..."

"Aw, no one uses those stupid numbers the township decided to stick us with. Buncha meddlers." She slaps her right buttock and guffaws again. "That's Queen Lizzie that you're on, folks."

The road got its nickname thirty years before because of a "bossy boots of a dame" called Elizabeth, Brenda explains. This woman's husband was a roads inspector, conducting a survey.

"She brought hubby his lunch every day, wanted to keep an eye on him, everyone said...and she bossed the road crew when she came up too. Said they should plant lots of spruce trees because it was too windy up there," Brenda takes a deep breath. "Ah yes, a real queen she was, that Elizabeth. But they did plant the trees. You have a whole lotta trees?"

We nod in unison.

"Well then," smack, "you're on old Queenie's road."

She hands over a slip of paper for us to take to the back of the building to pick up the hardware cloth. Her rear wobbles as she takes Logbook Man's credit card and rings the charge through. Then she turns and looks hard at us, her expression speculative again.

"The Wilkinsons musta been awful glad when you guys came along," she says with a quiet chuckle this time.

"How come?" I ask.

"Well, the place was on the market for months and months. That house has one big reputation around here, eh? No one would touch it." Another chuckle. "Too old. Too much work, eh? You guys sure are brave."

"But," I object, surprised, "we heard that there was an offer in before ours that was too low or something…."

"Oh yeah, they did get one offer from some young hippie guy. Just one. But it was for a ridiculous amount and he wasn't really serious about buying the place, eh? And …" she hands over the credit card slip to Logbook Man, "that Gordie McTavish is kinda hopeless at selling real estate anyway. You buy from Gordie?"

We nod in unison.

"Well, he only went into real estate this spring, eh? He used to be a clerk in the county office. Bought himself a wig and decided to get a new life. He'll be trading in his wife next." Her buttocks jiggle up and down as another roar of laughter reverberates around the building. "But Gordie's always so wrapped up with that barbershop stuff, eh? Did he try to sell you tickets?"

I nod, feeling instantly guilty. The realtor who sold our house in the city ordered us to transform it into a Hollywood film set—a task that proved so arduous, it became a major preoccupation for several weeks. As a result, we completely forgot our pledge to come up to Fernfield and attend Gordie's concert at the Legion.

"Well, I hope ya didn't buy any tickets," Brenda says. "He's a nice enough guy but …" she raises her eyebrows and looks mischievous, "… they say he can't sing a note."

The weather holds. It stays mild. A swarm of ladybugs hatches and flies around in a confused state in the trees, settling on our shoulders and getting into my hair. I'm surprised to find that they bite. Hard. But a few days later, they miraculously vanish. When no rain comes, we congratulate ourselves on our luck. And we avoid discussing Brenda's shattering revelation that far from being a hot piece of property, eagerly sought after, our new home was in reality as unwanted as an abandoned child.

There's no point in rehashing the whys and wherefores of buying this place. It's a *fait accompli* now. We aren't going back to the city, whatever individual misgivings we have. And there's work to do. The maples around the house are suddenly dropping their leaves in handfuls when we return from Fernfield. Soon they'll be piling up, obscuring the holes of those pesky critters. We crawl on our hands and knees around the perimeter of the house before it gets dark, checking every centimetre for places where the critters might be getting in. "Four holes. I found four!" I announce triumphantly. Logbook Man discovers five. In every instance, the bushy tails have made cunning little tunnels into the soil, often obscured by shrubs or long grass or piles of leaves. And these entry points lead down to more holes clawed out between the piled up stones that constitute the house's foundations.

Time to get cracking then. Logbook Man gets out his big new black and orange spade acquired at the LumberMart and examines it, running his hands lovingly up and down the shiny shaft. This spade—a pricey one made in Finland—will put less strain on his back than cheaper kinds, Brenda says. And we believe her. Brenda has a canny approach to selling LumberMart's wares. She's already convinced us that she wouldn't mislead anyone simply to make a buck, so we've spent a ton at her establishment, especially on the hardware cloth. It's stacked in rolls beside the front entrance to the house, looking like fencing to keep protesters out at some G8 summit.

"Want me to help?" I ask gingerly. It's going to be hard work installing this wire barricade and I'm still aching from removing the carpet.

"No, I'll do it. Good for me to dig. Therapeutic," Logbook Man says. "You go make some money."

Money—a lack of it—is a constant millstone around our necks. Although we sold the city house for a reasonable price and have a good rate on the mortgage to purchase this huge property thanks to the machinations of Ms. Iron Pants Kowalchuk, our wreck of a house is clearly going to swallow every penny we can make.

The next morning, the squirrels exit the premises to gather nuts as usual. We watch them out of the windows. Then Logbook Man gets busy with the spade. He digs and digs. Deeper and deeper. The two cats watch too. They're fascinated. Patrick has finally been persuaded to venture outside and clearly has high hopes for this new and promising-looking litter box. I stay indoors, trying to concentrate on phone interviews with Employees of the Month for a telecommunication company's staff magazine as the spade keeps going *tock tock tock*, outside the window.

"Sorry. Repeat that, if you don't mind, Rob. You said it was a case of prioritizing the objectives for the new switching equipment..."

Tock. Tock.

In three days, a trench about a metre deep emerges around the entire house. The hardware cloth is stapled into position the next day, after the squirrels have exited, then Logbook Man refills the trench and we wait, hearts in our mouths for scuffling sounds. There are none that night. Nor the next. Nor the one after. Zip. Nada. We've done it. We've defeated the little bastards. Locked every one of them out. Yippee. We open another bottle of wine to celebrate, then he collapses exhausted into bed.

The squirrels are now, in fact, congregating in the branches of the black walnut tree. They're all grey ones, fat and prosperous looking. Yet every morning, they chitter anxiously. It's obvious that our resident critters are wondering what their next move will be, with cold weather on the way and no attic in which to hibernate anymore. Occasionally, one scampers up to the house, does a quick circuit, then hurries back to the tree, perplexed and calling noisily to his buddies. But I feel no remorse. Not one bit. Watching them I realize that I have metamorphosed into one of those people despised by urban environmentalists, because now I think nature needs to know who's boss, not the other way around. Where wildlife is concerned, I've become as heartless as the cats. When Tilly, lurking in long grass at the base of the tree, catches an unwary squirrel and tosses it about, then chews its head off, I do wince a little. The sight of its mangled corpse lying on the lawn isn't pretty. Yet later, as the reality of what our hunter cat has done sinks in, I pat her on the back full of praise, and encourage her to go out and repeat the performance.

And the cage erected around our house is finished in the nick of time. Two days later, the snow comes. Very early.

Six

There is something magical about the first snowfall of a Canadian winter. As a young immigrant to this country years ago I thought that, and I still do. Our cold season drags on far too long. The rigmaroles of winter get tedious— the snow tires, the bag of road salt and jumper cables stashed in the trunk, the special kind of windshield wipers, the scraper kept prominently on the dashboard, the salt-stained boots, the scarves and wool hats, the mittens that need to be constantly replaced because I inevitably lose them—those facets of winter are a time-consuming nuisance, the older I get. Yet the first dump of white never fails to cast a strange spell. Noise is somehow swallowed up, even in the city, when it snows. A hush descends. And those initial snowflakes seem so clean, so white, so perfect that in Montreal back in the early 1970s, I couldn't stop marvelling at them. Like all newcomers, I watched the flakes fall on my

thick grey winter coat entranced, amazed at how intricately constructed—and individual—they were. I stuck my tongue out
like a kid to taste the snow. I danced around a fire hydrant
on the sidewalk. I climbed the mountain behind the downtown area and made a snowman with a Vietnam draft
dodger called Charlie, who'd driven up to Canada from Florida
and was as astonished to be surrounded by such whiteness as I
was. And even years later in Toronto, I still found enchantment in that first
real brush with winter every time it happened.

But now I'm experiencing this first snow in a way I never have before—
out in the country—and how different it feels, because of the openness and
space. A snowflake falling on a coat is usually the first hint of an impending
snowstorm in Toronto. Yet here everything—the sky, the landscape, the air—
gets drawn in, subtly changing with every hour. On the twenty-eighth day of
September, only a couple of weeks after the move and so early everyone is
taken by surprise, the buildup begins. A duvet of cloud, dove grey and cottony,
blankets the sky behind the pond at breakfast time. The cloud stays motionless all morning. By noon, the air has magically thickened. Everything is silent
and still, as if held in check by some irresistible force. There's not a breath of
wind. The treetops no longer swish, the tall brown grasses down in the pasture
which normally undulate a little even on the calmest day, stand idle. The squirrels have disappeared into the woods—either that or they've gone into hiding, high in the black walnut. They don't chitter anymore. No insects are flying
around outside the living room window. The cats decline to go outside, as if
they know what's coming. An expectant feeling cloaks my whole world.

And then it starts, at two in the afternoon. Big, soft flakes, light as goose down. They looked strange descending slowly on to the lawn, which is still as green as Ireland. Yet in minutes, the grass becomes coated in a thick fleece of white. So do the chair cushions on the deck and garden tools and my flip-flops and a brightly striped towel draped over a chair, which I've left outside after swimming in the pond only days before. The snow doesn't stop. It keeps falling, falling, falling, the flakes drifting this way and that, like a beaded curtain swaying after someone has passed through it. The movement is hypnotizing. I can't stop watching. Nor can the cats. They sit by the living room window in the bright light that's pouring in, because of the whiteness outside. They stare out, seemingly entranced as the wisps continue to plummet out of the sky, bending the small cedar trees in the garden double and turning the shrubs into hummocky shrouds.

At dusk, we're still watching when something stirs in the shadows down the hill, near the dogwoods. The cats sit up straight, alert, curious. Whiskers twitch. A buck with antlers is struggling through the snow up towards the house. It's the first time I've seen a deer since moving in, and it looms very large in the fuzzy landscape. The animal seems as surprised by this early blizzard as I am, because it galumphs along clumsily beside the split rail fence. Making progress is difficult for deer in deep snow and this one clearly isn't happy about what's happened. Then it spots me in the window, and with a sudden spectacular leap heaves itself high into the air and over the fence. Away my graceful visitor goes, kicking up a cloud of snow with scissoring legs, hurtling down the hill into the safety of the shadowy woods, white tail bobbing up and down like a piston.

The coat on this buck is already thick and greyish brown. Yet the summer wardrobe of deer is a sort of tan. It looks prepared for the months ahead. I realize with a start that I'm not. I don't have a stick of firewood.

A monster oil furnace inhabits the bowels of the house, so Logbook Man and I won't exactly freeze without firewood. Yet the furnace is a cantankerous companion for the cold nights ahead. Old and rusty, it fills the place with the stink of oil and doesn't seem to heat any room up much. But the most tiresome aspect of our basement behemoth is the noise. It roars like a 747 taking off at the airport when starting up. The floors shake. The first time we fired the furnace up a week or so ago, the cats were so scared, they ran and hid under the beds. Then the beast settled down into a steady rumble almost as intrusive as scuffling squirrels. It keeps us awake.

So wood is the way to go. No question. A glowing cauldron of heat, quiet, constant, comforting, in the grey enamel woodstove in the kitchen. That's what we want—and like a lot of transplanted urbanites, we have thus far entertained rather romantic notions about setting that process in motion. We decided, on moving in, to use our own trees. Definitely. After all, there are forty-eight acres out there, surrounding three sides of the house, and most of that acreage is wooded. We have enough wood to last both our lifetimes. Blowdowns can be hauled out first. Logbook Man planned to chainsaw these into suitable lengths for the stove, then stack them outside the kitchen door and, when these ran out, move on to the standing trees. It all seemed so straightforward and promising when we arrived. And our wood is good. Much of the cache that awaits us down the hill is dead elm, wiped out by the terrible disease that's destroyed almost every elm in North America. Elm is a hardwood, one of the best for burning, and ours is dry, not green. We'll be really cosy.

There's just one snag to this plan. We can never seem to find the time to haul the dead elms up to the house, let alone cut and stack them. And the truth is, no fantasizing urbanite suddenly cast adrift in the country can. Cutting firewood is laborious, time-consuming work. Usually what's required is to plan two years ahead, felling the trees, drying the lengths of wood the first winter, then sawing these into stove lengths and finally splitting them before the second freeze up starts. Yet like everyone else, we're too busy earning the money to pay the mortgage on our new acquisition to spend hours hauling dead trees out of the woods. And with precious days wasted on tackling the squirrel invasion, we never even got around to doing a tally of our dead elms before the snow began. Now Logbook Man is away again earning money—and here I am. A greenhorn from the city at the tail end of the first big dump of winter, looking at an enchanting woodstove. And I have nothing whatsoever to put in it.

"Sorry, we're sold out. Try us again next year."

"My dear, you should have called in August."

"Well, now that's a shame. For you, not me, ho ho. Someone took my last bush cord yesterday."

I make some calls. The local paper, the Fernfield *Advertiser*, contains a number of ads placed by locals selling firewood. "Seasoned hardwood. Bush or face cords," one says. "All maple fireplace logs. Cut and split," proclaims another. "Good firewood. We'll deliver and stack it for you," offers a helpful type. Yet none of these folks has any wood left. It's alarming. My fantasy is disintegrating. Depending on the basement behemoth will be a trial, to say the least. The constant rumble all through a long Canadian winter is going to drive us both nuts.

One ad remains in the classifieds. In small type, it lists a telephone exchange that doesn't sound familiar, indicating that this particular woodsman lives miles away up north. Two disconcerting words "delivery charges" tacked on to the bottom of the ad are a definite deterrent. They mean his offerings will be costly. Yet options are running out. I call the number.

"Yiss, ve haff goot firewoot," says a male voice, after the phone has rung at least twenty times. "And sorry for ze delay, madam. I voz outside cotting."

"Hardwood?" I ask hopefully.

"Yiss, madam. All hardwoot. All goot. Dry. You vont?"

"How much?"

He names, as anticipated, a high price. Cash only. I gulp. Then shrug.

"Sure, I'll take two bush cords."

"And zair iss delivery charge too, off course."

"Yes, yes. I understand."

"I sink sixty dollars, for vair you are. Maybe more."

Yikes. The total cost is going to equal more than a year's worth of furnace oil. Perhaps this is a lousy idea. I look out at the snow. It lies in big mounds on the deck, completely covering the chairs now. And the basement behemoth is rumbling with the disconcerting sound of subway trains passing underneath a building I once lived in, back in Toronto. Another gulp. Stratospheric price or not, this man's wood is going to be necessary.

"Vee come tomorrow?" he asks.

"Fine."

They arrive in a big old white truck splattered with mud on the sides. The truck wheels make deep tracks in the new snow as it jerks down the driveway and I worry that they might get stuck. His name is Roman. Danuta, his poker-faced missus, sits in the passenger seat clutching a metal cash box. A big brown mole clings to one side of her punched-in nose. She has a blank, unfriendly stare. Roman is stockily built, tucked into dark green coveralls and a grubby grey windbreaker, with a white toque that needs washing perched comically on top of his head. He has strands of woolly grey hair poking out from under the toque and faded blue eyes that dart about eagerly. He is quite the most spry senior citizen I've ever met.

Roman and Danuta immigrated to Canada from Poland in the 1950s. After climbing nimbly down from the truck and extending a callused hand with the top of the middle finger missing, he explains that they lived out in the bush while he worked for a logging company. Then they went into town "for a vile" and raised their son who now has a family of his own. But this town, wherever it is, didn't suit Roman. He worked in a factory making light fixtures, where he lost the finger tip. And when their son left home, back they went to the bush. Now, in their eighties, they are still living there, a long way north of where I live, felling, chopping and hauling firewood. The son, named Peter, has recently paid for them to have a phone line put in.

"Vairy expensiff for Peter," says Roman, shaking his head. "But iss goot. People can call us now."

"Yes," I say. "I'm so grateful to find you. And that you still have some fire-wood."

"I alvays haff voot. I alvays cotting voot," he says proudly. "And my birth-day in December. I am eighty-four." He flexes his wiry arms like a wrestler and looks as if he expects a compliment.

"Well, that's amazing," I say. "Good for you."

"Da, da, cotting voot keeps person young," Roman says, shaking his head up and down. "Young people nowadays, zay watch too much TV. Vee neet to move our bodies. Keep everysing going down here."

He gestures in the region of his crotch and winks.

"I'm sure that's true," I say and laugh.

"Da, da."

Danuta is still ensconced in the truck, staring at us out of the passenger window. She looks cross. Her round face is the colour of tapioca pudding and a red and yellow flowered head scarf is tied in a knot under her chubby cheeks. Like some babushka in the Russian steppes, this woodcutter's wife appears ready to go out and harvest the potatoes. The mole on her nose sticks out in the winter light like a big muscat raisin. I marvel that people like this couple still exist in Canada—so determinedly rural, so self-contained, so immune to the unrelenting forces of urbanization.

Danuta isn't a talker. She blows her nose on a piece of old Kleenex and then continues to stare. Her expression indicates that she thinks it's high time Roman stopped showing off about his fit body and gets busy moving the wood out of the truck.

"Roman," she calls out bossily. "Zee voot. Zee voot. Vee haff other deliveries to make."

Something else follows in Polish which I take to mean "Quit gabbing, you horny old goat. Let's get our money off this dame and get outta here."

"Da, da, Danooootaaaah," Roman says, his eyebrows lifting up into the strands of grey hair as he shoots me a look that says see-what-a-henpecked-husband I am. He winks again.

Scampering over to the old truck where Danuta sits enthroned, he exudes the energy of a twenty-year-old. He yanks on a big metal lever. The back of the truck slides upwards and out cascade my stove logs in a messy heap, plopping into the wet snow.

And they look fine as they fall. Goot voot, undoubtedly. Mostly maple, from the appearance of their greyish bark. Just as Roman promised. I count out a depressingly large wad of tens and twenties, hand them over to Danuta and watch as she silently counts them again in her fingerless mittens and stashes the wad in the cash box.

They depart without saying a word to one another. Her expression remains surly as the truck groans and fusses, climbing back up to the road, churning even deeper ruts into the driveway. A snowplow has been by while we talked and tossed a great heap of white stuff into the entrance, yet Roman clearly sees this barricade not as a hindrance, but an exciting challenge.

"Da, da," he yells excitedly. "I go. Truck go goot. Don't you vorry, madam."

He reverses with a frightening crash of gears. Then *kerdunk, kerdunk*, the truck moves forward again with jerky motions, right through the drift. Roman guns the engine, sticks a hand out of the driver's side and waves. Danuta remains motionless in the passenger seat staring straight ahead. And then they're gone.

Back indoors, a note of their phone number goes into my address book. It seems likely the way things are going that the woodcutting acumen of randy old Roman might come in handy again soon.

But a couple of days later, there's another surprise.

Seven

The snow melts. Bam, just like that. As fast as grass going through a goose. Overnight, the temperature shoots up eighteen degrees and an annoyingly perky weatherwoman on the TV (which has been reluctantly installed in the living room, at the insistence of Logbook Man) attributes the phenomenon to a high pressure front emanating from the southern U.S. Whatever the reason, the lawn is abruptly restored to its bright green self and the snowstorm seems like no more than a mirage. Little yellow-winged insects appear out of nowhere and start flying about under the trees. The squirrels come back, rushing to and fro, arguing over the green tennis balls under the black walnut. Chickadees make their unmistakable *chick-a-dee-dee-dee* chant in the silver maple and in the old apple trees down by the pond, a blue jay flashes about, squawking its head off. A red-winged blackbird hops up and down on the split rail fence, pecking at shrivelled berries the colour of wine on a redcurrant bush. Our move here was, alas, too late for me to pick the berries and they are rotting in the surprisingly warm sunshine.

The air feels summery in the garden. So much so that I don't need a jacket. The cats even come out and sniff around, having quickly discovered it's more comfortable outside than in, because the basement behemoth has gone into sleep mode. Indeed, the only tangible evidence of our first brush with winter is down in the pasture and in the flowerbeds. Goldenrod, *Rudbeckias*, Michaelmas daisies and the once elegant urns of Queen Anne's lace lie in blackened heaps. Sensual silky threads on milkweed stalks have clumped together and turned to mush. Two small cedars were snapped clean in half by the heavy, wet snow while brown leaves of perennials lie spread-eagled on the ground, no longer recognizable as plants. They look like piles of messy blond hair in need of a shampoo.

This abrupt turnabout in the weather is a lucky break, the opportunity to do some tidying up and plant a few things before the freeze-up inevitably comes. Experts say it's always preferable to put shrubs into the ground at this time of year, because then they have a headstart and you don't have to sit around twiddling your thumbs until the following spring, waiting anxiously for post-winter wetness to subside. In the past, in the city, I've never got around to planting in fall. Yet now I'm bursting with enthusiasm to take their advice.

I head into Fernfield under a wonderfully clear sky, without a smidgen of cloud. There's a garden centre on the outskirts of town which has a "25 per cent off everything" sign blaring on its high white notice board by the main road. Perfect. I want shrubs. Lots of inexpensive shrubs. I load six *Euonymus alatus*, commonly known as burning bush because of its fiery crimson red foliage in fall, four cutleaf sumac, and several spireas on one of the little open-sided carts provided for customers at the entrance gate. The place is virtually empty, so I take my time picking out specimens, checking their shape with maternal care as I wheel the cart around. And I daydream. So much of gardening is daydreaming. Wishful daydreaming, often not achievable in reality. Yet the hard truths about growing things up here in the frozen north are yet to be discovered and these purchases I've selected are all easy to grow, so confidence about planting them fills my heart. They will be just the ticket to expand the garden and shrink the lawn so it's not so overwhelming.

At the cash desk, however, a young woman in a dark green apron looks doubtful.

"You say you have deer up there?" she says, inspecting my choices with a worried frown. "Much as I'd love to sell you all these shrubs, I have to warn you about the deer. They chomp euonymus to the ground. And my gosh, if you put in these young sumacs...." She rolls her eyes. "There's nothing deer like more than nibbling those."

"Oh, I think they'll be all right," I say airily.

"You're sure you wouldn't like potentillas instead?" she persists. "Or perhaps a barberry?"

Ms. Green Apron explains earnestly that deer won't touch those two shrubs because they don't have a top row of teeth and thus are unable to chew anything hard. The sharp twigginess of potentilla bushes is anathema to them, like humans biting on steel rods. Ditto for the barberry bushes, whose branches are stippled with sharp spines.

Yet I hate potentillas. Such dinky little flowers, so prissy and ineffectual, like embroidery on old-ladyish sweaters. And barberry, striking though it can be with such brilliant red foliage, sounds like more trouble than it's worth. Shrubs with spines will tear my hands to shreds because I often like to rip off gloves while working in the garden, all the better to feel the wonderful crumbliness of soil in my hands.

She shows me a potentilla, but I stay firm. After all, I've been visited by only one buck. And it appeared way down by the split rail fence, then abruptly took off when it noticed me standing at the living room window. Deer surely aren't going to be trampling around the couple of acres up around the house that I intend to cultivate, because there's too much for them to eat down in the woods.

"Thanks, but I'm going to stick with these," I say, gesturing at what I've picked out on the garden cart.

She smiles, shrugs and helps me carry everything to the car.

I also splurge on a hundred and twenty tulip bulbs, because the garden centre is selling red and yellow Apeldoorns. They're an unremarkable variety but have been around for years proving their worth. Apeldoorns are as tough as old boots. They will survive anything, multiply happily and give me the same kind of spring splash of colour that Monet had in his garden at Giverny outside Paris. The cantankerous old Impressionist painter fell in love with the combination of red and yellow after seeing swaths of tulips in those colours growing in the Dutch bulb fields—and although they're overdone now, used far too often by gardeners, I've never tried this planting scheme myself. So I'm as excited by the prospect as Monet was. Maybe next year I'll even sit on under a parasol in the garden doing paintings of my flowers, the way he did.

I spend two satisfying days finding a home for these purchases in the existing flowerbeds and await the arrival of Logbook Man back from the city. It will be exciting to show off what I've done and discuss other more ambitious plans for the garden.

"Lasagna," I say firmly. "I want to do lasagna."

"Good. When? Are we having some for dinner?" he says, smacking his lips and grinning.

"Well, maybe, but right now be serious, please," I say. "I'm talking about lasagna for the garden."

We're standing outside in the waning light of October, mugs of tea in our hands. The pale yellow afternoon sun filters through shrivelling leaves of the black walnut onto the lawn, where grass is finally starting to go brown in patches, as if as reluctantly acknowledging the end of summer. And though the lawn doesn't know it yet, I'm scheming to end its life. Permanently. Having a football field of trimmed turf out the back of the house has become annoying, because it's dull and uninteresting and a bore to cut. My fingers itch to reduce the lawn's size by half, and introduce much bigger flowerbeds.

The lasagna method is how I'll accomplish this task. It is not as crazy as it sounds. Lasagna gardening has become a hot new trend as gardeners everywhere decide to make a lawn smaller—or get rid of it completely, replacing turf with plants. "Going lasagna" is basically a lazy person's way of removing all the grass, I explain to Logbook Man. Instead of digging out all the turf sods and getting half crippled in the process, you pile up layers of organic material at least a foot thick, and then wait for the grass underneath to die off. Added to that, the best time to do it is in the fall, so the material can slowly break down over the winter and early spring, before the gardening season starts the following year. So why not now?

He nods, likes the idea. And he's drawn even more to the prospect of laying out these ideas for flowerbeds on paper. Doing meticulous drawings of projects has always been Logbook Man's passion, even if the actual execution of such ventures often falls by the wayside, a victim of procrastination. In the evening, as enthusiastic about reducing the size of the lawn as I am, he draws designs for four very big curving beds that will mimic the contours of the pond down the hill and cut the size of the lawn in half. He adds paths wide enough for our garden cart to separate these beds from each other. Then with the weather staying warm, we lay out his shapes on the grass the following day using lengths of orange plastic tape.

"Looks great," he says. He turns to me with a satisfied grin. "You like?"

"Yup," I say. So we get started.

The first step is to recycle a mountain of newspapers, wetting them so that they'll break down easily, then placing a thick layer over the whole lasagna area. And what malicious pleasure there is in spraying the garden hose over photos of politicians and Celine Dion with her Svengali husband, then stamping all over their faces in our rubber boots. I spot Roberta Bondar and her photographs of the Canadian landscape in among the soaked pages of newsprint and feel a twinge of guilt about subjecting the country's first female astronaut to such disrespectful treatment. Yet unlike the others, she would probably delighted to know that her printed work is being returned to the earth in this fashion.

Next, we set about raking up every leaf we can find in the garden to pile on as another lasagna layer. Then, it's the turn of six bales of peat moss which we lug back from the garden centre. Dried grasses and flattened stalks of Queen Anne's lace and *Rudbeckia* from the pasture come next, chopped up with a machete and garden shears so that they'll break down easily. Yet even after all this layering, there still isn't nearly enough organic material to achieve the magic fifteen inches that will kill the grass. We need some hay. But where to find it? Although our house is surrounded by farms, we're still very much outsiders from the city. I don't feel familiar enough to venture up one of the long farm driveways around here and ask if we can buy some of the occupants' hay bales.

Flocks of Canada geese keep passing high in the sky, flying south as we build the lasagna beds. Overnight it seems that the leaves take flight too. The poplars and maples behind the pond become a brilliant bonfire of golds, yellows, and oranges, then start dropping. Quickly. The air when we get up in the mornings feels crisp now. The basement behemoth kicks in again and then stays on, grumbling away to itself. A jacket becomes necessary outside.

It's too chilly to work without one, although mercifully, there hasn't yet been heavy frost.

When Logbook Man has to head back into the city to work, I abandon the lasagna beds even though they're not quite finished.

Something else beckons. The firewood.

After the snow melted, the pile of logs brought by Roman looked twice as big as when he dropped them off. In fact, the firewood has seemed so intimidating, we've put off stacking it. Yet it's perilous to postpone such chores in Canada. The express train of winter is always lurking somewhere up the line, ready to roar in. The sky looks the colour of pewter most mornings now. The thermometer hovers near the freezing mark when I get up. It's time to acknowledge the approach of the train and stop procrastinating.

A woodstove makes for arduous work. The logs feel like stone blocks on Easter Island as I heave them one by one into the garden cart, then drag the cart over to an area under the eaves of the house. We've decided to store the wood there so it will be easily accessible from the house when the snow piles up. My middle-aged muscles protest loudly. Staggering back to the pile for the eleventh load, I promise myself that I will jump into the hottest bath possible in no more than ten minutes. After one more foray to get firewood, it will be permissible to retreat indoors, rip every piece of clothing off and plunge my aching body into the old, pink bathtub. And accompanying a long soak there, my knees hunched up because the tub is a ridiculous size, way too small for even a shortie like me, will be a fortifying glass of vino.

Yet the fantasy disintegrates—interrupted by a young boy. He appears like a ghost under the spruce trees beside the house. Pale face, fair hair and utterly silent. In fact, I practically collide with him as, head and shoulders bent forward, I drag the cart along, back to the woodpile. He's about ten. Round cheeks, wide earnest eyes, a Batman T-shirt in lurid red and black, dirty sneakers that look too big for his feet, his expression as solemn as a priest's. In front of him, he awkwardly cradles a shallow basket containing something wrapped up in a white tea towel. This thing, whatever it is, nearly falls out on to the ground as we bump into one another.

"Well hello," I say uncertainly. "Where did you appear from?"

"Um, over there." He indicates with his head towards the trees on the other side of the road. He blushes and looks down at the basket. He is paralyzingly shy.

"You live around here then?"

"Yes." He doesn't look up.

"That's nice. And what's your name?"

"John," he says gravely. He thrusts out the basket still without looking up, clearly finding it hard meet my gaze.

"And my mo . . . mo . . ." he stumbles over the words, tips of his ears turning almost as red as his Batman logo ". . . my mmmo . . . mo . . . thought you might like to have these."

I fold back the tea towel. Inside are muffins. Golden brown and still warm.

"Well, how lovely," I say, cradling the basket, feeling awkward myself.

Having no children of my own, I'm uncertain how to behave around kids, always wary of the inevitable sniggers behind cupped hands. And with my filthy woodswoman clothes and hair sticking out, I must look like one of Macbeth's witches to this reluctant child.

"Thank you, John," I say, recovering. "That's very kind of her. I'll go inside and enjoy one of these muffins right now, with a cup of tea. Please tell your Mom...."

He interrupts.

"Please excuse me." His abrupt change in tone is a shock, because he now speaks with an authoritativeness and a formality far beyond his years.

"My mother also wonders if you'd like to come over and have supper with us tonight?"

The words are articulated carefully, with all the poise of a boarding school boy addressing his roommate's parents on graduation day.

"Yes, I'd love to," I say, surprised. "Thank you, John."

I thus meet Ann, my nearest neighbour and first friend in the country. And I'm grateful. One of the ironies of urban versus rural living is that in the city we can occupy an apartment for years and never even say hello to the person living on the other side of the wall, only centimetres away, and such anonymity is welcome. Yet in the country, even though homes are far apart, often separated by enormous fields and swaths of woodland stretching for miles, lives of neighbours become inevitably linked precisely because of the isolation. There is a desire to connect, if only at a distance. It is comforting to know that you are not alone out there.

This invitation from Ann has come at exactly the right time. I'm eager to have a conversation with someone other than myself. A quick shower replaces the idea of a long bath. She lives a ten-minute walk away, up the hill on the other side of the road. Her house, a boxy white modern one, is hidden by the thick stand of roadside spruce planted years ago to keep the road inspector's wife happy. Fields of ripened soybeans, gold and burnt sienna in the evening light and looking far too wet to harvest after the sudden snow, surround the house. Ann is a widow with four children, all under eleven. Her brother, who has a farm a few kilometres away works both her land and his. Her husband died suddenly a few months before.

"He had heart problems. He had a sudden attack while he was away on business and it killed him," she reveals in a matter-of-fact way as we eat. "Would you like some more scalloped potatoes?"

Ann seems very brave. And very busy. She has a big vegetable garden, she makes her own jam, she takes care of her kids, she works at a university an hour away in a large town. She is a microbiologist. With her scholarly spectacles and neat straight hair parted in the middle, I can picture Ann poring over glass slides smeared with some incomprehensible bacteria, then jotting down notes on a pad beside the microscope in her neat handwriting.

Warm and helpful, Anne makes a point of not mentioning her husband again. She clearly wants to move on from her devastating loss. We talk about the freakiness of the recent snowstorm and the kind of flowers and vegetables that will grow well in our clayey soil as three young kids scream around the dining table, interrupting and bringing over toys for us to look at. John, who at ten is the eldest, seems to have forgotten his shyness and is eager to engage me in a discussion on splitting atoms, then looks disappointed when I confess that I have no idea what he's talking about. Ann rolls her eyes, says "John's a bit precocious," and promises to dispatch him across the road again with a peony—it's the time of year to plant them and they do well here, she adds. And she insists that her brother would be happy to bring us some bales of hay along with a truckload of bird manure, if I want to start a vegetable garden in spring, because on his farm he raises pigeon-like birds called squabs. He sells these to Chinese wholesalers in the city and is always looking for ways to get rid of the mountains of avian excrement that such an enterprise engenders.

"Oh I don't know if I want to bother him. He sounds as busy as you," I say politely.

"It's no bother," Ann replies with a wry laugh. "All farmers are delighted to get rid of their poop. They have so much of it, it becomes a real problem. If some gardener comes along wanting manure, they're delighted."

Indeed, farms generate so much poop her current project for the university is a study of manure management. Ann is looking at ways to recycle animal wastes more effectively, so harmful pathogens don't leak into the groundwater.

This practical down-to-earth woman also keeps her word about the hay. The following morning her brother, whose name is Don, calls to confirm that he has some hay and do I want it? Well, sure. Then later on in the afternoon, he shows up at the wheel of his cream-coloured pickup, oblong bales of hay piled in the back. Don is a big man with broad shoulders and a booming voice. He has the relaxed manner of one who spends a lot of time outside and likes the life. His face is wrinkled and suntanned as he shakes my hand and introduces himself. Then as he unloads the hay from the pickup, he keeps shaking his head, adamantly refusing to accept payment.

"No, no, please," he says, appearing to be mildly insulted and holding his hands up in front of his face as I proffer two twenty-dollar bills. "We don't take money from friends. And you're a friend, aren't you?"

Well, yes, I guess I am now—a friend of these people in the country. A new friend. It's a pleasant thought. The tension and anxiety about the last few weeks start to slip away. Moving out here and leaving the city behind no longer seems like such a crazy idea.

As I clip the twine off the bales and spread mounds of hay over the lasagna beds, I realize something.

I am beginning to feel at home.

Eight

Blustery weather blows in. Rain buckets down all night, swinging and slapping against the roof. The mysterious leak that surprised us on our second night opens up again. Plop. Pause. Plop. I hear it before dawn—an intermittent sound, like someone dropping small stones down a well. Groping my way to the living room from the garage bedroom, I discover a puddle spreading all over the oak dining table. A saucepan comes out of a cupboard and is placed directly beneath the hole to catch the drips, then I stagger back to bed. Yet within an hour I'm up again, wielding a cloth and pail. The saucepan is full to the brim already—and the water is murky and smelly, as if someone has used it to wash a muddy car. It's spilling over the sides.

This leak is serious, dammit. A roofer will have to fix it. And soon. We can't wait any longer for Logbook Man to do the job. He never likes getting tradespeople in, always protests that it will be cheaper and better if he does the job himself. Yet the weeks have trickled by and the roof has simply been forgotten. Now he's away in the city again and the hole has somehow enlarged itself. The drips are bigger and not so far apart. I keep glancing anxiously at the ceiling, then out at the grey landscape, hoping that the temperature will drop in the same dramatic way that it rose a week ago. Once everything outside freezes in the grip of winter, the leak will surely stop and we can postpone doing anything about it until spring.

The rain has settled into a steady drizzle. Clouds like little grey battle-ships cruise along the horizon behind the pond. In the garden, wads of wet leaves from the silver maple and black walnut keep being tossed about in gusts then settling down on to the lawn. All their vibrant colours have drained away, as if they've been laundered in the water dripping into the saucepan. Every deciduous tree I can see is losing its leaves. Soon they'll all be bare, summer wardrobes razored from their branches by the flailing rain and wind. The beautiful view outside my window is becoming ugly and depressing.

It feels comforting to be inside the house now. And fairly warm. Lives turn inward during Canadian winters and I enjoy the sensation of being en-closed within solid walls, turning my back on the elements outside. To be for-tified against the cold is to enjoy it. I am finally learning the art of operating a woodstove properly. Before going to bed, I now know it is crucial to build up a good base of red hot embers. Only then do you cram a massive log into the firebox. I've followed this formula with one of Roman's biggies on a cou-ple of nights, and it's working like a charm. With the damper turned down, the logs lasted right through the night. So the only task after getting up at dawn, cold and stiff, is to top up the fire with some new split lengths of maple. There's no tiresome crouching down with sticks of kindling, matches and torn strips of newspaper, not anymore. The stove is working as it's supposed to and I'm simply its willing helper. I feel ridiculously pleased with myself for mastering the art of operating this piece of equipment, because it means I am acquiring the skills necessary to survive in the country. The glowing orange window in the stove remains steady hour after hour, tempering the disappointment of discovering that the roof leak has started up again.

The fire goes *plick, plick* as logs crumble and shift in the firebox. I love this sound, so gentle and soothing. Apart from the dripping into the saucepan, I can hear nothing else in my blissfully quiet house. I am alone yet not lonely. It's been surprising to discover that isolation isn't such a bad thing. I even revel in the sense of being cut off, with no radio, no TV, no nothing. Since moving up here, I've stopped listening to the news. Bad things in the world always seemed to stay bad and I've reached an age where I just don't want to hear about them anymore. How much more satisfying it is to listen to the woodstove crackle and contemplate making a pot of soup. A big cauldron of some flavourful concoction of vegetables and herbs can sit on the woodstove all day, sending up solitary bubbles now and then and wafting wonderful smells throughout the house. Then it will be ready to savour by dinnertime. I get out a bag of onions and some carrots and potatoes and put the chopping board on the counter.

The onions are at the semi-chopped state when the phone rings. Shit. Who is this? I ignore it for a while. Logbook Man rarely calls when he's away in the city now. He hates phones and we communicate by email. It's cheaper and quicker than playing telephone tag. And I'm not expecting anyone else to get in touch. This person calling is probably just some telemarketer. With their chatty Cathy voices, either disembodied or real, they are as omnipresent in the country as in the city, I've been dismayed to discover. They call most days with recitations about deals on aluminum siding, credit cards and time shares in resorts that I would never want to visit, even if they paid me to go. I mentally beg whoever it is on the other end of the line to go away. And if the person refuses to do that, let the call go to voice mail. I'll pick it up later.

The phone doesn't stop. The caller hangs up, then calls again. He or she repeats the process. Twice. It's insistent, insufferable. I'm tempted to pull the jack out of the wall. But then I put the chopping knife down mildly alarmed, realizing what I don't want to acknowledge. Someone is clearly trying to reach me or this wouldn't keep on happening. But who? Could Logbook Man have been taken ill or been injured in a car accident? Is this an emergency? Reluctantly, I pick up the phone.

"Well, hello, stranger. You ARE there, after all."

Oh no. Omigod. Not him.

"Sandra?"

I take a deep breath. It's Tim. Real estate mogul Tim.

"Um, hello, Tim," I reply cautiously. "Yes, I'm here. But I…um…" what the heck, I don't care if my words sound rude "…but I wish you wouldn't keep calling me Sandra. My name is Sonia."

"Well, sorreee," he says, his voice smooth as custard. "Sorreee for that. How are ya, anyway?"

"Fine," I say in a clipped voice.

"Good. Got your number up here from Janice, your old next-door neighbour. Miss the city?"

"No, not really. Just, um, sometimes." Yes, Bread and Roses's chocolate cupcakes. I do miss those. Sitting in the café at this moment, munching on a cupcake would be infinitely preferable to submitting to the encounter that is inevitably ahead.

"Well, listen up, SONIA," Tim says, putting heavy emphasis on my name, as if I'm some fussy old coot who has to be humoured. "Believe it or not, I'm right in your neck of the woods. Down at this—what is it? Bellweather Lake. I'm calling you on my new cellphone."

So what? I'm tempted to say. And please go away, Tim. While his insistence that we make an unconditional offer on the house no longer rankles—I love being here, I'm glad we'd bought the place in spite of its dilapidated state and no longer care if we could have acquired it for a cheaper price by attaching some conditions. But Tim is the kind of guy I dislike. Aggressive, greedy, exploitative. Phony and insincere too. And removed as I am now from the bragging oneupmanship of life in Toronto, it seems that I can comfortably close the door on such people. I don't want to see him. Friendship with Tim isn't friendship, just an endless round of him showing off how he has the upper hand.

"Thought I'd drop by," says Tim, as my heart plummets in unison with the rain outside the window. "Have something here to show you guys. Yeah, something preee...ttttt...yy exciting. I think you'll like it."

"Well, Tim . . ." I demur. "I don't know, I'm kind of busy and I was just about to . . ."

"Aw, c'mon," he says in a wheedling tone. "You can spare a few minutes, cancha? I'd like ya to see this. You should really take a look. Your retirement could be very bright with what I have sitting here in my hot little hands. And from the map I have—" he pauses, obviously checking something—"I think I'm only minutes away from your place."

God. So close. Should I just run away and hide? Pull on my wellies, not even bother to wash the smell of onions off my hands, hurry into the woods behind the pond in the pouring rain? It isn't a good idea to try and escape in the car. The poor old Toyota is on its last legs now. It takes ages to splutter into life once the ignition key is turned and if I do that, Tim will undoubtedly appear in the driveway, then charge down in that great big SUV of his with the kangaroo bars on the front. He'll deliberately block the exit before I can get out. Either that or he'll see me heading down the road towards the lake and insist that I pull over.

Thin drizzle is falling steadily, leaking out of the eavestroughing and streaking down the glass of the living room window. The woods, or what I can see of them, look dark and unwelcoming. Trunks of poplars in the foreground are silvery with wetness. Not a good time to go down there. It will be slippery and dangerous underfoot and the woodstove feels so warm.

"Well, all right. I GUESS you can drop by," I say, drawing the words out in the way Logbook Man does when he's annoyed about something, hoping Tim will pick up on the hint that I don't want company. Yet all the while I know he won't. Guys like him have no idea what hints are. They're as immune to subtlety as politicians are to reining in public spending.

"Come on up," I say wearily. "We're the first property on the left as you drive up from the lake. I'll make coffee."

Raindrops glisten on Tim's black leather jacket as he slides like a seal in through the front door. Yet he's isn't soaked, not by any means. The familiar immaculately ironed jeans look bone dry underneath the jacket. Same goes for the polished Ferragamo shoes ornamented by shiny doodads on the front. People like Tim never allow themselves to get caught in the rain. They're like cats, cunning about everything, including the weather.

Depositing a big black umbrella in the hallway where it promptly makes a puddle on the hardwood floor, he shakes himself off and runs a hand over clipped dark hair. He is handsome in a TV-celebrity kind of way. A bit cruel around the mouth and his eyes are too small, so deeply set under his eyebrows that they look like bits of shiny black coral. Yet Tim is undoubtedly the kind of guy I'd have dropped my knickers for once because (it's unfortunate but true) in spite of feminism, young women are ineluctably drawn to men with an aura of hardness about them. Then we eventually grow up and learn better. Tim and I do the quick air-kissing routine. He's wearing an aftershave that smells like peaches mixed with air freshener and as a whiff of the stuff assaults my nostrils, I feel immediately relieved that Logbook Man is away in the city. Strong perfumes always give him violent sneezing fits. He is no longer polite when people who squirt these concoctions all over themselves come visiting.

Tim seems in a tremendous hurry to get out of the hall. But of course, he would be. It's not because of the rain or the fact that he's feeling wet and cold. Tim is in the business of Making Money from Real Estate. Being nosy comes with the territory. Without asking if he needs to remove his shoes, he heads straight into the living room, his face wearing that appraising look that realtors always have. Twitchy eyes dart around the room, taking in the saucepan laid out on the dining table to catch the water drips and a big crack in the wall above the woodstove. I can almost hear a calculator clicking in his head.

"Soooo…." he says, his lips curling up in a thin smile. "So this is your new place. Mind if I…."

"Sure." I shrug.

He pokes his head into the old Victorian part of the house, raising his eyebrows at the peeling particleboard and holes in the baseboards, then climbs quickly up to the attic bedrooms, hard shoes sounding awfully loud in the quiet house. The cats, sleeping in their box seats by the woodstove look up, mildly alarmed. Hurrying back downstairs, Tim glances briefly at the view, but it clearly doesn't interest him much. He fixes his gaze resolutely on me, the smile evaporating.

"Phew," he says. "If you don't mind my saying so, Sandra, it looks like you guys have bought yourselves a ton of work."

I bite my lip. A drip goes plop into the saucepan in front of us.

"Yes, the house is pretty old," I concede, taking a deep breath and pouring hot water into the Bodum coffee maker "But we don't care. We like it.

We're going to fix it up when we can. We think we'll probably start the renovations next..."

But Tim isn't listening. His mind has already moved on to more important matters. He starts fiddling with the locks on his black leather designer brief case.

"Well, that's good. Good for you, Sandra," he says dismissively, looking up. He's impatient for me to finish this little speech about our plans to gut the Victorian part of the house and rebuild it. He places the briefcase on the dining table at the other end from the saucepan and presses its gold locks. They open with a dramatic snap. He pulls out a folder.

"Just take a look at this," he says, handing the folder over with the bright taut expression of a salesman showing off a new model at a car dealership.

The brochure is shiny white, printed on expensive stock, with a raised border of gold and green. A thick wad of paper inserts is tucked inside. The cover photograph shows a slim middle-aged couple grinning from ear to ear, both with startlingly white teeth. She has blond hair cut in a bob, her lips painted scarlet. He looks like an ad for Grecian Formula. Golf bags are slung over their shoulders and behind them is some very green grass, backed up by an architect's rendition of a long, four-storey condo building in pinkish brick.

"Launch your brand new life!" proclaims the advertising copy printed under the couple. "Here, at Port Forty Nine, Our Five-star Active Adult Community! World class private golf course. Boating paradise. Spectacular units with 50 ft. balconies. Great real estate investment."

"It's up in Collingwood," says Tim, hardly able to contain himself with excitement. "We're co-developers of the project with a financial buddy of mine, name of Sanjay. Caron's up there right now, meeting with Sanjay and the architects and they're going over the plans for the building. I'm on my way up myself. Lifestyle communities are the way to go now, and being as you're getting older . . ." he shoots a sly look at me ". . . I thought I'd do a bit of a detour, come by and give you guys a sneak peek. Don't want you to miss out on this. It's truly an awesome deal. The units are going to be incredible, no expense spared, you'll see. You'll love the kitchen, Sandra. Marble counter tops from Italy, top-of-the-line cabinets. And if you buy now. . . ."

I examine the brochure politely and hand it back to Tim.

"Yes, lovely," I say. "Great-looking building, Tim. Good luck with your project."

He rubs an ear and regards me expectantly, eyebrows raised.

"Well, waddya think? You guys interested? It would be a terrific investment, ya know. And if you decide you don't like the place down the road, you could always sell. Adult lifestyle is hot now. So hot," he sighs with the pleasure of a lover ". . . and this project we're doing, well, it will keep on going up in value, I guarantee it. Such a great location. And the golfing up there is the best . . ."

"But we aren't golfers, Tim," I interject. I debate launching into another little speech, about how I loathe every aspect of golf, because of the overwatering and chemicals required to create all that unnaturally perfect grass. But there's no point. It would be like talking to the wall of his condo building.

"A boat then? It's a great place for boating. Right on Owen Sound," he says a bit lamely.

"No, we're not boaters either. Sorry."

"Well, ya know," Tim's voice rises a notch, his cheeks go pink. He's starting to get irked now at my refusal to be interested in his Port Forty Nine. "You guys should be very careful about pouring a wad of cash into a d...." he nearly says "dump" but catches himself in time "...a place like this. I mean, it's not a high demand area or anything, up here. You're surrounded by all these fields and um, FARMERS...."

He almost spits the word.

"But I like farmers," I retort, angry myself now. "They're nice people. Very genuine."

Generous, too. I think of Ann and her brother and the free bales of hay, which are now strewn over the lasagna beds.

Tim ignores the remark. He waves a hand in an irritated way at the view outside the big picture window.

"I mean, what do you guys have up here? Fifty acres?"

"Forty-eight."

"Mostly bush and stuff? Looks like a swamp down there to me." He peers out suspiciously.

"Yes, there's some swamp at the back of the pond. It's been designated, um...." I chuckle now, hoping to lighten the atmosphere in the room which has suddenly become taught as a trapeze wire "...a significant wetland. That's Ministry of Natural Resources bureaucratese. Means we can't ever build on it. We've signed an agreement with the Conservation Authority that it belongs to the Grand River watershed and is protected in perpetuity."

Tim snorts.

"Yeah, well that's precisely what I'm talking about, Sandra," he says. His

TV celebrity face is screwed up with annoyance now, as he realizes he's not getting through to me. He looks mean and ugly. "You can't build on this land. It's never going to appreciate in value like our condos up in Collingwood."

"I don't care," I say doggedly.

"No one's going to be interested in developing this area at all, in my estimation. You're pretty much ..." he taps the window in such an agitated way the cats look up from their box seats once more "...off the high-demand map. This is rural. Always will be. There's no market potential in a place like this. None at all." He snorts again and shrugs. "This is the real sticks."

"Yes, I know," I say, hoping that my smile looks serene and Buddha-like. "That's why I like it here."

Utterly perplexed now, Tim doesn't stop shaking his head.

After he departs, spraying drops from his wet umbrella all over the coats hanging in the hall, I notice that he hasn't even touched his coffee.

The rain stops in the afternoon. An hour or so later, the dripping stops too. It gets dark. I close the curtains and restock the stove with some split logs. They flare up nicely. I'm about to settle down on the sofa with tea and a book on starting seeds when Logbook Man's key turns in the front door. He sometimes does this, shows up unexpectedly, and after the long drive up from the city in the dark, his face looks pale and creased with fatigue.

"Well, surprise," I say.

"Yes, I was sick of being in the city working. I needed some air," he says. "And I did email you. Your computer not on?"

"No. I had a visitor today. Didn't get around to doing any writing."

A solitary plop lands in the saucepan on the dining table as he shucks off his jacket.

"Not that roof again," he says in a weary voice. "I know, I know, I should have fixed it. But there's SO much to do in this place."

He climbs on a dining chair and, extending hands above his head, jabs at the drywall where the leak is coming from. There's now a big damp patch in the high ceiling, although most of the dripping has subsided with the rain. I wish this particular plop had waited to fall until Logbook Man had got settled in and relaxed with a cup of tea. He looks frighteningly tired. As he stands on tiptoe, fiddling around with a fingernail, a flake of cream paint flutters down from the hole like a leaf falling off the silver maple in the garden. It lands on his glasses. A chunk of drywall comes next, precipitating a gush of dirty water right into his mouth.

"Ow! Ow!"

He hops around on the chair as if stung by a bee, gagging and spitting out the water. He pushes up his glasses and wipes his eyes with the back of his hand. "Shit. This stuff is absolutely filthy." He spits again. "I'm going to get some awful disease now for sure. Get me a towel, will you?"

I hurry over to the kitchen sink and grab one.

"We're going to have to fix this before the winter," he says, jumping off the chair, rubbing the towel over his face and sticking it in his mouth and sucking on it.

"I guess we are, yes."

"Well, can you call somebody tomorrow?"

"Sure, but I thought you wanted to fix it yourself...."

"Forget it. I just don't have the time."

He rinses his mouth out at the sink, then drinks a cup of tea that I pour out quickly. We sit down at the dining table and start to relax.

"So who was the visitor?" he says companionably, human again.

"Tim."

"Tim who?"

"Tim Hedley, remember? Our old neighbour, the guy in real estate."

"Oh yeah. That guy." He grimaces. "What did he want?"

"To sell us a condo in Collingwood."

"Yeah?"

At that moment, a scratching noise erupts in the ceiling above where the leak is. We sit listening in silence and look up, hearts sinking. The animal, probably a squirrel, shuffles around noisily. It's clearly been disturbed by Logbook Man fiddling with the ceiling. We stare at each other. We realize an awful truth. All the bushy-tails weren't banished. At least one has been barricaded inside the house. With us.

Logbook Man doesn't get up and start banging on the ceiling this time. His sigh is long drawn out and desperate.

"You should have said yes," he says accusingly.

"To what?"

"To that Tim, of course." He gets up and shuffles into the kitchen to throw a log into the woodstove.

"Right now, I'd love to be living in a condo."

Winter

Winter comes in with pinching toes
When in the garden bare and brown
You must lay the barrow down.
        —Robert Louis Stevenson

Nine

She stands absolutely still. Frozen to the spot. A waxwork figure at Madame Tussaud's. Her eyes are big and melting, the colour of dark chocolate. The nose is wide and wet. Comically huge ears stick out in a peculiar way from the sides of her bony forehead.

Up close, a deer is a strange creature, more goofy-looking than beautiful. Jokey Christmas cards depicting Rudolph with his silly red nose aren't far off the mark. And here is my first experience of the real thing out in the wild. Barely a metre separates us. We are standing in the dense woods at the back of the pond. She stares. I stare back. Her body is so close, individual coarse hairs on her grey-brown flanks are visible and I can smell her strong, animal scent. She has a round taut belly that keeps heaving up and down as she breathes. I try not to breathe at all. Neither of us wants to make the first move.

Logbook Man and I have been out in the woods most of the day, hacking, slashing, chopping. He's swinging an old machete, legacy of our days in Costa Rica. I'm wielding brand new steel loppers from Switzerland, bought at huge expense because they seem essential now. Move to the country and you quickly discover that you need more tools than an auto mechanic. The soaring club has closed for the season, the logbooks are shut too, neither of us is, for a change, overloaded with work assignments, the scary word "condo" hasn't come up again. He's also managed to patch the roof leak temporarily with some tar paper shingles along the south side of the chimney. We've decided there's no point in calling in a roofer—not when we're intending to undertake drastic surgery on the house as soon as we can afford it.

A twist of white smoke curls from the woodstove up into the sky as we work. It leaves behind a scent that wafts agreeably into our noses. Nothing can quite match the smell of wood smoke. It's somehow primeval, harking back to our caveman origins. I love the way this maple fragrance, pungent and sweet, even reaches us down the hill from the house, where we are trying to impose a bit of order on the almost impenetrable growth that's springing up everywhere. Taking action has become imperative. Indeed, I have started to wonder if we're going to wind up living in Sleeping Beauty's castle, the growth is so thick, and there'll be no handsome prince in ballet tights materializing to change everything with a magic kiss. We have to get this mess under control ourselves.

It won't be easy. We're already learning one of the first lessons of life in the country: that Mother Nature isn't necessarily benign. She quickly turns into a rampaging monster given half a chance. Keeping her at bay takes strong muscles, a definite ruthlessness and constant vigilance. Urban environmentalists love to fantasize about wild untamed nature—and we certainly did our share at the beginning. In fact, the wilderness quality of these forty-eight acres where no one has farmed for years were one of the reasons why the place seemed so irresistible. Yet rural residents know all about the dangers inherent in such a philosophy and their unfashionable wisdom is only just beginning to dawn on us.

Great swaths of unkempt dogwood bushes are galloping all over our neglected land, their crimson tentacles elongated and skinny from growing too close together. Tangles of deadly nightshade and wild *Clematis sibirica* looking like huge unravelling balls of knitting cling in the dead apple trees and dense stands of buckthorn. They also lie in heaps on the ground, waiting to trip unwary humans up. And we have way too many trees. Hundreds of poplars, maples, spruce and cedars were planted by the previous owners in a provincial government reforestation scheme that provided free saplings to privately-owned properties in the early 1980s. Now those saplings have grown up and their progeny have self-seeded everywhere, resulting in a higgledy-piggledy sort of forest that's jam-packed, spindly and unhealthy. Branches dangle everywhere, ready to poke eyes out. Safety glasses are a necessity. A pleasant hike in the woods is impossible.

Yet the white-tailed deer have adapted. Although deer prefer open fields plus some sparse woodland for cover when they need it, we keep seeing their tracks everywhere in this mass of uncontrolled vegetation. They've been ripping bark off the trees, exposing the bright green cambric layer underneath and there are flattened-out areas where they sleep in groups. Yet they remain as elusive as shadows. Sometimes a group of five or six appears just ahead of us, browsing in the undergrowth as we prune and chop—vague grey shapes bunched together, barely visible in the sinking sunlight of late afternoon. Then one of us steps on a dead twig, or the loppers go *snick-snick*, and the deer erupt, banging on the ground with their hooves. One of them emits a weird loud prolonged snort, the characteristic behaviour of deer when enemies are approaching, and with a collective bounce of white tails like Playboy bunnies they're off.

Yet this deer hasn't heard me coming. I know it's a female because she has no velvety bumps of antlers developing on her head, and the does, when not nursing young, tend to browse alone.

We watch one another, transfixed. It's as if we're playing a game of chicken. Who will move first? Not I. One of my feet is aching, twisted in an odd position while stepping over a fallen poplar trunk when the deer and I bumped into one another. I will the ache to go away. A big fly crawls down her forehead. It reaches her eyeball, clambers over its rounded surface and stays there, yet she makes no attempt to twitch this irritant off. She just stares. Motionless. It's what deer do when you surprise them, and there is something uncanny about looking for a long time into the eyes of a wild terrified animal. It seems like minutes that we remain there watching each other. Then a twig cracks and in a flash, the deer has turned. She crashes through the undergrowth, tail flailing up and down, tangling herself up a clump of dogwood in a desperate bid to get away.

It was Logbook Man who broke the spell. He was standing right behind me, machete in hand and he stepped on the twig. The deer smelled him even as she missed me. His face is red and sweaty from the exertion of hacking at the dogwoods. His eyes look bright with excitement.

"See that?" he says.

"Yes." Wow, yes. My heart is beating fast.

"Close, eh? What a beautiful animal. We should set a camera up out here so we can take some pictures."

The hunting season is approaching. In our area, according to an advertisement in the local paper, white-tailed deer can be "taken" during a time slot lasting a week towards the end of November. Accompanying the paper this week, tucked inside the tabloid pages, is a brown and green flyer. "Sixteen pages of must-have guns, bows, ammo, calls, optics and more," it says on the cover. I take a look inside, curious. The range of equipment offered to hunters is wide-ranging, the terminology baffling. "Bonded Sabot Slug, lime green polymer tip backed by 385 grains of muscle".... "Best varmint rifle, long known for out-of-the-box accuracy".... "Mini digital reloading scale with a 1,200 grain capacity".... "sg-x small game head, lethal penetration that will give you peace of mind"...

Peace of mind from lethal penetration? Yikes. There are scent wicks, cotton gun socks, shotgun bore brushes that look like giant Q-tips, leather belts with slots for bullets and a terrifying-looking knife that is, the flyer proclaims, capable of cutting through bone in seconds. Political correctness clearly hasn't penetrated the hunting world either. Many of the guns on offer are made by a company called Savage Arms, whose logo is an Indian chief in a feathered headdress.

The flyer makes me a bit queasy. Like almost everyone else who's accustomed to living in a city and buying prepackaged meat that bears no relationship to any living animal, I hate the thought of hunting. Although I personally know no hunters, I have an inkling of the kind of people they have to be. An individual who runs around with a gun is a something of a Neanderthal, uneducated, lacking in compassion and respect for nature. That such folks can take pleasure from stalking wild animals and then killing them seems abhorrent and unnecessary, a relic of our more primitive past. Hunters are often careless and dangerous too, shooting their guns off at anything that moves. An incident in rural Quebec, where I lived briefly in the 1970s, provides proof of such sentiments. A well-known naturalist was shot as he went for a walk on his own property in the Eastern Townships. He bled to death lying under the trees and the perpetrators, drunken yahoos who'd consumed a case of beer before going out, were not even prosecuted.

I don't want this happening on my land.

November creeps in. The days are cold now, the sky clear and blue. A thick white frost coats the lawn and the lasagna beds every morning. My footprints break through this layer of ice as if I'm stepping on meringues. The pond has started to freeze, little crimped ribbons of bubble wrap running around its edges. At the compost heap, dumping out the tea leaves, my breath whooshes out and it's no longer possible to stick a spade in the flowerbeds and plant any more tulips. The Canadian earth stands hard as iron just as in the old Christmas carol. It's prepared for the bleak midwinter now. Yet there is still no snow.

One morning as I fork over the compost trying to prevent the heap from turning into a frozen lump as immovable as Everest a small beige pickup turns slowly into the driveway. It has several stickers on the side windows and the rear fender. I can discern one. In big orange letters it says: "Hunters make better lovers." A chunky man of about forty gets out. He doesn't look like a Romeo, but is typical of people who live in the Fernfield area. Sandy-haired, medium height with a barrel chest and muscular legs. His face is round and chubby and there's a fairly generous stomach zipped into his dark windbreaker. He has a purposeful demeanour as he strides over, hands tucked into his pockets, an approach that makes me feel mildly apprehensive. Since he's a hunter, I wonder if there's a gun tucked into one of those pockets, or in the truck.

"Hi, cold morning, eh? I'm Harlan," he calls out, pretending to shiver, turning up the collar of his windbreaker. His smile is warm and friendly. "Harlan McFarlane. Pleased to meet you."

I like the euphonious sound of such a name. As he extends a hand, I relax a bit. He seems without guile.

"I'm one of your neighbours. I live with my wife Maggie down there," he says, shrugging a shoulder in a southerly direction, towards the lake.

I'm agreeably surprised. He seems like a nice guy. This neighbour of mine clearly isn't some bloodthirsty bully bent on browbeating me into letting him hunt on the land.

"Nice to meet you too, Harlan. It's good to get to know your neighbours out here," I say.

"Yes, it is," he agrees. "And it's a great place to live, eh?" He takes a gulp of the crisp air, exhaling a white cloud. "We're lucky out here."

We exchange a few words about the space, the wide open fields, the bush that lies in great uncultivated swaths around the fields, the infinite wilderness that lies north of us in the Canadian Arctic. Harlan explains that he was born in Fernfield and works in construction, pouring concrete floors for homes in new subdivisions that are springing up in towns all over southern Ontario. He's ambivalent about the developments, wishes they didn't have to keep mushrooming everywhere, yet resigned. It creates badly needed jobs, he says, as it is difficult nowadays for anyone in the area to make a living solely from farming.

This introduction over, he regards me intently. I feel myself being sized up. He's obviously making an assessment of his new female neighbour and since he's doubtless heard I'm fresh from Toronto, is clearly wondering if I'm a liberal anti-hunting type.

"How do you feel about hunting on your land?" he asks, after a long pause.

"Um, well ..." I say slowly, playing for time, wishing Logbook Man was around for moral support. "We're ... well, I have to tell you that we're not really keen on it, Harlan."

I smile awkwardly.

He smiles back. He seems unruffled. He's been expecting such a response.

"Fine then," he says pleasantly. "Not a problem with me. I understand how you feel. But if you change your mind, you let me know. I hunt deer. I like to use a bow and arrow. And I'd be glad to come on your land and do that," he pauses, shifting his gaze to the woods behind the pond as if he can spot a likely quarry down there, "...but with your permission, of course."

"Yes, well, I'm really sorry," I say, staring down at the woods myself to avoid looking at him, groping for something suitable to say "but we sort of think that we'd like to keep our place as a wildlife sanctuary. You know, somewhere animals can go and feel safe."

Conscious that my words sound citified and sappy to a hunter who's lived in this area all his life, I decide not to waver. No way. It's important to get on with the locals, to blend in, to make sure you don't come across as some arrogant condescending twit from the city. I'm constantly aware of that necessity since moving out here. Yet the concept of hunting is hard to get my head around. I keep thinking of my female deer, the doe who didn't move when we met down in the woods. She was so gentle-looking, so scared.

So captivating to watch, and maybe shoot pictures of. But not to kill. As I talk with Harlan, I hope that she and the big buck that struggled up the hill during the snow storm will get together. Produce a fawn or two. Bring their offspring down to the pond next year, so I can watch. If that's naive and sentimental, I don't care.

Harlan nods and turns to go, seemingly unbothered by my reaction to his desire to hunt. He asks casually if there are muskrats in the pond.

Muskrats?

"I don't think so," I say. "I haven't seen anything like that swimming around."

"Most ponds around here have them," he goes on in a soft voice, "and they're real nuisances, eh? They dig holes in the banks and make everything collapse. I do a deal with some folks around here, you know. I trap their muskrats, they grant me rights to hunt on their land."

He raises his eyebrows in a questioning way. Getting no reaction, he pulls at the collar of his windbreaker again and says he has to run. He and his wife need to go into Fernfield today to have passport photos taken. They are going on a trip to Alaska, a tour organized by some naturalists. They hope to see grizzly bears.

"We want to photograph the grizzlies, not hunt them," he adds pointedly, giving me a close look as if I'd been thinking otherwise.

"Well, have a good trip," I say.

"We will. And if you see muskrats in spring and you're interested in coming to an arrangement about them...." he starts heading over to his pickup "you just let me know, eh?"

"Sure." But I know it won't happen. I won't be calling Harlan. My first en-counter with a hunter has left an unexpectedly favourable impression, but deer are not going to be shot on this land.

Another hopeful hunter drops by, knocking on the door one evening as I prepare vegetarian black beans to eat with tortilla chips. He's also a neigh-bour. He lives over on the next concession road and his fifty-acre property backs on to ours, on the western side. Dan is taller and trimmer than Harlan. Older too. He has a roguish smile. A Jack Nicholson with hair, I decide. And a bit of a flirt.

I invite him in for a beer. He says "Sure, great. Never say no to a lady," and plunks himself down in the living room, grinning broadly. He's a pilot with a major airline. A man high in the sky at the controls of some vast jet plane is a sexy image for women and I can immediately picture Dan up there, flirt-ing with the flight attendants. And judging from his conversation, he seems to have led a pretty wild life, which included lots of female company. He started out in the bush up north flying float planes for logging companies, where he had an aboriginal girlfriend. Then he worked in the Caribbean and "partied all the time" he recalls with the nostalgic sigh of one who realizes he has grown too old to swallow copious amounts of cheap rum every night. Now he's settled down in this area, where he was born and where he loves to hunt—always deer, every November. Nothing else. He gets a guy at the supermarket in Fernfield to do his butchering, then he puts the meat in his freezer. It feeds him and his Argentinian girlfriend Caterina all winter. There are loads of deer around here, according to Dan. Suddenly serious, he explains that farmers complain about the deer constantly. They wreck the cornfields, cause all kinds of problems. Hunters are doing a public service culling some of the animals, he insists. And some of the weaker animals will die of starvation in the winter anyway, if they aren't weeded out.

Unlike Harlan, Dan uses guns. He implies in a way that doesn't come across as macho boasting that he's a pretty good shot by now. His quarry are almost always felled with one shot, right to the heart. They don't suffer.

He looks thoughtful for a moment as he sips his beer.

"That Harlan McFarlane been around?"

I nod.

"Wow, that guy sure is quick to get his oar in," he says, annoyed. "He has the hunting rights all sewn up with everyone who moves in around here."

He takes another sip. "Yeah, crafty Harlan manages to get to all of you real quick."

"Well, he didn't get to us," I say. "I told him no."

Dan's face brightens. Perhaps he's going to get the nod instead? As I explain my personal feelings about hunting, he looks impatient. Getting up to go, he thanks me for the beer and says much the same thing as Harlan. If I change my mind, I should give him a call.

With a sexy grin, he disappears into the dark night.

Logbook Man doesn't like the idea of hunting either. He's a city-bred softie too. Only a week ago, he found a black and white cat scavenging for old crusts of pizza in the flying club's garbage bin. So he brought her home, where she's settled in with the predictable confidence of a cat who knows a good thing when she sees one. This newcomer has already taken charge of the two tabbies and is bossing all of us around. We've named her Sparky because she's so feisty. Now Logbook Man comes home for the weekend and assures me that I've done the right thing about Harlan and Dan.

"I don't want hunters here," he says. "All that blood, hauling the carcasses out, God, I just couldn't cope with that." He shudders. "Let's keep our place as a wildlife preserve and leave all the animals to live in peace."

"Right. Let's."

We go out into the woods again. With the winter solstice barely a month away, the pale yellow sun is low in the sky now, slanting knifepoints of light between the trees. It feels good to be taming the land, creating a trail on which to get some exercise. I'm from England, a nation of walkers who regard trails throughout the countryside as sacrosanct, and I haven't liked being barred from my own woods by the rampant vegetation. It's frustrating to be confined to the garden up around the house, the small pasture and an area around on the pond. I like being able to take a proper walk out there. Along the trail we're making, Logbook Man figures out where he might put a tripod, then install a camera with a time-release mechanism. As I stand watching him, I wonder if my female is watching us from somewhere. She's undoubtedly close. It's been surprising to discover that deer like a touch of civilization as much as humans do, for they are already using the trail instead of floundering through the bush. Their tracks go back and forth, footprints clearly visible among the fallen leaves and on the hummocky mounds of bright green moss. Yet there are no deer around today. The only wildlife in evidence is one grey squirrel, which has ventured down a poplar trunk from a drey constructed of twigs high in the tree. The squirrel starts rummaging around and regards us with suspicion. I feel a twinge of sympathy this time. It must be one of the bushy-tails that we ejected from the house. Now the poor little critter is clearly worried that it might be in for another eviction notice.

The hunting starts a week later. Volleys of bullets—*bang, bang, bang*—reverberate through the wooded areas all around us at random hours. Most of the shots come before dawn or in the evening, but there are a few in the daytime. Whenever a gun goes off, I jump. Then I wince. It seems as if every able-bodied male in the county is out with a gun firing away. Some volleys seem to be really close, on the property south of us where the woods blend into ours. The proximity makes me worry about my female. I hope she's survived, that she's been quick and smart enough to flee. Hunting of does is not allowed in Ontario, where only bucks can be taken, except in areas where deer are deemed too numerous. Yet remembering the drunken yahoos in Quebec, I'm sure someone will ignore the rule. And I feel a kinship with this animal, the one that was so vulnerable-looking, so transfixed by my stare. What will she do if she encounters a hunter? Undoubtedly she'll freeze again and get herself shot. In fact she's probably already been felled by someone out in the woods, then chopped into pieces with that ghastly knife I read about in the flyer. Parts of her are lying wrapped in brown butcher's paper in a freezer, that's for sure. I hate being here while this is going on, worrying about my doe. When a writing assignment calls me into the city, I feel grateful for the first time to be getting out of the country.

Harlan drops by a few days after it's over. He smile and chats, his bulky frame in the dark windbreaker filling the front doorway. I try to picture him lifting a gun and firing—and I can't. He seems like such a gentle guy. He says yes, the hunting was good this year and hands over a gift basket. It contains deer sausage, a bottle of his homemade red wine, some local cheddar cheese and crackers. The following day, Dan shows up too, holding an offering in his gloved hands. It's deer hamburger meat. It comes from an animal he shot on his own property. The pebbly-looking meat is stuffed into a long plastic bag coloured in the beige, dark green and brown camouflage outfit of hunters. It says: "Not for Sale. Wild Game. Custom Processed." on the side of the bag.

I'm squeamish about eating either of these gifts. We don't eat a lot of meat anyway, and as we're both opposed to hunting it seems hypocritical to partake in the spoils. Yet I was brought up never to waste food. Throwing out what our two neighbour hunters have brought along seems rude, silly and wasteful. So we reluctantly eat both kinds of meat. Harlan's sausage is spicy and a bit oversalted, yet his wine is good. Full-bodied. Well made. The hamburger goes into a big shepherd's pie, made with garlic, onions, lots of mashed potatoes, plus a few shakes of Worcester sauce. And it's delicious. The flavour is strong, yet not gamy as I'd expected wild meat to be. I have to admit I like the taste. So does Logbook Man. Not accustomed to being served such hearty fare at home—most of our meals are vegetarian—he declares that it's the best shepherd's pie he's ever had. As a measure of his respect, he doesn't smother his plate in ketchup. He wonders if we can get some more of this meat from Harlan and Dan.

But I wonder, sitting at the dining table, if we are eating the deer that stared at me.

Ten

Logbook Man is on the phone from the city. It's unusual for him to call. He sounds worried.

"You never put the TV on or answer your emails," he says in an accusing tone. "So I guess you haven't heard?"

"About what?"

"The storm. There's a huge snowstorm on the way. You haven't seen it on the news?"

"Nope."

"Typical. You really should stop behaving like a hermit and watch TV sometimes. You need to stay up to date with what's going on."

"Why?" I ask flippantly. "I like being a hermit."

"Be serious, please. This is no joke. It's a biggie. They're calling it the snowstorm of the century."

I shrug. Is it really true? Logbook Man has a flair for the dramatic. And weather forecasting, once the domain of earnest middle-aged men in suits, has become just as silly and shallow as everything else on TV, the announcers perpetually trotting out dark, designed-to-scare pronouncements that seldom match the reality. So I never watch, never pay attention. And come on, how can there possibly be a storm coming? The sky is brilliant blue and filled with sunshine. The temperature is hovering near the zero mark. It's remarkably balmy given the time of year.

I'm at the dining table, sitting beside the big picture window on a late afternoon. It's the first week in December. The woodstove is still performing admirably and three cats lie in box seats next to the firebox. The newcomer, Sparky, is snoring faintly lying on her side, black and white legs stretched out in front of her. She is the picture of bliss now that she has a proper home. Indeed, we all feel tranquil and warm in this newer part of the house. I hardly ever go into the old Victorian part now that winter has arrived. Nor do the cats. It's too chilly, too drafty in there, the dilapidated holey walls a depressing reminder that the place needs drastic surgery. And besides, there's no need to anyway. Worlds shrink dramatically during Canadian winters. This scaled-down interior I inhabit, consisting of the living/kitchen/dining room plus the bedroom in the former garage, is a more than adequate space in which to spend the cold months.

An oblong white palette box lies open on the table. Tubes of watercolours are scattered about and there's a big sheet of 140-pound paper stapled to a board propped up on my lap, with the beginnings of a painting on the front. The juices have started to flow again, after a long layoff occasioned by the move. The wintry light looks so captivating. At this time of year, when the sun slips down behind the zigzag split rail fence leading to the pond, the shadows on the weathered wood lengths become all wiggly and curvy, in ribbons of purple, pink and grey, overlapping one other. And the sky above the fence turns to faded rose laced with streamers of scarlet. From such hues are successful watercolours made. The effect of the waning sun's rays has fascinated me for a week. Now I'm finally getting around to capturing it on paper.

Yet spousal warnings of dire weather on the way are set to thwart the process.

"The storm is travelling through the midwest," says Logbook Man, urgency in his voice. "It's already killed eight people in Chicago, mostly in car accidents. But one guy's roof blew right off as he was lying in bed. All the roads are closed there, it's total chaos. And it's predicted to hit southern Ontario sometime tonight. What are you doing? Painting?"

"Yes," I say, irked by the interruption. All artists hate being stopped in mid-flow, especially when the work is going well. And this painting is.

"Well, I'm sure it's a lovely painting," he says sarcastically, "but you'd better quit. Right now. Because I'm not coming up from the city. I have a ton of work and if I do come up, I know I won't be able to get back here tomorrow. There'll be too much snow. So you'll be up there alone, probably snowed in for days because of the high winds. Do you realize that?" He speaks like a schoolteacher, his customary tone whenever I resist treating the possibility of imminent disaster as seriously as he does. "Make sure you get a lot of firewood in, won't you, and fill the bathtub? If the power goes off, you won't have any water because the pump won't work. And nor will the furnace."

Nag, nag.

"Yes, yes, I know about the pump and the furnace," I say wearily, dipping my big No. 10 brush into a yoghurt container of water, aching to get busy with a loose wash on the sketch I've drawn out lightly in pencil.

"Well, just do it then, please. Go fill the bath. Stop painting. Right now," he orders. "And for fuck's sake," he adds, "if you don't believe me, listen to a local radio station or something. They'll have news about the storm."

He slams the phone down. I get up from the table and reluctantly fiddle with the buttons on the radio. But there's no news. Not a whisper. If a storm is heading in our direction, the folks in Fernfield seem in no hurry to share any information about its size or time of arrival. Country music whines from a local station for twenty minutes, interspersed with commercials for the best deals on trucks this century at Walt Weber's Auto. Another channel from a nearby town offers more of the same. I shut the radio off and try to call Ann. Surely she'll know if there's going to be a storm. But the phone rings and rings, then voice mail clicks in. She often takes the kids to visit her mother in a town a few miles away. Perhaps she's gone over there. I hang up.

The sun is fading rapidly now, disappearing behind the spruce trees lining the road. Purple twilight, that most painterly time of day for water-colourists, has started to close in. Nothing feels ominous about the night ahead. No clouds are gathering on the horizon, not even a hint of one is in evidence. Has Logbook Man exaggerated? He's prone to look on the gloomy side of life. To be sure, I turn on the computer. I check email first, pick up two anxious messages from him about the storm, then go to the Environment Canada website.

The words "Snowstorm Watch" in big red capitals spread out across the screen, followed by a few terse words about the "possibility of high winds and heavy snowfall accumulation."

Hmm. Only the "possibility?" Not the "certainty?" How to interpret this cautious declaration? Seriously? Or with a shrug? The folks at Environment Canada are a canny lot. They never really commit themselves, always managing to hedge their bets, doubtless wanting to dodge angry reactions from the public if their prognosis proves to be wildly off base. I conclude that I'd better hedge my bets too. Slipping on boots, I go outside. It's dark now. There's no moon and we haven't got around to installing outdoor lights. I walk smack into the wooden posts supporting the compost heap as I try to find the garden cart. Ouch! The force of the collision practically knocks me out. Rubbing my forehead and cursing like a trucker into the blackness, I continue to stumble around, and over by the old woodpile my groping hands eventually locate the cart. I haul it back to the stack under the eaves and bring three loads of firewood into the front hall. Then I stagger inside to the bathroom and fill the pink tub with cold water. Remembering Logbook Man's insistence that I should watch the weather news, I try to turn the TV on. It doesn't work. I need the remote, but the damn thing is nowhere in sight. He doubtless put the little grey gizmo down somewhere when he was up for the weekend because he's the only one who watches TV now. But I can't find it. I scrabble around half-heartedly looking for the remote under some newspapers and a pile of his aviation magazines, but it's gone missing.

I shrug. All this effort is probably totally unnecessary anyway and I'm exhausted. I grab a bowl of soup, load up the woodstove and flop into bed.

It starts just before dawn. A roaring noise outside the bedroom window that's like a jet flying low overhead. Then the realization hits. You ninny, that's no plane up there. It's the wind. Constant, unrelenting, blowing hard from the west, buffeting the house with a fury that's frightening. Every window on that side of the house is rattling as if it's about to be blown out. The entire house creaks and groans in pain. The silver maple outside the bedroom window is thrashing around like a demented rag doll. Its branches keep banging and breaking against the roof, then sliding off with a clatter. I am suddenly nervous. What if the tree smashes into the roof right on top of me? Or the whole roof gets torn off like that guy's roof in Chicago? I think of him lying there, abruptly exposed to the elements in his jammies. I fantasize that the whole thing is going to happen all over again, with me playing a starring role, and that after I've been blown away and dashed to pieces in the woods, someone in the media will come up with a cute headline like "Fernfield Female Flips Her Lid."

I get dressed and go into the living room. The sky, so clear last night, has turned the angry colour of dishwater streaked with grey scum. The trees behind the pond are grey in the early morning light. Everything is grey and brown like some Dutch master's etching in the Rijksmuseum in Amsterdam.

Whitecaps are whipping across the pond's surface as if it's the Atlantic Ocean. The black walnut is getting pummelled from its right side and leaning heavily to the left, branches flailing around like palm fronds in a hurricane. Twigs keep flying around, hitting the living room window. A length of split rail lifts itself in the air then drops to the ground noiselessly, because the roaring wind drowns out every other sound. An empty brown plastic garbage bin is rolling crazily around the lawn.

The snow starts as I boil the kettle for tea, muttering thanks to the gods that the power hasn't gone off. Great white sheets, the kind of snow I've never seen before, appear from nowhere and start whizzing horizontally across the grass outside. The sheets swoop close to the ground, then gust up again like sand in a desert storm, twirling around and around down to the pond. Then they abruptly spring up into the air again in great explosions of powder. The early snowstorm back in September seems silly, wimpish, now, nothing more than a caricature of winter with its orderly flakes tumbling so prettily to the ground. That storm wasn't real life. This one is. Nasty, brutish and un-doubtedly not about to be short, by the look of it. The sheets of snow keep getting thicker, the gusts more forceful, the roaring of the wind louder. The pond and trees dissolve into a swirling mass of white, like some northern version of the Nefud Desert in Lawrence of Arabia. I fantasize that Peter O'Toole might pass by on his camel at any moment, ice encrusting those beguiling blue eyes instead of sand. He'll be mumbling through chattering teeth about Aqaba. Stoking the stove, I feel as humbled by the power of nature as he was in the movie and regret being snippy to Logbook Man.

He calls just before nine.

"You okay?" he asks anxiously. "Power still on?"

I tell him yes, I'm fine. I apologize for not taking his warning seriously and he says with a laugh that nothing is happening in Toronto yet apart from a bit of wind. And he wishes he was with me.

"So do I," I say.

"Stay warm, then," he says, his voice soft. "Take care."

After he hangs up, the electric clock in the kitchen makes an odd clicking noise. Once only. Yikes, does that mean the power has gone off? I flick a light switch on. Nothing happens. Yes, dammit, there's no electrical current now. That means the basement behemoth will no longer rumble into action when I run out of wood for the stove. And what about water? All I have is the stuff in the bathroom, and I never got around to cleaning the tub before I turned on the tap. Can I drink that water even though there's a rim of grime around the tub? I try to call Ann again. The phone doesn't seem to be working. I feel a bit scared now. My heart sinking, I realize that there are no batteries for the radio and precisely three thin decorator candles in a drawer of the kitchen cupboards, one already half used. It's not exactly the way a Boy Scout would behave.

Should I battle the blowing snow and trudge up the driveway to the road? I could perhaps flag down a passing car and find out what's going on. News travels fast in Fernfield, especially where the weather is concerned. Farmers are always stopping their pickups in the middle of roads up here, nonchalantly holding up drivers behind them as they exchange information about weather conditions. "Dry for the next twenty-four hours, Joe," one calls out. "Yep, takin' off the soybeans today," is the satisfied response. Then they chuckle, share a joke about something or other and eventually move on. And now, with this storm, any one of these friendly guys who always wave when they go by is bound to know how long the power failure is expected to last, and if it's widespread, or simply that a tree has fallen locally and knocked the power out to houses on the concession roads in the area.

But then I chide myself for being ridiculous. What a twerp, what a total greenhorn you are. The road at the front of the house will be closed. So will the road down to the lake. And the highway that runs alongside the lake. In fact, every damn road from here to the farthest reaches of the province is probably closed by now. No one, not even farmers in big four-wheel-drive pickups, would be dumb enough to venture out in weather like this.

I am alone, isolated in the country during the storm of the century. And I will just have to sit it out.

The wind roars all day. The snow keeps flying around, splatting against the windows and building up around the sides of the house. It becomes boring after a while. I need something to do. Venturing outside isn't an option, not with the snowshoes buried under massive drifts outside the back door. And in this non-stop wind, my face will flash freeze quicker than a bag of peas. I keep feeding the woodstove with Roman's logs. The living room stays fairly warm and it's not difficult to heat up the soup left over from last night on the stove's grey enamel top. So far, so good. Spooning up the hot liquid at the dining table, there's nothing for it but to read a book. I start a paperback picked up at fundraising sale held by the local arts centre. It's about a woman who bought a ramshackle olive farm in the south of France. But she's irritating, this pampered Ms. Prissy. She keeps whining about an unexpected frost knocking out her precious olives.

In the late afternoon, the light evaporating, I'm still reading the book on the sofa and it's starting to get chilly. So I go into the garage bedroom for another sweater and skip smartly back beside the stove again. Yikes. Without the electric baseboard heaters going, it's like a walk in freezer in there. Yet the attic bedrooms prove to be even worse. Ribbons of snow have dribbled in under a couple of the sash windows on the west side, right where I saw the cracks in the fall. And there's a heck of a draft blowing in too. I shiver. In fact my thoughts about gold rush prospectors lying frozen in their beds weren't too short of the mark. It's as cold as an unheated Yukon log cabin in the attic right now. The only bearable place in the house for the night is clearly going to be by the woodstove.

I haul a single mattress down the stairs, find some blankets, light a candle, read more about the olive farm woman. She keeps complaining about the climate in the south of France. She's boring. She should get a grip. She should try Canada. I slam the book shut, irritated by her musings. The three cats cuddle up beside me on the mattress. We don't sleep well. The wind is relentless, roaring non-stop throughout the night and I keep jerking them and myself awake, obsessed that the stove might have gone out. There's a frightening bang on the roof sometime in the early hours and I shut my eyes tight, scared that a branch has punched a hole in the roof. But when I summon the bravery to look up, the ceiling above us is still intact, just creaking and groaning. And the windows continue to rattle. A thundering snowplow goes by on the road as dawn nears. It sounds like a steam-powered train, all clanks and bangs and flashing lights as it barges through the deep drifts. I wait, heart in my mouth, scared to get up, wondering about what is going to happen next. What if the pipes in the basement freeze? Or the roof blows off?

Yet it doesn't happen. Nothing happens. The pipes survive. So does the roof. So do I. The storm roars away to torment folks in the Maritimes and by 9 a.m., the power is back on. The phone miraculously works again. The sun is even shining. The wind subsides. And the snow, massive mountains of the stuff, is piled up against the glass of the living room window, looking so white it's blinding. I squint as I fold up the blankets and haul the mattress back upstairs. Yet the brightness after the gloom of yesterday is exhilarating. It's the best thing about Canadian winters, this brightness, so uplifting to the spirit after a storm. No longer cowed, I'm even jubilant, eager to go outside and check out what's happened. The plow clanks noisily by along the road again, flashing a red light through the spruce trees as I get dressed in parka and boots. A great whomp of the white stuff falls into the front hall when I open the door. There's an incredible amount of digging to be done, that's clear, yet the big green plastic scoop that Logbook Man insisted on buying a few weeks ago is nowhere to be found. I sink into a drift up to my hips trying to find it. As I scrabble around, mitts and boots fill up with snow which promptly melts, freezing my fingers and toes. Then after the scoop is finally found near the back door, I have to retreat into the house again to don Logbook Man's gloves and boots and warm up by the stove, because I can't stop shivering and my extremities are turning numb and blue. What are the symptoms of frostbite? I don't even know. So ignorant about survival in the Canadian wilderness, that's me. What a soft life I have led, ensconced in the cosy confines of the city. I make myself go outside again even though it's awkward moving around in Logbook Man's too-big boots and I'm still feeling very cold, because I simply have to do some cleaning out. I scoop and scoop. The snow piles up each side of a path I cut to the road. The house starts to look like Dr. Zhivago's cottage in the Urals, with just the top storey and roof poking out. And what tiring work it is. Breathless, I go inside to take a rest again and hear the phone ringing. It's Ann. She's spent the night at Don's with the kids.

"Do you want Don to come by and give you a blow?" she asks. This expression, new to my ears, sounds rather risqué.

"Yes, please," I say with eagerness. Whatever a blow is, I can't wait for this big muscular guy with the booming voice to come over and deliver it, I'm so exhausted from digging myself.

I stagger up to the road to wait for Don. The snowplow has cut a path through the blowing drifts, but there are such mountains of white on either side that it's hard to see where the road begins and ends. It looks dangerous. I'm glad I don't need to drive anywhere. And there are no tracks of any vehicles going through the snow yet, apart from the giant treads pressed in by the plow. No one else is clearly venturing out either. Don eventually comes. There's a welcome chug chugging noise and his old green tractor appears between two dark green spruce on the other side of the road, a great spray of snow like a fountain leaping into the sky in front of him. He's been cleaning Ann's driveway. Now it's my turn.

He does the job surprisingly quickly, cutting a wide swath all the way down the driveway, like a knife cutting through a white angel food cake. It looks impressive. I offer him coffee, but he laughs and shakes his head. Other people need blow jobs too. He's going to be busy all day. He heads off along the road as the snowplow rumbles into view again.

Logbook Man makes it in just before dark, patches of white clinging to the front of his little car which has somehow managed to nose its way through the drifts. He marvels at the cleaned-out driveway.

"Wow. This is great," he says with a whoop. "I expected to have to dig and dig all night. Who did this?"

"Don. He came by this morning and gave me a blow."

He laughs and raises his eyebrows.

"That sounds funny," he says.

"I know, but it's what you say up here," I say, laughing myself, so happy to see him. "It's the lingo. Rough drive?"

"On the roads around here, yeah," he says. "But the storm completely missed Toronto. Went north of us. You watched the TV news, I guess?"

"Nope," I say smugly. "I couldn't. The power was out."

The following day, we discover that the wind brought a visitor. Logbook Man hears a mewling sound when he goes outside to get more wood and there's a black cat perched on the logs under the eaves. It is coughing and painfully thin, the fur on its back matted together in a lump as if it's carrying a backpack. We have no idea how the cat got there, although a trail of paw prints goes towards the barn.

The cat, a young male, is starving. We bring it indoors, provide some food and a litter pan in the basement. As he holds the protesting cat down, I administer a haircut, removing the entire backpack of fur so that this newcomer winds up looking like some big, and very ugly, black rat. And like Sparky, Blackie settles in quickly. Within a week, there's another box seat positioned by the woodstove. Four cats now. And the winter proper has only just started. As I clean out their litterboxes, I wonder: what will January bring?

Eleven

Christmas nears. I discover distinct advantages to living out in the boonies. There are no crowds of shoppers out here. No homeless men in Santa hats cadging contributions outside the liquor store. And I don't hear even once the *parum-pum-pum* of that awful little kid with the drum. As the TV stays permanently in the off position (at least when Logbook Man is away in the city) the celebrities grinning like morons beside fake Christmas trees can be skipped too. It feels liberating to be cut off, to escape the enormous invisible bubble that descends over almost the entire world at the time now known euphemistically as "the holidays." The bubble traps everyone inside in a complicated tangle of tinsel, tension, sentimentality and guilt, but by an accident of fate, a tear in its side has provided me with a means to crawl out. How wonderful it is. I am walking on air, nonchalant for the first time ever about this anxiety-inducing time of year.

Yet trouble looms. Mum likes Christmas. She always has. She gets weepy over carol singers from Kings College, Cambridge on the TV and will expect some kind of get-together. So I organize one, feeling quite sanguine about the prospect this time. And perhaps because the members of our fractured little family are enchanted by the idea of a fairy-tale "country Christmas," or simply because I am more relaxed myself, this celebration proves more successful than such gatherings have been in years. There are no arguments. No door-slamming incidents. No resentments raised over the turkey and mashed potatoes. Although Mum has to sleep downstairs in the old part of the house right next to the suspicious holes in the wall—she's become too frail to climb the attic stairs—she pronounces herself "snug as a bug in a rug." Then excitedly hoping that we all get snowed in, she falls asleep and is snoring in minutes. On Christmas Eve snow does fall again, but gently this time, making the house and everything around it look impossibly lovely, like some Currier and Ives card of bygone days. I bake passable mince pies. Brothers-in-law don't roll their eyes when I put on a CD of Bach's Christmas Oratorio. Strapped into snow-shoes for the first time in her life and looking younger than her seventy-six years, Mum stamps out a careful path around the snow-covered lawn, giggling all the way, falling over only once and exclaiming that she'll simply have to send a picture of this to her friend Kay back in England. We all listen to Alan Maitland reading "The Shepherd" on CBC radio.

And we go to church.

"Church?" Logbook Man almost chokes on a mince pie at the prospect. "You want to go to church?"

Brother-in-law Number One shakes his head in amazement too. They are scanning the *Holiday TV Guide*, seeing if there is anything other than movies featuring Jimmy Stewart to watch.

"Yes, why not?" I say jubilantly, filled with a rare burst of bonhomie about the season of good cheer. "We can see the lights in Fernfield on the way in, sing some carols, give thanks for our good fortune. It will be...." I pause, groping for the right word "...spiritually uplifting."

Brother-in-Law Number Two, nibbling on a tortilla chip, puts his hands up and backs towards the fridge.

"No, no, not me. Please," he begs, as if he's about to be frogmarched off to the Inquisition. He opens the fridge door, takes another beer out. "Haven't been inside a church in years," he says pulling off the bottle cap. "God and I had a permanent falling out long ago."

We leave the heathens behind. Only three of us pile into the old Toyota bundled up in parkas and scarves, Mum squeaking out "Hark the Herald Angels Sing" from the back seat. She peers with excitement out of the window at the white fields as the car heads into Fernfield. Above us, the deep purple sky looks huge, the moon bright. Ribbons of stars twinkle obligingly. I drive, turning the heater up full blast. There are no complaints about cold feet.

And if other curmudgeons about Christmas lurk in Fernfield, they've all been locked away for the night. The whole town looks as if it has embraced the holiday spirit with gusto. Outside just about every house there are lights. Lights hanging from eavestroughing, lights draped over shrubs, lights wound around and around trees, lights encircling doorways. Lights in blue, red, green, golden yellow and white. Big lights, small lights, icicle lights in little crooked lines, great big spotlights. The latter illuminate massive inflated Santas who compete for attention on snowy lawns with cut-out reindeer and Stars of Bethlehem hung wonkily from flag poles. The orgy of light is almost blinding. The hydro bill will be huge, I think.

The Presbyterian church, our destination because it is one of the few holding a midnight service, stands on a hill above the town. It looks a forbidding place in the daytime—Scottish, built of local grey stone, with a graveyard at the back. Yet this night its big stained glass window shines a warm welcome through the darkness. The light reflects on the snow-covered pavement in soft patches of blue, red and yellow, and illuminates our eager faces as, with other church-goers, we scrunch up the hill in our boots, arms linked together, pleased to be out like this on Christmas Eve.

There is a surprise at the end of the service. The minister, a youngish man with ginger hair and freckles and a voice that sounds raspy from too much preaching, announces that he has a treat in store for the faithful gathered below him in the pews.

"Ladies and gentlemen, we're delighted to bring you the Fernfield Four," he says dramatically, twirling around like a magician in his white cassock and waving an arm at a black curtain on one side of the church.

Four stocky men with barrel chests bound out. The shortest, barely reaching the height of the tall altar, is Gordie McTavish. He's wearing a grey tuxedo with satin lapels. A pale pink frilly dress shirt peeps out from under the jacket and his black patent shoes shine under the altar lights. The other three are garbed in the same uniform. This quartet from the era of Norman Rockwell grin and bow at the congregation, then take deep breaths and launch into a bob-a-dee-doo-dah-bob-bob-bob version of "Oh Come All Ye Faithful."

I haven't seen Gordie since buying the house. He's still wearing his ill-fitting red wig and there remains something rather touching and vulnerable about him. His role is to trill the high notes, which is clearly an effort. Beads of sweat stand out on his shiny forehead, the falsetto comes dangerously close to cracking. Yet Big Brenda down at the LumberMart wasn't very generous. Although barbershop singing seems an odd choice for a Scottish church on Christmas Eve, Gordie is good. A more than competent performer.

I slip a twenty-dollar bill into the collection plate.

Logbook Man's Christmas gift to me is flannel sheets—king-sized, thick and dark green, along with a striped Hudson's Bay blanket. I buy him a bread machine. All three are indispensable accoutrements for anyone foolish enough to swap the comforts of the city for a ramshackle house in rural Canada in wintertime. By January, the snow has settled into a steady pattern. A few centimetres, sometimes more, fall every few days. The wind blows too, often hard, either from the west or north. There is no repeat performance of November's nightmare, yet it's cold. And bleak as a Dickens tale. The drifts pile up. It takes hours to dig out. The house never feels warm enough, even with the woodstove and the basement behemoth going non-stop. The problem is the old Victorian part. How charming the grey clapboard looked from the outside in July with the white gingerbread trim—yet how deceptive. The interior lacks sufficient insulation. Even worse, it leaks like a sieve. The gaps under the windows where the snow came in are now plugged with torn-up strips of fabric, but this doesn't help much. Drafts of chilly air keep finding their way in through holes in the particleboard and the electrical outlets. These entry points are so numerous that drapes I sew and hang up in front of the windows—and then keep permanently drawn in an attempt to thwart the cold air—billow out into the room when the wind blows.

In the damp garage bedroom, which has no basement, we spend long mornings lying snuggled in the fleecy flannel, listening to the bread machine in the kitchen go through the conniptions required to create "Basic Wholewheat Number One." We love the sound it makes, rather like a train chuntering along, with a big whomp in mid-cycle. And we marvel at the perfect loaves that come out of its tall aluminum container with absolutely no effort on our part. Back in the city, I sneered at bread machines with the condescension of all urbanites who have every possible convenience, including good fresh bread, at their fingertips, yet out in the country our mechanical kitchen magician is proving infinitely more useful than a computer.

"The person who invented this thing should be awarded the Nobel Peace Prize," declares Logbook Man, biting into a slice of fresh raisin bread he's just made, on a particularly dreary morning. "What's more peaceful than a good loaf of bread?"

What indeed? Our loaves are a lifesaver, because trips to the supermarket in Fernfield have become like an Arctic expedition now. The driveway is constantly plugging up with snow. I don't want to keep asking Don for a blow job, so we have no choice but to dig the stuff out. Endlessly. And once the digging's done, the car windows need to be scraped off and the end of the driveway cleared out all over again because the snowplow has just clanked by. In any case, supermarket bread, plastic-wrapped, pappy and tasteless, palls after the caraway rye and French baguettes of our urban existence. It's simpler and tastier to just stay home and bake bread ourselves.

So like squirrels we hibernate through January. And the cats join us— four of them now—hogging the best part of the bed and squabbling over territory or lying in their box seats by the stove. Ours is a quiet sedentary household and enforced idleness inevitably encourages reflection. It also— if you aren't too old to think optimistically about the future—prompts an orgy of planning. We come to two decisions during those long sleepy days. First, we need a snowblower. Second, it's time to stop dilly-dallying, bite the bullet and renovate. The project will be huge and expensive, that's becoming more and more obvious as the winter drifts by. Our faded Victorian lady demands more than a facelift. A total disembowelment, a gutting, a brand new interior is the only way to bring her back to life. Yet if we intend to stay in the country—and there's no going back now—we have no other choice.

Thus starts the Search, the most frustrating aspect of owning an old home anywhere in the world nowadays, city or country. Who can we find to take on this job? What will it cost? And given Big Brenda's discouraging revelations, is there anyone out there willing to say yes?

Ann drops by with homemade muffins, and supplies a few names. She reveals that she once lived in a picturesque old house in a nearby village with her husband before their kids were born. Yet she's now quite content with her less aesthetically pleasing but functional alternative.

"Old houses are often more trouble than they're worth," she says sagely, biting into her blueberry and banana. "We found that. You're better off to build a new one."

Well, yes—and no. Many people in the country follow that route, unsentimentally abandon the home that their family lived in for generations, and erect a new home beside it. There are plenty of old farmhouses attesting to this sloughing off of history around Fernfield. The rejects often stand forlornly beside the ugly upstarts, windows boarded up with plywood, back porches crumbling, red brick falling off. It's a sensible solution and usually made for financial reasons, yet the dismissal of the past makes me sad. Although we haven't had a long connection with our Victorian lady, I've grown attached to the face she presents to the world. After more than a hundred years braving the elements on this dusty gravel road, she's as enmeshed in the landscape as the fields and trees around her. She has to stay.

So we need a renovator. Bob's Home Services is our first try. A nervous man of about fifty with protruding ears and a face like crumpled brown paper, Bob works by himself. He has a tic in his right eye and talks all the time about winders.

"I do winders," he says. "Good winders. Quadruple glazed. Fit real good, my winders. Looks like you could use some new winders here."

He walks over to a sash window in the old part of the house and taps it with a nicotine-stained finger.

"Very old winders," he says, shaking his head. He utters the cough of a heavy smoker. "Useless winders these. You'll need all new winders."

"Yes, we know we need new er … windows," I say. "But we're looking for someone to take on the whole renovation, Bob. We want to completely redo the interior of the house, but keep it looking the same outside."

I smile. "Can you do that, do you think?"

Bob looks stubborn, lips set in a straight line. He peers in the downstairs rooms again and shakes his head. He taps the window ledge, clearly anxious for a smoke. The eye tic abruptly goes into overdrive, giving him a rather crazy look.

"I have the best winders. I can give you good winders. All kinds. And that's what you folks need. Good winders." He folds his arms defiantly in front of him, as if daring us to challenge his assessment of the situation.

Bob gets crossed off the list. The next candidate laughs. Out loud, right into the phone. "I know that house. No thanks," he says aggressively and hangs up. Two others don't respond to messages. Discouraged, I dig the car out and drive into Fernfield to visit on an outfit called Heavenly Home Makeovers. Perhaps a personal appeal, as opposed to simply making contact by phone, will persuade this company to show an interest in our project. A lumpy woman with bleached blond hair, who looks as if she could use a makeover herself, is sitting at a desk in the front office. She shakes her head, says to come back next year.

"We're fully booked," she snaps, hardly bothering to look up. She returns to painting her fingernails purple.

Two companies running ads in the Fernfield Express make appointments to view the house. Yet on the designated days, their representatives don't show up.

We have one last resort: Big Brenda.

"Well now, I thought you folks might be having a few problems, eh?" she says, her dark eyes twinkling as she sizes us up again. "Ah, the difficulties of fixing up old houses. But it sure is good for us." She lets out a bellow of laughter. "Keeps us in business, eh?"

She slaps her bum.

The LumberMart is quiet, post-Christmas. Big Brenda's bellow echoes around the cavernous warehouse of a building. A woman in a blue parka with embroidered geese on the back is poking around in a box of rusty paint cans marked "40 percent off." Leaning on the counter at the back, three middle-aged men mull over the high price of pine planking with mournful faces.

"Ridiculous," says one, shaking his head. "I mean it's just ridiculous, Dalton. How come it's cheaper for you guys to bring the stuff in from Brazil than to get it from B.C.?"

"Dunno," says a man with a brush cut standing behind the counter. He's wearing the same kind of red T-shirt as Brenda and keeps looking at his watch as if he's getting bored with the conversation and counting the minutes till he can knock off for lunch. "That's just the way it is, guys. Sorry, but it's globalization, I guess. We don't have no choice in the matter."

The other two look at one another and shake their heads in unison, like spectators at a tennis match.

Brenda, up on her raised dais, frowns at the mention of the word globalization and stares sharply down at the trio, as if she doesn't like this kind of talk. I realize that she isn't simply an employee of the LumberMart. She owns the place. Turning back to us, she rummages around by the cash desk, pulling out a couple of business cards. Then she hands them down from the dais.

One is for the company with the purple-clawed receptionist. And I've already received a negative response from the other one.

"Nope, we've tried both of those," I say, sighing. "They're not interested."

She thinks for a few moments, finger on her lip, one hand resting on a plump buttock. She has surprisingly elegant fingernails, painted the same red as her T-shirt. I wonder if all the women in Fernfield have a fetish about manicured nails.

"Well then," she says, suddenly beaming. "I think you're just going to have to get hold of Stoob."

"Who?" says Logbook Man.

"Stoob." She clasps her hands together as if the path to enlightenment has hit her like a thunderclap. "Yes, Stoob. Stoob would be perfect for you guys. His name's Solly Steubenhoven really, but everyone around here calls him Stoob. He's a guy who likes old houses, eh? Regards it as a challenge fixing them up, restoring them to how they looked before. Only takes on jobs he likes."

She taps her nose now.

"Yes, Stoob."

Seemingly immensely satisfied with this conclusion, she pulls out a memo pad with the words "LumberMart: Build with us" printed in red on the top, and scribbles a number on the pad.

"Stoob doesn't have a business card, or at least I don't seem to have one here," she says, rummaging around again beside the cash desk, chuckling to herself. "I don't think Stoob's big on business cards. Doesn't need them, I guess."

She tears off the sheet of paper and pushes it at Logbook Man.

"You call Stoob," she urges. "He's the one. And when ya need stuff for the reno…" her big laugh echoes again around the store "…come and buy from us, eh? I'll give ya a good price."

"Sure," he says. "And thanks."

As we push open the plate glass door, her voice rings out again through the building.

"Stoob'll do good for ya. Real good. I know he will. He's a meticulous builder, ya know. He's a Mennonite."

There are many Mennonites living in the area around Fernfield. Some have been a fixture for more than two centuries. The first wave, I learn from a local library book, were Swiss, who came to Canada in covered wagons from Pennsylvania following the U.S. War of Independence. Others migrated northwards across the Niagara River at the beginning of the nineteenth century. Then it was the turn of Ukrainian Mennonites to stake a claim for the cheap, fertile farmland on offer, and to build new lives in a climate similar to their own. Now the descendants of these polyglot settlers have split up into more than twenty groups, and most Mennonites, the book says, don't look or behave differently from anyone else. They wear the same clothes, drive the same cars, have the same kinds of houses, send their children to the same schools and work at the same jobs.

Even so, the Old Order Mennonites continue to stand out. We often see them. Their black buggies hug the sides of rural roads, pulled by horses that incline their heads nervously when ten-wheelers roar by. The buggies sometimes stop at the roadside, their occupants sitting solemnly, always garbed in black, with bunches of gladioli in glass jam jars for sale on a bench in front of them. Men on bicycles in white shirts and dark caps, old-fashioned suspenders holding their trousers up, cycle around the area too. They make us feel like weaklings, these tough young males, for they seem to go from farm to farm on their bikes in all kinds of weather, even snow.

Yet the most visible evidence of Mennonites are the women. Many shop, I'm surprised to discover, at the Fernfield supermarket: lumpy pale-faced matrons for the most part, hair concealed under lace caps secured to their heads with big bobby pins. And in an age where most females wear pants or close-fitting skirts, their shapeless Plain Jane dresses in pale blue or pink tied with bows at the back and falling past their knees can't help but be noticed. Nor can Mennonite children, who never scream around the supermarket or grab things off shelves as other kids do. Instead, they obediently trail around after their mothers. Most of them are very blond, with close-cut hair, and they wear subdued, wistful expressions, as if bewildered by the bright commercial world that they aren't permitted to be part of.

A small, uncharitable part of me has noted that these plainly garbed women aren't quite the purist housewives celebrated in mythology about Mennonites. Noticeably absent from their shopping carts are the big bags of flour, whole cabbages and other cues that wholesome meals are being cooked from scratch in their homes. Indeed they seem to buy less flour than I do, with the bread magician in the kitchen needing constant refuelling. Instead, these Mennonite mothers, like modern mothers everywhere, load up on plastic-wrapped Wonder Bread, potato chips, pre-made cakes, big cheap cartons of ice cream and cans of Coke. I wonder if any of them bother to bake their much-vaunted shoo-fly pie.

We get a commitment by telephone from Solly Steubenhoven that he will drop in, and curiosity sets in. I feel the vague apprehension that all outsiders have about ultra-conservative religions that they can't quite fathom. Is this Stoob an Old Order Mennonite? If he agrees to take on the job of renovating our house, how will it proceed? I picture him showing up in a black buggy with a squad of muscular young men in suspenders in buggies following on behind. Will this team then leap out and get the whole job done in only a few days, just as Mennonites famously do whenever one of their number wants a new barn?

Whatever is ahead, it's exciting. I count the days before he comes.

Stoob arrives in an old beige truck like Harlan's. He's a slim middle-aged man, quiet-spoken, wearing blue jeans and an enormous puffy blue parka that makes him look like a lampshade. He sloughs off the parka and hangs it up in the entrance hall without waiting to be asked, as if he's been here before. His face looks rather cherubic—unlined, the cheeks pink, lips pursed in a sort of rosebud. Dark curly hair which shows no signs of thinning around the temples frames this visage. We shake hands, the lips crease into a sort of smile, and when I confess that I wondered if he was going to show up in a buggy, he raises an eyebrow.

"Whatever gave you that idea?" he asks, a flicker of annoyance registering on his face as Logbook Man shoots me a reproachful look. "There's all kinds of Mennonites, you know. I'm not Old Order."

I blush at the tactless stereotyping, but our potential renovator doesn't notice. He quickly gets down to business, revealing that he's already intimately acquainted with this house because he's been friends for years with the previous owners. In fact, Stoob built the long high-ceilinged living room—the only comfortable place in the entire house—that we're sitting in.

"The hardwood floors still look good, don't they?" he says, kneeling on the floor by the dining room table to stroke the wood with the pride of a craftsman. He smiles to himself and stands up again. "They were one heck of a job to install, you know. That's the problem with old houses, getting everything to fit. But they do look good."

We tour the rest of the house and the smile fades.

"Gee, this place is in rough shape now," he says, black hair bouncing up and down as we climb the attic stairs. "I hope you folks realize that you'll have to gut the whole thing. There's nothing here worth saving."

He takes in the avocado walls and ceiling, the dented particleboard, the wads of cloth stuffed under the old sash windows. Down in the basement, he taps the old rumbling furnace and shakes his head again.

"Heap of junk," he decides.

"Well, do you think it can be done?" I ask.

"Um...." The response is doubtful. "Sure, any house can always be renovated. I can do it for you, but...."

"And you'd be able to keep the outside looking as it does now?" I interrupt eagerly, seizing on this hint of an affirmation like a dog grabbing a bone.

"Yes, probably," he says. "But it's going to cost you a bundle, you know."

"Yes, yes, I know that. But you're willing...?"

"Sure. I can give you an estimate, if you'd like one."

That settles things, I think. Logbook Man looks quizzical, then terrified.

Stoob returns twice, armed with a measuring tape and a clipboard. He goes around the entire house, inside and outside, taking notes, dismissing the suggestion of an architect to draw up plans. Architects just get in the way, he says. He hates having to work with "those people." With an old house like this, we'll be better off without anyone around meddling. He waves off offers of coffee.

A week later, he places a single typewritten sheet of paper on the dining table. The numbers on the sheet make us gasp.

"Could be more, could be less," he says in his soft voice, running a finger down the numbers, oblivious to the look of consternation that passes between Logbook Man and me. "It's impossible to tell at this stage. And I wouldn't be able to start till spring, of course."

"When in spring?" I ask weakly.

"Yeah, it would be good to know so we can, er . . . make plans," says Logbook Man frowning, his mind clearly on the bank.

"Don't know. Can't say," Stoob gives an offhand shrug, the gesture of all people in the business of renovating houses. He's not going commit himself. He's too canny for that. He stares out of the window at the split rail fence, now almost completely obscured by snow. "Nice view you folks have here," he says absently, "I've always loved this view."

He gets up to leave.

"Weather up here could foul things up," he concludes. "We could have storms in May. Often do here. And I have other jobs pending. Lots of people coming out to the country from the city now like you, wanting to have these old places restored. I'll leave the estimate, shall I? You can think about whether or not you want to go ahead...."

Logbook Man and I stare at the figures, then at each other. It's now or never. We both know that. He shoots me the twisty little smile again, the smile I remember from the day at pond. The smile that always means yes.

"No, we don't need to think," I say. "We'll do it."

We gulp in unison.

The Search is finally over. Now the Wait begins.

Twelve

The weather changes in February. It gets much colder. The whole of northeastern North America is gripped by a deep freeze. Logbook Man, raised in Montreal, accustomed to bone-cracking winters, hates this development. He keeps saying he wishes he'd been born in Texas, even though everyone carries guns down there. He's becoming soft with age like a bag of potatoes kept too long in the cupboard, I think. But I don't say so. One morning, he tiptoes into the living room in his jammies to check the thermometer outside the back door. Minus thirty-two degrees Celsius. A low whistle follows. "That's inhuman," he says, coming back to bed. Cold feet tentatively approach my back. "There's no way I'm getting up to do anything today."

Minutes later, the phone rings. It's the production woman at his art studio. She's young and ambitious, already at work on this icy day even though it's barely 7.30 a.m. Does he want a work assignment in the city lasting about six weeks? Does he ever. Suddenly imbued with uncharacteristic eagerness to work himself, Logbook Man leaps out of bed like a teenager off on a hot date. He dresses in a flash, pulls on parka and boots over the pyjamas and hurries outside to check if he plugged in his car last night. Luckily, he did.

"What's the work? Something exciting?" I ask, knotting my bathrobe, yawning over the teakettle. I peer out at the sun through the kitchen window. It's a fingertip of brilliant scarlet, only just starting to peep over the horizon.

"Nah, boring stuff, we're redoing the Canadian labels for an American office supplies company. The usual," he says, grabbing a cup of tea.

"Why the big hurry to leave then?" I say, mildly miffed by his haste.

He ducks the question, heads for the shower. Barely ten minutes later, poised by the back door with the big black bag he carries his computer hard drive in slung over his shoulder, he stops only to catch his breath.

"Sorry," he says. "Sorry I have to leave you like this."

Yet he doesn't look sorry. Not in the least. He's grinning all over his face.

"I'm just so happy…" he says, peering at the thermometer again. "I'm just so happy to be getting out of this fucking place."

His car glints in the early morning sun at the end of the driveway. It sputters and jerks, protesting at being prodded into action during such bitter cold. Then off he goes down our frozen road, a puff of white exhaust smoke rising in his wake. The car disappears around a bend and Logbook Man is gone.

I am alone again, in the country.

Yet I don't mind. Solitude suits writers and extreme weather has its advantages. January was grey as a Norway rat and windy. Now, in tandem with the plummeting temperatures, the snow has stopped and there's not even a breeze. The days are bright. Wonderfully bright. With the sun's rays bouncing off the snow and into the living room, everything is bathed for a few hours a day in glorious sunshine. It feels warm indoors, in spite of the sub-zero temperatures outside. I don't need a sweater. The cats seize on patches of the sun on the floor and armchairs. They guard them jealously, rolling on their backs, purring. How cats do love sun. They should all live down south. Not so indoor plants. I move my precious amaryllis flowers, lifesavers of Canadian winters, to the back wall of the living room fretting that their spectacular trumpets of scarlet and pink will wither like burst balloons in this abrupt onslaught of brilliant light. The sky is so blue. Deep blue and bottomless. It reminds me of the Bahamas, where I spent my impressionable teenage years. I have never forgotten the blue down there. So intense, so enveloping, you feel yourself getting swallowed up in it. But why is the sky at its bluest in Canada when the temperature dips so low? The scientific explanations are never wholly satisfactory. If cold weather makes the sky blue, it seems contradictory for the same thing to happen near the Equator.

A writing assignment sits in a folder on my desk. It has been there since right after Christmas. More Employees of the Month slated for their moment of glory in the telecommunications company's staff magazine. I fire up the computer, dispatch the job quickly, go outside, strap on snowshoes. The cold air feels energizing. Medical mavens nag in the media that taking great gulps of air during extreme cold is dangerous, particularly at my age, because it can lead to heart seizures. Yet who cares if I drop down dead on this amazing morning? What a wonderful way to go. I defy the doctors of doom, breathe in deeply, revel in the kettles of steam that come out of my mouth. I am eager for exercise for the first time in weeks. If you're bundled up warmly and nimble on your feet, nothing beats a walk on the coldest days of the year in Canada. The snow is so crisp underfoot. The air sharpens the senses, bringing everything into focus. It is how winter should be.

The snowshoes sink into the deep drifts. It's like walking on pillows. Whopping great feathery pillows. Aided by these cradles, I stride right over the split rail fence feeling like some powerful giant. I'm off to the woods. Above, the sky looks as if it has been scratched all over with skates. The source of the scratching lies to the southeast over a hundred kilometres away. Huge numbers of aircraft take off every morning from the airport in Toronto, yet usually too much humidity and pollution clutters the atmosphere for their vapour streams to be visible. Today, however, the plumes of white are sharply defined against the Arctic blue. I wonder vaguely if Dan the deer hunter is up there, steering a silver cigar tube in the direction of Beijing. I feel no envy for my pilot neighbour as the aircraft rises higher and higher, hurtling westward, sending a long scratch out across the sky in its wake. On a marvellous morning like this I'd much rather be down here.

Animal tracks criss-cross the snow. Raccoons have been out when the weather was milder, seeking water at the pond. Their footprints look like tiny human hands. Some other unidentifiable smaller animal, a weasel or a marten maybe, has left its mark too around the pond's silver perimeter and there are the sharp, knife-like indentations of wild turkeys. I'm dying to see these clumsy birds roaming free on my land, not naked and trussed up ready for Thanksgiving dinner. There are thousands of wild turkeys again in Ontario, thanks to a government restocking program, yet thus far they've been as elusive here as the extinct passenger pigeon.

The turkeys' feathers are long and elegant, in shades of nutty brown, tan and cream. I've picked up a few in the woods. They hark back to earlier times, prompting thoughts of Samuel Pepys dipping a quill pen into an inkwell and leaning over some heavy carved Elizabethan desk of dark oak to scratch in his diary. I want to do the same thing—write trenchant words with a pen made from one of these feathers. Such an instrument would surely provoke more thoughtful scribblings than a computer. I resolve to make myself a pen by the end of the winter.

Although the turkeys are in hiding, not so the rabbits. I've watched them out of the window. Now a grey jackrabbit as big as a small dog hops into view, then turns tail and hurries back into the safety of a spruce tree's over-hanging boughs after hearing the scrunch of my snowshoes. And I don't spot a single groundhog coming out a burrow to see its shadow, so clearly the end of winter is still a long way off. None of these canny rodents is foolish enough to venture out in such intense cold. Yet a trail like a looping skein of wool on the surface of the snow runs from a purple coneflower seedhead to the tip of a ribbon grass leaf, which gleams gold in the sun. Then another big loop goes back to the coneflower again. Clearly field mice are out questing

MIDDLE-AGED SPREAD 🐾 173

for food, although their actions seem foolishly brave. Why don't the dumb little critters stay protected under the thick blanket of snow like the ground-hogs? Some rodents are winter savvy but not these. It would surely be less chilly for them to scurry around beneath the white stuff instead of making trails on top.

In the woods, deer have sunk deep into the drifts, leaving hoof prints as big as those of cows. And there are blood stains along the trail. Perhaps a stray cat has been pursued by a predator and finally eaten. With dismay, I detect traces of cat-like greyish fur in a pile of coyote poop. The coyotes howl habitually at night—their noise is bloodcurdling—and cats have a rough time in the country, quickly using up their nine lives, unwanted by anyone except for catching mice in barns.

Extending the trail, I work up a sweat with the loppers and a pruning saw. Branches keep snapping like pistol shots in the cold air. The debris piles up in satisfying heaps. The American gardening writer Stan Yarbrow once opined that "...slashing through another evergreen, I felt the hot-knife-through-butter sensation that is one of chainsawing's guilty pleasures." I experience the same thrill now. As sawdust from the poplar saplings trickles into the snow under my tools, it feels exciting to be wielding power over nature. This trail now extends halfway around the property. Our identity is being im-printed on the land. Let the environmentalists tut-tut all they want. The slash-ing and cutting, getting rid of all the excess vegetation, is sheer delight.

Yet outdoor pursuits inevitably pall in the winter air. Once the weak win-ter sun starts descending, so does the mercury in the thermometer, often with the speed of a sprinter. Wet with perspiration and exhausted, I shiver back up the hill, noting that no comforting spiral of smoke is rising now from the chimney above the house. The woodstove has nearly gone out.

I toss another log in the firebox to fire it up again and on impulse clean off the car and head into Fernfield. Like Logbook Man, I'm suddenly gripped by an urge to get away—and to visit a store on the main street for some winter fuel of my own.

Fernfield is fat. It's undeniable. Overweight people outnumber those who fit descriptions like "lean" and "slim" in this country town. While farmers steering their monstrous machines around the soybean fields look trim and well-exercised for the most part, in Fernfield proper it's a hugely different story. The women waddle, if they walk at all. Yet mostly they don't seem to bother. The local citizenry do what citizens of small towns do across North America. They get in their cars and drive everywhere. The most popular destination in town is the drive-thru window at Tim Horton's. There's a non-stop traffic jam outside this establishment every day as cars and pickups wait in line, engines running, drivers tapping steering wheels, impatient for a fix of their sugar-laden double-double and donuts. In Fernfield, fat isn't a dirty word. It's the norm.

There's a palpable "who cares?" attitude to the whole issue of excess poundage out here, and it's rather comforting as I head into town late on this winter afternoon, with the sun almost down, in search of a fix myself. I have a sudden craving for chocolate, a great big slab stippled with almonds to savour solo on the sofa on this very cold night. So my destination is the second most popular place in Fernfield, a store on the main street called the Chocoholic. Back in Toronto, I'd have felt incredible guilt undertaking such a journey. I probably would have chickened out and not gone at all, because in cities, everyone is so obsessed with being thin. How, I wonder do, restauranteurs cope? "Yes, ma'am, we did use butter in the quiche. And whole eggs too. And cream. It's how quiches are made and if you don't like it, I suggest you shove off." Such a response must surely be tempting. Yet out here, there's no need to worry about urban hipsters nibbling their fat-free biscottis and looking on contemptuously as I waddle into the Chocoholic. I am overweight myself now, having piled on pounds in my late forties, yet that *avoirdupois* around my hips won't earn me a second glance. Being among the Fernfield fatties is liberating in middle age. In the country, you are what you are, and no one cares if you have a double dollop of ice cream on your apple pie.

The store has a few customers browsing around even though it's about to close. But then it's always busy at the Chocoholic. The place is a tasteful shrine to the virtues of the cocoa bean, painted in delicate hues of beige, apricot and, of course, chocolate brown. The wares are classy too. There's no cheap candy bar stuff on offer. Behind the glass counters sit rows of hand made chocolates with labels like Tempting Truffle, Sizzling Strawberry, Pecan Paradise and Chockfulla Cherries. And if tastebuds aren't activated by a see-through box of those, wrapped in a bow of beige satin, there's a cornucopia of temptations to choose from elsewhere in the store: chocolate mice, chocolate cows, chocolate dolphins, chocolate letters and numbers, cream-filled chocolate eggs, cats, dogs and horses fashioned from dark, milk and white chocolate, chocolate-dipped coconut clusters, splats of pecan toffee with blobs of chocolate melted into the centre. The selection seems endless.

Soft Muzak ripples through the store. My mouth waters. I'm hungry after all the exercise out in the woods with the loppers. The girl behind the counter, plump and pretty, wears a silky beige dress with a cream apron and has a name tag in chocolate-coloured type that says "Debbie." She is on the phone when I approach the counter. She's telling somebody that she has to pick up Ryan from daycare and that she's bringing home marshmallows. As I wait to be served, I wonder if the marshmallows are destined for Ryan and if he's plump like his mom. I suspect that he is. I picture him, a chubby little fellow in rompers with sticky fingers poking the soft white squares. She gets off the phone and beams, apologizing for keeping me waiting and insists that I try something called Peanut Perfection because she loves it herself and knows I will. She seems like such a happy person, this young woman whose size engenders frowns of disapproval nowadays and hints that she should go to Weight Watchers. As she hands over my sample, I think of a Jersey cow, round, sleek, golden. And very maternal. I wonder if the store's owner hired her because she looks so perfect for the job of selling chocolate. The proffered peanut toffee and chocolate concoction is disappointing. It sticks to my teeth and is far too sweet, but I buy some anyway because I don't want to disappoint Debbie. She carefully places my purchase in a bag along with some dark chocolate with almonds, the kind of confection that I prefer, and a sample of something else called Choco Rocko, "because you like nuts, ma'am." Beaming again, she hopes I'll drop by again soon. Heading home, I feel bathed in the warmth of this young woman. I'm glad I pushed guilt aside and went out to the Chocoholic.

The fire has gone out, dammit. I didn't stoke it up properly before going into Fernfield and now I have to put my boots on again and flounder around outside in the bitter cold in search of kindling. Not just any kindling, however. I am becoming an expert at the fine art of fire-lighting, picking and choosing wood with the discernment of an oenophile assessing fine wines. Birch twigs and bark are best by far to get a cold stove going. Pine, cedar and dogwood bits and pieces work after a fashion too, but only if they are very old and dry. Poplar, basswood and spruce? As bad as cheap candy bar chocolate. Then once the fire has caught, split lengths of dry maple—pinkish brown stripe running through the grain of the wood—are utter rapture, like nibbling on dark chocolate with almonds from the Chocoholic.

As the fire starts roaring again, I greedily eat chunks of my purchases, then make some tea. There is mail to be looked at. We are now getting our letters delivered to a box positioned at the top of the driveway. This convenience is the consequence of a chat Ann had with Marg, the apple-cheeked postmistress in the little village down the hill. Ann didn't want to drive down there anymore to pick up mail. Nor did we. And Marg capitulated. Two boxes positioned side by side on the road would be sufficient, she agreed, to warrant her helper doing a little detour in her car from the lake road to ours every weekday morning. I'm grateful to them both. It's a thrill every time I walk up the driveway to the box now, except there is never anything inside the box to read. Not now that everyone uses email.

A big envelope has come from Tim. It contains bumf about his development in Collingwood. "In case you change your mind, Sandra," a note attached to the folder says.

Shall I toss the whole package into the woodstove? How good to watch flames licking around the sides of this brochure through the little window in the stove's belly. How satisfying to witness at least a minuscule piece of Tim's greedy grabby world going up in smoke. But no, the shiny, plasticized coating is a deterrent. It might gum up the chimney.

I bury the envelope and its contents somewhere in the middle of a mountain of newspapers. Logbook Man mustn't see this brochure, not in his current mood of disenchantment with country living. Some day, when I get around to it, I'll haul the lot off to the dump. And I'll tell him about the brochure from Tim. But not now.

A person afflicted by cabin fever can find plenty of indoor pursuits to while away the winter hours if so inclined. The mail brings a course guide from the department of continuing education of a big college in a nearby town. The college has recently opened a branch in Fernfield. I browse through the pages, now sipping a bottle of wine I've opened, feeling the pleasurable warmth hit my stomach. I could enroll to make a stained glass mosaic trivet. Or hand-paint garden stones. Or produce a rustic birdhouse with the sign "Home Tweet Home" on the front. There is a even a course dedicated to messing around with liquid chocolate. Aha. Should I try that? "Students will fashion Easter bunnies for their loved ones, then pack them into cardboard boxes decorated with butterflies they paint on the boxes themselves," the brochure says. Hmm. It all sounds a trifle too precious for me. What about boning up on the art of wreath-making with spent grape vines then? And if I want to make a weekend of it there's even a dream exploration workshop on offer at a local bed and breakfast. Participants, the guide says, should show up with "a glue gun and a smile."

To do what exactly? Glue themselves to the bed so they can dream out the rest of the winter, smiling beatifically? The brochure doesn't say.

More wine seems infinitely preferable to any of these endeavours. I refill my glass, shove another maple log into the firebox and settle down on the sofa with a book about starting seeds. And then I feel rather sick. It's all that chocolate.

Thirteen

"Yes?" A little gnome with spectacles and a face like a walnut shell is peering shortsightedly at me through a half-open door.

"I'm your neighbour," I say brightly.

"I know who you are," he says.

Well, of course he knows. Old-timers like him know everything. It's the way country life works. The jungle drums beat fast along rural roads. Every inhabitant is observed, discussed, dissected with a toothcomb, chuckled about, sometimes regarded with contempt. Lives are an open book—as wide open as the rolling soybean fields. There's no such thing as keeping secrets in the country. If you're shagging your sister-in-law, old-timers will know about that tryst in her Honda parked off Concession Road 25 before you do. Drinking problem? Your preferred tipple and the number of bottles you purchase a week will be duly noted at the liquor store in town. You gamble? Watch out. Eagle eyes will spot your every move at the slots.

And if you're new and a bit exotic, i.e., from the city, so much the better. The gnome at the door of this trim white bungalow is clearly cognizant of a few facts about me already. I can tell that from his face.

It is another bright morning. And very cold. The icy road shines like an unrolled length of tinfoil. My head aches. I'd like to blame the piercing light but mostly it's the consequence of consuming too much wine accompanied by all that chocolate. I fell asleep on the sofa, exhausted from the slashing and lopping, the seed-starting book abandoned on the floor. Now my middle-aged body feels fragile as an amaryllis flower, as if the stalk propping it up is about to collapse. Yet like some fit climber on Everest, I have strapped crampon-like contraptions on to the bottom of my boots and ventured out again, onto a surface that's as slippery as a skating rink. I have decided to shake off the hangover by walking a kilometre or so down our road to meet this man. He has eggs for sale. Good free-range ones, I've been told. I'd like to get some. And I already know about him and his brothers, the eccentric Beattie Boys, because I've been listening to the jungle drums too. Ann has filled me in on the lives of these four reclusive men who happen to be our other closest neighbours.

The Beattie Boys are all bachelors. None ever married. They once farmed a property close to hers with their parents, but now they live in the trim white bungalow. People in Fernfield refer to them as "the Boys" because that's what rural single men are called, even the old ones. And these brothers are certainly old—but not as old as I expected. What's more apparent is how excruciatingly shy they are. The one who answers the door looks to be about sixty. He relaxes a little when I tell him I'd like some eggs. I am invited in to stand on the front door mat as he shuts the door carefully and says with the awkward giggle of someone much younger: "Better keep the cold out, eh?"

I identify myself. He nods as if I didn't need to do so. He knows my name. Probably my middle name too for that matter, and my date of birth and how often I take a bath. Country people know everything about each other. The living room where I stand waiting for my eggs is small, immaculate, modest, with net curtains at the windows. A ticking grandfather clock dominates the room and there's an old oak cabinet containing mismatched bone china tea cups. Two other men look up as I hover awkwardly by the door, while the man who let me in goes away into the kitchen. One lies on a brown corduroy La-Z-Boy, doing a crossword puzzle. The other is sitting on an old sofa eyeing in a disinterested way the kind of small cheap TV that was around in the 1970s. There's a game show on. These two are carbon copies of their brother—same spectacles, same round faces, same balding heads with a ruff of hair around the sides, same wrinkles.

The brother who answered the door comes back carrying a dozen eggs in a styrofoam carton. He bustles about, opening a drawer to get out a plastic grocery bag. He has a womanly air and is wearing an apron, like a farm housewife taking care of her family. Ann has told me that this Beattie brother, the youngest, does all the domestic chores. The others loaf around a lot and pay him rent.

"This here is Bill," he says, waving at the crossword puzzler. "And that's Bob." Both men nod in a wary way but don't say a word or get up.

"We have another brother, Bert who ..." A note of hesitation enters his voice now, and he frowns. "...Bert's moved out. He has um ...a place of his own now."

"And I'm Bark," he concludes, smiling shyly. "Well, it's Barker really, but everyone calls me Bark."

The smile lights up his face. He seems nice. I like him, even if his name doesn't really fit. I have the urge to make a silly joke, to say something like "Woof-woof, that's a mighty funny name for a shy little guy like you," but I restrain myself.

"It's a pleasure to meet you all," I say. "Thanks for the eggs."

With careful steps along the frozen road I head home, protective of my fragile purchase in its plastic bag.

The sun starts to go down. Swaths of apricot and orange spread across the sky. On a table in my office the painting palette sits waiting. So does a row of brushes, placed in a neat line to dry. My half-finished watercolour—the one I started when the November storm blew in—is still on the board, face turned towards the wall because I can't bear looking at it. I have ignored this painting, once so promising, for months. And now it's too late, I fear. Although the cold February light is sharp, the murkiness of preceding months no longer a hindrance, the shadows on the split rail fence outside aren't anywhere like what they were in November. That the fence is partially buried by snow now proves one deterrent, but the position of the sun is wrong too. It has shifted. What I see out of the window is not what's there on the board. And I can't recreate shadows in my head. I'm not clever enough. Yet it is worth a try.

Expectation always exceeds reality in art. The results are never quite what you had in mind. Even so, expectation is also half the battle, because from it springs the courage to attempt the task in the first place. Without the anticipation that the results will be at least be half-way decent, every creative effort is doomed to failure. And I secretly know this painting is doomed. It never works, going back to a half-finished watercolour. The spontaneity has gone, the moment lost. Yet I sit down anyway, because I always do. It's a competitive urge, a family thing, this desire to get a painting right instead of abandoning it. I come from a family of artists and we've always tried to one-up each other. So I grab a brush and dab away. And dabbing is the worst way to work with watercolour. This one is wrecked in seconds. Too much ultramarine mixed with burnt umber equals mud. Awful, fucking mud. I fly into a rage, rip the paper off the board, tear it in pieces and stomp madly around the house, another inherited trait. My painter grandfather would jump on his battered hat when paintings didn't go right, once astonishing Laurence Olivier who was posing for him.

Yet here I have no audience but the four sleepy cats, who look up from their box seats by the woodstove, mildly interested in this sudden rant, then settle down again. The anger dissipates. I feel lonely, isolated now. Suddenly a great ache for human company sets in. How comforting the city would be, with the bright lights in stores and people walking along the street and

Logbook Man to share a cup of tea with. The banal, accumulated rituals of cohabitation are a source of strength that grows deeper the longer we observe them. They keep us grounded. If I were in the city, I could pour out the story of this painting disaster to him—and he would treat the matter casually as he always does, calm me down, pour a second cup of tea, say I must try again. It feels wrong to be out here in the boonies like this, separated from my spouse. On my own, not part of his world.

Yet isolation teaches independence. It has to. I tell myself to move on, do something else—because what choice do you have, you ninny, stuck out here in the middle of nowhere? The self-administered pep talk works. I go down into the basement and the painting fiasco is immediately forgotten. Optimism returns in the shape of green fuzz. My seeds are sprouting.

It is easy to get hooked on seeds. Seriously hooked. I once had a gardener friend in the city called Joe who fell hopelessly in love with seeds. Every winter, he started hundreds and hundreds of them, in flats, recycled milk cartons, old styrofoam containers, plastic pots, anything he could lay his hands on. You couldn't move around his little downtown house for fear of tripping over containers of sprouting seeds. They covered the living room sofa and every tabletop. They took over the bedrooms, filled the bathtub, were squeezed in around the toilet. And Joe's seeds all grew. They flourished, in fact. Then when spring came, he hauled the containers outside and promptly forgot about them. He never could find the time to plant those seedlings in his garden or even to give them to anyone else. So they sat flopping and gasping for water in the hot sun on his deck until they shrivelled and baked to death. And then he threw them all out. It happened every spring. The fun for Joe was in collecting the seeds themselves, examining them, planting them—and trying to make them sprout.

Seeds are like that. Such objects of fantasy and excited speculation. I wonder if I'm going to wind up like Joe because I can't resist them either. Logbook Man hung four rows of grow-lights in the basement when he was up here for a weekend and I have planted seeds in plastic trays, far too many trays, under these lights. I want my babies to develop into big strong seedlings that can be transferred outside in spring. I have visions of masses of plants, arranged in the undulating drifts that writers in British horticultural magazines always urge as the only way to garden. My football field of a lawn will disappear under this tidal wave of flowers and fantastic foliage. I will create a garden that's the envy of everyone in Canada, and grow vegetables worthy of a farmers' market too. And in the meantime, these pinpricks of new life, these plants in waiting, have me enraptured. It is the effect that seeds have on everyone who bothers to look at them closely. And it happens because they are not all the same, but wildly, spectacularly different. Some seeds are that classic shape we're accustomed to thinking of, i.e., like a grain of rice, yet they also can be round, lumpy, long and flat, square, tubular like sausages, or even shredded. They may be remarkably big or so minuscule you need a magnifying glass to inspect them. A few smell funny or look like weird little bugs. At least one has a sinister appearance.

I've planted up a whole flat of *Nicotiana sylvestris* seeds because I love its intense tropical scent, like jasmine in the Caribbean of my childhood. I am determined that this perfume will waft everywhere in the garden come August. And although this kind of Nicotiana, commonly known as wild tobacco, grows over two metres tall, its seeds are as tiny as fine coffee grounds. It's the same with perennial poppies. From small do great—indeed, enormous—things grow. Yet with one fragrant herb called sweet cicely, the opposite applies. The plant is middling size but sports big bullyish seeds, torpedo-shaped and over a centimetre long, with such warlike casings they must be cracked with a pair of pliers if they are to sprout. *Verbascum* seeds are hard too, and perfectly round, like the silver balls that decorate Christmas cakes. Those of *Calendula* come in little segments and remind me of an orange, while the seeds of sunflowers are striped like mint candies. However, the trophy for elegance in the seed stakes goes to *Gaillardia*, the blanket flower, whose offspring resemble little vases with tufty bits and pieces poking out the top.

Castor bean seeds are the ones that make me nervous. They're the equivalent of the evil witch in fairy tales—unnaturally shiny, dark, shaped like Japanese beetles. And indeed the progeny of these particular plants can be deadly. Castor bean seeds contain ricin, a compound which terrorists have discovered has the potential to wipe out an entire city if they can find out a way to get it into the water supply. Yikes. Does this stuff rub off on hands, I wonder? Scared to even touch my castor beans, I handle them gingerly with surgical gloves on. I probably should toss them out, yet a few are sitting in flats anyway, because I love the look of the plants themselves. So big and exotic, capable of making a dramatic statement in a beautiful expansive country garden. As mine is going to be.

And in the meantime, these seeds, such obliging little companions for a long Canadian winter, are starting to sprout. On top of the flats, I detect a hint of green. To a gardener, it is the most exciting feeling in the world. So uplifting in the middle of this boring winter, I want to sing.

Bark's eggs are brown and satisfyingly heavy. They have rough shells, widely differing in size, with big golden yolks inside. I make an omelette with them, savour how fresh and tasty they are, wonder about his hens, where he keeps them. The trim white bungalow seems to have no outbuildings. It's just plonked down at the edge of a vast field of white, with a big garage tacked on the side. There's nothing else around the place. What happened to their farmhouse?

And this other brother, Bert. What's the story on him? It's all a bit mysterious. There was a tenseness in Bark's voice when the brother's name was mentioned. A definite hesitation. Could Bert have gone off and done something that his siblings didn't approve of? Our brief encounter has left me curious. I want to find out more about the Beattie Boys.

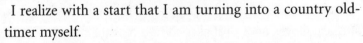

I realize with a start that I am turning into a country old-timer myself.

Fourteen

Winter drags on endlessly. The long, cold season becomes like a house guest who shows up for Christmas, is good company for a couple of weeks, but never gets the message that it's time to leave.

We stagger past the middle of March and the woodstove is still going flat out. I'll need replenishments from randy old Roman if this keeps up. Logbook Man seems remarkably content though. He sits at the dining room table, a sheet of newspaper spread out in front of him. He's sharpening the loppers and machete on a filing stone. And there are some old secateurs that he's taken apart and laid out in pieces on the newsprint in order to clean them—the kind of task that perfectionist men like him always take pride in doing properly. His assignment at the art studio ended and now he's eager to get to work himself on expanding our trail, using these tools. I watch him, relieved. His mouth is no longer permanently fixed in that bent coat hanger of annoyance. He hasn't whined once since he got home about all the work there is to do here, or how cold it is. In fact, he's said twice how happy he is to get out of the city.

I'm the one who's whining now. Everything still looks so bleak out there. A lot of snow has melted, leaving ugly after effects. The cedar and spruce trees around the edge of the lawn are no longer prettily cloaked in white. They look brown and dead, whipped into submission by winter winds. So does the silver maple. Blackened stalks of the purple coneflowers poke dispiritedly out of old shrunken heaps of dirty snow that only a few weeks ago were pillowy white hummocks where the field mice scurried to and fro in such fetchingly wavy patterns. Long brown dried-up grass down in the pasture is flopping around. And every time I try to go out with the compost bucket I nearly break my neck. Shiny patches of ice lie in wait on the pathway outside the back door. They melt in the weak morning sunshine, then freeze again at night. I slip. I slide. And wham, down I go on my rear end, tea leaves splatting everywhere. I hate this worst of seasons, the awkward, ugly time that's sandwiched between deep winter and Canada's brief fling with spring. It would be wonderful to go to bed and wake up to the warm caress of a summer morning, the birds singing. But no such luck, according to the weather forecast. There's another snowstorm brewing.

"Cheer up," says Logbook Man briskly, polishing the loppers. Their steel blades flash like a new frying pan. He snaps them shut with satisfaction. "The snow will melt quickly, you know. It's March the twenty-first tomorrow."

"So?"

"Well, that's the first day of spring."

I grunt and heave the thousandth log of the winter into the woodstove's firebox.

"That date doesn't mean a damn thing in Canada," I say crossly.

And it doesn't. The first day of spring is a meaningless marker here in the frozen north. It goes by, winter hangs on and on, there's no noticeable change. That's the norm. Yet spring IS apparently coming, and amazingly fast, according to a book I'm reading called *Cultivating Delight*, by an American writer, Diane Ackerman. She reports that spring travels north at about 13 miles per day. "That's 47.6 feet per minute or about 1.23 inches per second," she calculates. "It sounds rather fast and viewable." Ackerman, a gardener and botanist who lives in New England, says the thought of the new season approaching her home at the speed of someone taking a brisk walk always cheers her up. It has the same effect on me. I head down into the basement to check on the progress of my precious seedlings. They're doing well, and that's encouraging too. Logbook Man, humming to himself, goes out with the shiny clean loppers.

Dan drops by. He's brought another gift: more deer meat. A frozen slab of deep brown flesh with an enormous white bone attached to one side. This time, the wrapping isn't a camouflage bag, just clear plastic. Even so, it doesn't look like anything sold at a butcher's or a supermarket.

Yet I feel less squeamish now about cutting up and eating a part of a wild animal that probably roamed about on my land. In fact this offering seems quite exciting, bearing in mind how tasty the shepherd's pie was. A thick venison stew with lots of herbs and vegetables. Yes, that would be just the ticket, the perfect antidote to the grey, nasty March that won't fold up its tent and move on. Perhaps juniper berries could be added to the dish. Doesn't venison marry well with the berries of this evergreen? I have a hunch it does, I've read it somewhere, but I'm not sure how and where to find juniper berries in the middle of the winter. I ask Dan. He looks blank, says he always just roasts this cut of meat in the oven, sprinkling garlic salt on it. I gag at the mention of garlic salt. I loathe the stuff. Yet oven braising sounds like the way to go.

The snow starts falling in soft wet flakes outside the window. I pull a face. Dan stays for coffee, suggests with a grin that since the weather is lousy, we should warm ourselves up and put some rum in the coffee. Good idea, I say, hauling a bottle out from the kitchen cupboard. I like having Dan here. He's fun. But that's not the only reason why his presence puts me in a positive mood. With one of my neighbours standing in the kitchen there's the same sense of being grounded in the country that I had during the first supper I shared with Ann. Without such connections, life in rural Canada must surely be overwhelmingly lonely, an invitation to madness. Yet perhaps it's no worse than the city, where many people live alone surrounded by thousands of strangers, without uttering a single word to any of them. Loneliness is loneliness wherever you happen to be.

Dan pours a generous shot of rum into his own coffee and says he's been busy flying to exotic locales: Beijing, Tokyo, Shanghai, São Paulo, Paris. However, like Logbook Man, he's pleased to be back home in the country because he likes living in Canada best.

"It's the space," he declares, waving at the view. "I love having all this space around us. It's so crowded everywhere else in the world. We have so much land here. And of course...."

He flashes a broad grin.

"...Of course, there's lots of deer to be had out there."

He's a smooth operator, this Dan. I'm beginning to suspect that he's a bit of a rogue. He confesses that he had an ulterior motive in dropping by. He pulls a rolled up magazine out a pocket of his jacket. There's an article inside it that he wants both Logbook Man and me to read.

"'The Bambi Epidemic,' see?" he says, spreading the magazine out on the counter and jabbing a finger at the headline. "In Ontario, the deer count is about to pass half a million for the first time, an astounding ten times the level in the 1980s and a high that will propel the province into uncharted ecological territory...."

He leans forward, raising his eyebrows. He has an appraising smile and looks hard into my eyes. I feel myself blushing, then worry that I must look ridiculous. Yet this genial rogue does have an undeniable charm. Even though I'm past fifty and have graduated to BOMMIE (Boring Old Married) status, I'm not immune.

"Too many deer, see?" he says. "Are you sure you don't want..." he keeps on looking at me, eyes twinkling "...that you don't want me to go hunting out there?"

"Well, I don't know, Dan," I say, nonplussed. Am I being railroaded? Is this undeniably attractive guy trying to seduce me into tossing aside convictions about killing wild animals that I've held all my life?

"I think I'd like to read this first," I add primly, looking away, uncomfortable under his gaze. I examine the magazine, which shows a picture of a young deer gambolling in a suburban garden and pointedly sip my coffee, still without looking at him.

But Dan isn't about to give up.

"You'll make the farmers around here very happy if I do come and hunt here," he persists with the probing smile.

"Yes, but..."

"Okay, think about it." He leans back now. His tone changes. He takes a big gulp of coffee. He's clearly realized this is a waiting game. He has to bide his time, not move in for the kill yet.

"This here meat I gave you," he says. "It's the very best cut. Very tender. I know you'll both like it."

"Yes, thanks," I say, gulping down my own coffee.

He wipes his lips with the back of his hand and changes the subject. We talk about the dead elms on our property. He'd like to come in with his tractor and cut one down. I say that's fine, we want to get some firewood out of the woods too, maybe we can collaborate. He says yes, sure. As he gets ready to go in the entrance hall, I tell him with a chuckle that I met the Beattie Boys.

"What's the story on the one who left? Bert, I think that's his name?" I ask. "I'm just curious."

Dan shrugs. He pulls on an old dark green jacket and camouflage boots that come up to his knees.

"No idea," he says. "They're a funny bunch, those Beatties. Nice old guys, though. I guess they just drive each other crazy, all living in that little house and Bert decided that he'd had enough."

He leans forward and kisses my cheek, lingering a little longer than mere courtesy dictates.

Dan drives off. I can hear him going all the way down our road to the Third Line. He has a truck with an aluminum trailer that rattles like stones being rolled around in a tin can. After he's gone, I wonder about Harlan. Is he going to appear at the front door next? Will our other hunter neighbour try turning on the charm in an attempt to bring his bow and arrow on to this land?

No, Harlan's not the type. In spite of that bumper sticker about hunters making better lovers, Harlan doesn't look like a flirt.

Harlan will be more down-to-earth. He'll use straighter tactics. He's not a Romeo. Yet I suspect that he's every bit as cunning as Dan in the matter of securing hunting rights.

There's a recipe for "Great Venison Stew" in an old cookbook belonging to Mum. And yes, it does require juniper berries. On a gloppy morning, roads everywhere still a mess from wet snow, I venture out to Fernfield, eager to make this dish. At the big supermarket in the shopping mall, a teenager in forest green polyester pants and a matching bow tie is standing at the herb rack. He's stocking the shelves with the kind of little jars of McCormick's herbs that my mother used back in the 1960s. I haven't bought herbs packaged this way for years. I always get them loose at a health food store, or grow my own. I quiz the clerk about juniper berries and he looks perplexed. He runs his fingers along the line of jars with turquoise lids, then shakes his head. He calls an older man over dressed in the same uniform. They are both so eager to help, these employees of some big organization run by self-important executives who doubtless pay their underlings miserable wages and couldn't care less if they provide good service or not. I marvel at the trouble these men take trying to find the elusive berries. Everyone in Fernfield is always like this, irrespective of who they are or where they work. The friendliness of small towns is not a myth. It's one of the things I've grown to love about life here.

Yet the supermarket has no juniper berries. The men are profusely apologetic. I thank them, drive away from the big shopping mall down to the main street in Fernfield, which is as empty of shoppers as it usually is. I go into the health food store. It's housed in an attractive low white building with a poster about the virtue of glucosamine hung in the window. The owners are two women, as different from each other as apples and oranges. One is tall and skinny with legs going up to her armpits and a pointy sort of face, like an ostrich. She's called Sharla. The other, who fills a chair at the cash desk and is always sitting down when I go into the store, is a large motherly type who has breasts flopping down to her waist. She's known as Nana by everyone who comes into the store. And they're both as helpful as the guys at the supermarket, these small-town entrepreneurs who try so hard to keep everyone happy. Yet they have no berries either.

Half an hour away lies Ellerton, more sophisticated than Fernfield, a pretty town on a river, full of artists and fancy shops, which attracts a lot of tourists from Toronto. I rarely shop in Ellerton, because I can't afford a single thing they sell, and in any case, I have no need of nightdresses trimmed with Belgian lace or designer handbags or copper urns containing artful arrangements of dried imported flowers.

But I go there now. And in a store on the main street of Ellerton that sells cookware from France, I find what I'm looking for. Hard little berries, bluish grey, packaged in a tiny plastic bag. The price tag is quite high. They're probably imported too from somewhere like France. I buy two bags, drive home triumphantly and tell Logbook Man in an excited rush about my outing, trying to track down these hard-to-find berries for the venison stew I want to make.

He is lying on the sofa. He's exhausted from lopping out in the woods. He wakes up with a start. An aviation newsletter is spread out on his knees— a publication that invariably puts him to sleep in minutes.

"Junipers?" he says, only half awake. "Um.... I thought you said we had some things called junipers in the garden?"

I start to shake my head. Then I stop.

Omigod. Yes we do have these berries. A few of them anyway. There's one small juniper shrub up near the road, probably planted by the previous owners. I took a look at it last fall, noted a small handful of berries developing on the fuzzy blue green branches.

So I've made a wasted trip. Spent money for no reason. Blown bucks on berries that probably aren't going to be half as good as the ones I already have on the property.

Well, never mind. It's winter and my own berries are doubtless shrivelled and inedible. And the bought berries work well in my venison stew, which I've devised after consulting several cookbooks. The juniper gives the venison a unique flavour. In fact it's fantastic. I'm immensely proud of myself for making it. We eat two helpings apiece in big soup bowls with a loaf of fresh bread from our machine. We can't get enough of this thick dark brown stew, concocted from crushed garlic, onions, carrots, red wine, herbs and Dan's tender deer meat.

Outside the living room window, a centimetre or two of new snow has fallen. It looks like layers of grated coconut on the old hardened white snow that's lingering under the silver maple.

Yet the sight no longer seems depressing. Winter will go away eventually. It's just a matter of being patient, of biding my time till spring. And in the meantime, savouring a mouthful of stew, I realize that there are compensations to country life in Canada during the cold months.

Spring

Naturam expellas furca, tamen usque recurret
(You can drive nature out with a pitchfork;
but she will always swiftly return)

— Horace

Fifteen

It's finally April, and the world outside the living room window looks like some great wet dog exhausted after a long swim across a lake. The dog's matted hair—tangled heaps of goldenrod, Queen Anne's lace and grasses—lies flattened in the flowerbeds and pasture. And there's mud everywhere, along with lingering dribbles of snow under north-facing trees. The mud splats all over Logbook Man's car, making him fret that he needs to go the car wash in Fernfield. Like most males, he's meticulous about anything to do with his automobile. Yet he doesn't go. He's busy again at the art studio in the city, earning a welcome wad of money to help pay for the upcoming renovation. While he's away, I keep tracking mud into the house on my rubber boots and it becomes clear why most houses in the country have what are known as "mud rooms." Gobs of the stuff fall off, dry and crumble into the new

Persian carpet and the shiny maple floor installed so carefully by Stoob. Yet I leave it there. It's just too much trouble to keep sweeping the mess up.

The wet dog stirs. Down in the woods, I hear snow squeak and trickle as it drains away into the earth under the dead leaves. The clayey wet soil of the flowerbeds which has developed cracks and fissures over the winter makes a sucking noise like a plunger in a blocked toilet. One morning, a pistol shot rings out down the hill near the woods and I think with a shudder, yikes, hunters already? Then the realization dawns: it's just the ice cracking on the pond. And next morning, a great jagged slash runs from one side of the pond's frozen surface to the other, looking like a broken window pane.

The first bird sings high in the silver maple. A cardinal perhaps, and yes, there's a flash of scarlet up there among the bare branches. This bird has hung around all winter, even though I haven't fed it. There's no bird feeder outside because of the cats and in any case, experts say it's best to leave wildlife to its own devices, and not encourage unnatural feeding patterns. The cardinal's unmistakable whistle—*woo-eeeee, woo-eeeee*—followed by a noise like a child's rattle, is very loud. It wakes me up before dawn.

Logbook Man comes up for the weekend and after the dead silence of winter, we lie in bed listening, enchanted by the sound. Then on Monday, when he has to go back into the city and the bird wakes us again, he rolls over in the half light, looks at the alarm clock and says that he wishes the cats would go out and catch the cardinal. Because then the bloody thing would shut up.

After months of being cooped up indoors it is thrilling to be outside, checking for signs of life. I turn over the compost heap, which is a soaked mess of potato peelings, onion skins and other bits and pieces we've kept tossing in there over the winter. I wander around the wet lawn in a sort of giddy trance, taking deep breaths of the fresh air, examining and touching buds on plants and shrubs with the curiosity of a botanist. I pull haphazardly at dead foliage, making half-hearted attempts to tidy up. Is that a weed or isn't it? Hmm. Not sure. The truth is, all things, even weeds, seem bright and beautiful when spring is coming. Poplars, such rampant and annoying trees much of the year, look delightful in April, their sticky caramel buds opening up into fuzzy caterpillars that are sensual to stroke. I bring some poplar branches into the house and plunk them into a vase. Overnight, propelled by the heat of the woodstove, the caterpillars lengthen into the elegant fringe on a chenille shawl.

I am in love with this oh-so-short-season in Canada, when the earth miraculously seems born again.

Yet the cats aren't stirring. Not yet. Fastidious creatures that felines are, they have no intention of going outside and getting muddy paws. All four remain grouped around the woodstove, sleeping the days and nights away. I clean out their litter boxes reluctantly and one rainy morning I'm in the basement doing this odious chore when a loud hammering summons me back upstairs to the front door.

Two men stand stiffly outside under a black umbrella. They look like undertakers. Both have faces white as corpses. They're wearing black suits with white shirts and narrow black ties. No coats, though. And they are obviously cold. Rain is dripping off the umbrella on to their shoulders leaving damp, shiny patches. One of them is shivering.

"Yes?" I am as wary as Bark Beattie was the first time I showed up at his door. From the Bibles folded in their hands and carried close to their chests, I can guess why this pair is here.

"Have you thought about God today?" asks the taller of the two in a sombre monotone.

The other man stares, expressionless.

"Well now, I can't say that I have," I reply, goading them a bit. "The truth is, I've had my mind on more earthly matters this morning."

I brandish the scoop from the kitty litter box.

The joke falls flat. They look uncomprehending, not even puzzled, as if they're deaf. But of course. What did I expect? Zealots of any stripe, religious or otherwise, seldom see the humour in anything. To them, life is a Very Serious Business. I want to ask these two men if God ever tells them to lighten up, if he counsels his flock that a belly laugh is good for the soul.

And in fact I'm mildly curious about the pale, po-faced apparitions hovering on the doorstep. They are Jehovah's Witnesses. Adherents to this branch of Christianity have a much lower incidence of heart disease than the general population because they don't eat meat. Their vegetarianism is interesting; I'd like to discuss it with them, instead of answering prying questions about my attitude to a God I'm not sure exists. Perhaps they have some tips to impart on the matter of diet.

Yet the inevitable black briefcase, the kind of shallow briefcase that security men carry guns around in to protect U.S. presidents from assassins, is opened now by the taller man. Out come the copies of the Jehovah Witnesses' mouthpiece, the *Watchtower*.

"Sorry," I say quickly, putting my hands up, refusing to take a copy. "I'm not interested. I'm er … Jewish."

The men don't go. They stay rooted to the spot. The taller one who looks to be in charge opens up the magazine to the centre spread. Spread across it are two brightly coloured coupons for $10 off at Buck's Car Wash.

"You own the car wash in Fernfield?" I ask, astonished.

"Yes," he says, with a glimmer of a smile, seeming human for the first time. "Our family owns it. and if you take our magazine," he fingers the coupons, regarding me slyly, "…you get to keep these."

Well, now this is a turn-up. Car wash coupons. There's nothing Logbook Man likes more than washing his car. He's been wanting to go down to Buck's for ages. I accept the magazine, thank the men and shut the door, probably faster than I should.

And that night, when my spouse comes up from the city, he picks up the magazine sitting on the kitchen counter and his mouth drops open.

"What the heck is this?" he says. "The *Watchtower*?"

"Yes," I say, grinning. "You should look inside. There's something that will interest you in there."

"You aren't turning into some religious freak, are you, now that we're living out here?" he asks nervously.

"Just look inside the magazine," I insist.

"Not right now."

He throws the magazine back on the counter. In the living room he collapses on the sofa and picks up his *Aviation Safety Newsletter* from the coffee table.

"This is what I need to read. Have to read the reports," he calls out. "Don't bug me with that stupid *Watchtower* thing."

So I remove the coupons myself from the magazine and take them in, spousally solicitous, with a cup of tea.

Logbook Man's eyes gleam now. The *Aviation Safety Newsletter* is tossed abruptly on the floor. He's as thrilled as a kid getting a new iPod.

"Oh, wow," he says. "Wow. Car wash coupons! Manna from heaven. I hope you asked those guys to drop by again."

The pasty-complexioned preachers don't return. They've clearly written this household off as a lost cause. Instead, a very different kind of visitor shows up. As the ice melts in the pond, I become aware of an animal down there, moving around in the water. A persistent dark brown shape, with a broad head and body that's positioned partly above the surface. This creature swims purposefully from one side of the pond to the other several times a day. Then it keeps disappearing into a little black hole in the far side of the bank. Another creature slides along in the dark water too. It's a bit smaller than the first one. And I think I see more of them, lurking in last year's cattails.

Muskrats. So Harlan was right. Just as he said, the ubiquitous aquatic rodents have taken up residence in our pond. And indeed it's hardly surprising. Muskrats are probably the most prolific fur-bearing animals in North America, with the average female producing five litters of half a dozen babies, or kits, in one year. As a consequence, they're constantly searching for new territory to hunker down in. Our little protected body of water, spring-fed, surrounded by cattails and other vegetation, is undoubtedly a muskrat's idea of paradise.

Down at the trim white bungalow, getting more eggs, I receive confirmation that we have likely been invaded by these rodents.

"Yep, that sounds like 'em," says the brother called Bob, who is gradually warming up to me. He is oiling an ancient green lawnmower outside the garage when I arrive. "They're everywhere round here. And you better get rid of 'em. The sides of your pond is going to fall down if you let them muskrats stick around."

Added to that, I'm not exactly keen on swimming in the pond anymore, not with a bunch of big rats paddling around in there too. They could, after all, be right beneath me as I attempt my middle-aged version of the breast-stroke. And muskrats have big incisor teeth, two on each side. They can hold their breath underwater for over ten minutes while they scour around, searching for food. It's a scary thought. The pond is seventeen feet deep at the centre. It's pretty dark down there. They might mistake my toe for a tasty morsel. And what if Logbook Man goes skinny-dipping? We wouldn't want any male appendages to go missing.

"The folks who used to live at your place always had dogs," says Bark

Beattie as he hands over a carton of eggs, "and a dog will help to keep muskrats away, you know. But being as you have all those cats...."

His mouth turns down at the corners in a faint gesture of disapproval. Having an affection for felines, and what's more, letting them live indoors, sleeping by the woodstove, is unfathomable to these three retired farmers, who believe that a cat is useful for one thing only, and that's to live in a barn, catching mice. The Beattie Boys have a dog, everyone in the country does, and theirs is a big boisterous golden retriever called Jack, who likes sticking its nose in my crotch. Yet I don't want a dog. I've nothing against dogs, I like most animals, yet owning one would be too much like the responsibility of caring for a child. Although I'm going into the city less and less, committing to a canine just isn't in the cards.

Bark says good luck and gives me a brighter smile now that he's getting accustomed to my visits. I head back home to cope with the muskrats.

It seems as if I'll have to invite Harlan McFarlane back on the land after all.

On a wet weekend when he's home from the city, Logbook Man and I pull on rubber boots and trudge with some trepidation down to the pond. We've anticipated having to wade around in the still icy water looking for muskrat holes, yet it's hardly necessary. Evidence of their presence is staring us in the face. The big water rats have clearly been busy already. Very busy. At the eastern end of the pond, the bank that was concealed by big drifts all winter is now in danger of collapsing, just as Bob Beattie predicted, with deep indentations in two places. The animals have been burrowing into the bank, creating a muskrat Holiday Inn right under our feet. We discover further proof: three holes hidden in decaying cattails at the water's edge. And there are more holes on the other side of the pond. Under the small jetty where I sat with Gordie the previous July, drinking in the peacefulness and conversing with a frog, Logbook Man finds two holes that are larger than the rest.

"I guess we'd better call that guy Harlan," he says backing away apprehensively from the holes, clearly wondering if it's conceivable that an enormous muskrat might suddenly appear in the entrance and object violently to his presence.

"Yes, but we're in a difficult situation with this, aren't we?" I say.

Not eager to stay within close proximity of an army of annoyed muskrats either, I clamber up to the safety of the jetty and sink down on the old rickety school bench. This seat has been abandoned since we moved in. We've never bothered to do anything with it and now, after a winter of braving the elements, it looks ready to collapse the moment anything larger than a mosquito settles on its surface. It protests at the imposition of my ample rear end, but holds.

"What do you mean?" Logbook Man says, climbing up from the side of the pond and plunking himself down on the creaking bench too.

"Well, Harlan wants to hunt here. We can't expect him to get rid of the muskrats and then say no to him hunting, can we?"

"Should we offer to pay him to trap the muskrats?"

"No, I don't think so. That's not the way things work in the country. You do something for somebody, it's expected that they do something for you in return. It's the old barter system. Harlan told me that he has a deal with other people who have ponds like ours. He traps the muskrats, then he gets to hunt the deer on their land. That's what he'll want from us. You can count on it."

Logbook Man picks up an old shrivelled apple that's lying on the jetty and lobs it in the direction of the muskrat holes on the other side of the pond. He shrugs.

"So let's let him hunt here then."

"But I thought you were violently against hunting? You were insistent in the fall that you wanted to keep this as an animal sanctuary."

He shrugs again.

"I liked that meat we got from Dan. Perhaps I'm changing my mind."

"Yes, I liked it too," I say, remembering the venison stew. "And that presents us with another problem, you know. We can hardly let Harlan hunt here and then say no to Dan, can we?"

"Why not?"

"Well, it's bad neighbour relations. Word gets around. It will cause resentment once Dan hears about it, especially as he gave us that great cut of meat."

"Yeah, I guess so."

Logbook Man stares at the lopsided part of the pond, the area which now harbours a muskrat mansion. He throws another old apple into the pond. He breathes deeply. He looks perplexed. He hates handling situations like this.

It's going to be my job, I know, to sort this out with Harlan and Dan.

Life can get mighty complicated in the country.

Harlan comes. After the chilly reception I gave him in November when the subject of hunting was raised, I've wondered if he might decide not to show up. Yet the beige truck with the "Hunters-Make-Better-Lovers" sticker on the side window rolls into the driveway a few days later, after I call him. He heaves his chubby frame out. Harlan's kitted out for the task of catching muskrats in olive green rubber boots, a camouflage slicker and thick water-proof gloves that make his hands look like a giant's. He puts me in mind of an Atlantic fisherman going out for lobsters. Giving a wave, he walks around to the back of his truck and hauls out two frightening-looking traps in black metal which have chains hanging from one end.

"Kills 'em instantly, don't worry," he says, seeing the stricken look on my face as I approach the pickup. "Breaks their necks. Snap, like that," he makes motions with the rubber-gloved hands and grins. "It's painless, guaranteed."

He'll trap two muskrats with these contraptions, he explains. The proce-dure is to position the traps right outside the holes. The hapless animal exits and wham! it's off to muskrat heaven. And it will only take a couple of days, Harlan says with the assurance of one who has trapped wild animals many times before. Then he'll come back, remove their corpses and reset the traps.

"I used to sell muskrat pelts," he says in his soft voice. "Made quite a good business out of it. They're great for those fur hats everyone used to wear, the ones with ear flaps, you know? But then the anti-fur crowd..." he regards me in a challenging way "...well, those folks got busy meddling and no one wants muskrat pelts no more. Can't even sell them for a buck each." He snorts. "But that's life, I guess."

With a trap dangling from each of the huge gloves, he heads off down to the pond.

When Harlan comes back two days later to check his traps, I make a point of being busy around the front of the house, trimming shrubs. The thought of observing two brown furry bodies, flattened out and dripping with water, their mouths slack in the grip of death, makes me squeamish. I don't want to watch these doomed creatures being hauled up the hill to the truck, even though I'll be happy to see them gone. An out-of-control purple smoke bush near the front door badly needs attention anyway. It's a welcome diversion. Wielding the secateurs, I'm engrossed in the job while Harlan is down at the pond when a big mud-splattered pickup rattles into view. It's Dan.

He stops, the brakes slurp. Everything is still so wet. The truck gouges out deep ruts that make our road look like some logging track up north.

"Well hi there, babes. Long time no see. How's things?" he says, leaning out of the driver's window. He's wearing his pilot's uniform, a clean white shirt with navy blue epaulettes trimmed in gold. His cap lies on the passenger seat beside him. A muscular arm rests on the window frame. He looks sexy. It's that men in uniform thing. He seems to know it too. Dan flashes a flirtatious grin and I reciprocate even though I suspect that when he has that look, it usually means Dan wants something. Then just as abruptly the grin fades from Dan's face.

"Isn't that Harlan McFarlane's truck I see over there, down your driveway?" he asks, frowning now.

I swivel to look at Harlan's pick-up, which is barely visible through the spruce trees.

"Yes, we've discovered that we have muskrats, Dan," I say a bit sheepishly. "Harlan's getting rid of them for us. It's nice of him to do it. I wouldn't want to have to do something like that myself."

Dan snorts softly, as if he knows the real reason behind Harlan's willingness to undertake this unpleasant task.

"I guess that means you're going to let him hunt on your land now, right?"

"Yes, probably. But, um...." I flounder a bit, wish again that Logbook Man was around for support, because this is getting tricky. "You can come too if you like. We've, er, come to the conclusion that we don't really mind hunting. I think you're right. We should keep the deer population down."

He softens.

"Well now that's a switch," he says, arching his eyebrows. "Finally persuaded you, have we? We hunters aren't all a bunch of yahoos. But have you thought," he taps the steering wheel impatiently with a neatly clipped fingernail, "how your friend Harlan and I are both supposed to be hunting out there at the same time? That's dangerous, you know."

"Well, yes, I suppose it is." I'm uncertain what to say next. I blunder on. "But couldn't you ... couldn't you just work it out between yourselves? I mean, you hunt one day, he comes the next?"

Dan snorts again. Even so, he seems to want to stay on friendly terms, because a smile suddenly flickers around his lips. I take it as an indication that some juicy bit of information is about to be forthcoming.

I'm not wrong.

"Well, we'll discuss hunting later in the year, shall we?" he says, voice dropping to the pitch of one about to impart a secret. "Um, wanna know something funny, babes? Really funny. Remember that Beattie brother, Bert? The one you were asking about, who moved out?"

"Yes." I'm all ears. "What about him?"

Dan chuckles.

"Well, get this. The guy's just got married. He's seventy-six and he's found himself a bride on the Internet."

"You're kidding."

"No. Honest to God. There's all kinds of websites that you can go to now if you're looking for a wife and I guess Bert did that. He wanted to get hitched."

Dan says he knows it's true because he got roped into picking the bride up at Toronto airport. And Bert has rented himself an apartment in the north end of Fernfield. He moved in there a couple of months ago.

"She's from the Philippines," Dan says.

"Wow. What's she like?" I ask, wondering how desperate you have to be to travel half way around the world and hop into the sack with a wrinkled farmer old enough to be your grandfather.

"Well, I wouldn't call her a cutie," he says. "Kind of ordinary looking and she has a moustache. But she's young."

He has a wicked grin now.

"And I guess that's what Bert's after. He's taken her on a honeymoon to Niagara Falls."

Niagara Falls!

A gnome-like figure slides into the heart-shaped jacuzzi and crouches among the bubbles. A naked nubile slip of girl, all soft breasts, flowing hair and olive skin slips in beside him. She puts her hand under the water and....

Dan cuts my off wild imaginings. He has to go, he says. He's suddenly all authoritative, every inch the commercial airline pilot. He's flying off to Beijing in a couple of hours.

His pickup roars off down the road towards the lake, splattering mud everywhere.

Sixteen

Logbook Man has left a note on the kitchen table. He went off to the city early this morning, before I was awake. The note says "Look in the barn" but I'm suddenly nervous. He has a warped sense of humour sometimes and when you live in the country, being told to go out and take a look at something almost always means coping with evidence of a visit from the Grim Reaper. The mangled remains of a deer in the ditch, hit by a car in fall. Bits of brownish fur belonging to rabbits and raccoons killed by coyotes. Dead bats, their wings splayed out like little umbrellas, faces fixed in Dracula grins. A peculiar-looking opossum which ventured too far north, poor creature, and died of frostbite over the winter, its rat-like tail bare and bleeding. And decapitated squirrels and chipmunks, courtesy of the cats, who are finally wide awake and helpfully getting rid of the wildlife that has wreaked havoc in the walls and attic.

Such sights are the norm with the arrival of spring. Out here death stares you in the face and you can't turn away and pretend that it's not there. Mortality becomes banal. Yet not today. I'm feeling a bit guilty about the trapping of the muskrats. Harlan insisted on showing me one of the corpses while I was turning over the compost yesterday afternoon. I think he wants to educate this soft, citified dame in the realities of country life. And it was not a pretty sight, the stiff dead critter, eyes glazed and mouth open, big yellow teeth hanging out, a mark on its neck where the steel bar of the trap had sprung shut. I want a breather from the sadness of death. So I'm ignoring the spousal command to inspect this object, whatever it is, that's lurking unseen in the barn.

Our barn is located a fair distance from the house, on the edge of the road as it slopes down towards the Third Line, where Dan lives. A plain, boxy structure, it sits in long grass backed up by a stand of ash trees. Although the barn is old and weathered, it's not the kind of historic showpiece made of silver-grey planking that gets pictured in elegant country magazines, not by a long shot. Those barns have virtually vanished from this part of Canada, their finery stripped off by canny farmers and sold to urbanites to be reincarnated in basement rec rooms. Patched with recycled bits and pieces, mostly plywood and green plastic corrugated sheeting, our barn looks pretty derelict and has gaping holes in its sides. It even tips at a crazy angle, because some of the beams are rotting away. Unlike the previous owners, we don't raise sheep and indeed don't intend to try. The woods are crammed with coyotes which do dreadful things to sheep and their presence would mean more death than I can handle. So the barn is not on our list of things to repair.

It's already Logbook Man's personal fiefdom. The snowblower that we bought secondhand and the old lawnmower are stored in there, along with the mountain of tools that we're accumulating. And, of course, his big shiny motorbike. He putters about within the cavernous building, doing guy stuff. I rarely go inside.

Yet when he gets home from the city, he's still insistent that I take a look. And he's smiling as he speaks—an indication that whatever is out there is unlikely to be nasty—so we go over to the barn together. The surprise is mushrooms. Masses of mushrooms, all over the barn floor. They've popped up under his work table, next to the snowblower, between the tines of a garden fork, in the old rotted straw, beside the motorbike. They're all identical, these mushrooms—white and hummocky, with rounded tops. A few have started to open up, revealing gills that are pink underneath. The soft rosy colour stirs instant memories. I recall the *Agaricus campestris*, the meadow mushroom, that I collected as a child in Kent, England. They always grew prolifically in pastures where sheep and cattle grazed. My grandmother fried so many in bacon grease for breakfast that my sister and I, dispatched to spend summers with her, grew sick of eating them. Yet we still couldn't resist going out to forage for big dinner plate-sized specimens on crisp mornings when the fields were soaked with dew. And meadow mushrooms are delicious when picked fresh with those pink undersides. They are in fact the progenitor of the cultivated kind of mushrooms sold in supermarkets, yet far more meaty and flavourful. They've clearly popped up here because of the traces of sheep manure left behind in the barn by the previous owners.

"Wow, great," I say. "I'll collect some." Meadow mushrooms are one of the few fungi that I can recognize with any degree of confidence.

Logbook Man looks dubious.

"I just wanted you to take a look, because there are so many of them in the barn. I didn't mean we were to EAT them," he says nervously.

"Why not? They're really good, you know."

Realizing that I'm serious, he hurries indoors for *The Mushroom Hunter's Field Guide* and races back to the barn. I go in search of a knife and basket.

"It says here that *Agaricus campestris* fruits in late summer," he says "… and it's only May. So I think you're probably wrong about these mushrooms."

"No, I'm not," I say cheerfully, squatting down on the barn floor. "I know *Agaricus*. I'm going to cook these."

I cut into their white stalks. My mouth is starting to water. Already in my head these yummy little discoveries are being sautéed in butter and garlic. The last step is to add a handful of chopped parsley, plus a generous sprinkling of salt and pepper.

"But what if it's a …" Logbook Man turns the pages of the fat mushroom book. He looks like an old-time preacher with a Bible, standing above me in the barn, evening sunlight coming through a crack in the planking and lighting up his dark hair "… what if it's a destroying angel, an *Amanita verna*. Well, it could be, couldn't it? The Amanita mushroom shown here looks a heck of a lot like one you say you're used to eating. And it says that the *Amanita* fruits in June."

"It's barely May," I grunt.

"Well, perhaps these are early coming up. Global warming is affecting everything. The cycles of growing are probably getting mixed up. You really should take a look at this picture."

He stabs at the page and gasps.

"My God. The *Amanita verna* is deadly poisonous," he reads out. "Listen to what it says here. 'The symptoms are delayed, making the application of first aid useless. It is why this fungus has been accorded the name Destroying Angel.'"

He bends down and shoves the book under my nose.

"Take it away, please," I say crossly. I don't want to look at the picture.

"These are not amanitas. I know that."

My heart is set on eating these mushrooms as I continue to carefully cut and place good specimens in the basket.

"How can you be so sure?" he persists.

"I just am. I can tell by the pink undersides."

"What's that an indication of?"

"*Agaricus campestris*, the meadow mushroom," I say doggedly. His constant questioning is becoming irritating.

"Yeah?"

"Yes, really."

He stands and watches as the basket fills up.

"You people from England are always so cocky," he says after a minute or two. "You always act like you know everything."

"Well," I shoot back. "We pay more attention to nature than North Americans. We aren't raised to expect everything coming in a plastic package at the supermarket."

Whoops. This is dangerous territory now. He's insulted me. I've insulted him. A bout of spousal sparring is surely about to ensue, because when two different nationalities have to co-exist, verbal battles about cultural backgrounds are inevitable. In our case, snarkiness about Canada versus England rears up with predictable regularity. Yet surprisingly, he doesn't pick up on my jab this time. He's too worried about the mushrooms.

"No, really," he says, frowning. "What if we get paralyzed or something?"

"We won't. Believe me, we won't."

"Well, sorreeee," he says, slamming *The Mushroom Hunter's Field Guide* shut with a decisive bang. "You can kill yourself if you want, but I don't intend to eat any."

As a parting shot, Logbook Man kicks at a little cluster of the mushrooms, so that broken off pieces of white and pink fly into the air and land on his motorbike. He brushes them off crossly and stomps out of the barn.

The meadow mushrooms are given a miss. Even I don't want to eat them now. There would be no pleasure in cooking up a gourmet dish and sitting down to savour them solo. Not with Logbook Man poised by the phone ready to dial 911, watching for signs of paralysis at every mouthful.

Observing fungi that's popping up all over the property seems safer and less likely to lead to marital discord. And there's quite a parade, thanks to the wet spring. Aided by the mushroom book, I identify *Sarcosypha coccinea*, whose brilliant scarlet cups look like little shallow dishes of soy sauce placed on tables in Japanese restaurants. These mushrooms are a harbinger of spring in northeastern North America, usually appearing under hardwood trees. Mine have chosen to show themselves in wet leaves beneath a maple. A weird-looking fungus with a top that's like sticky brown toffee seems to be the *Steinpilz boletus* much admired in Poland. It prompts me think of Roman and his grumpy missus. Are they out collecting mushrooms right now? They look like the types to do such a thing. And Roman would certainly be drawn to the cluster of *Phallus ravenelii* poking up near the boletus. These mushrooms are well named. They resemble big erect penises so perfectly that I laugh out loud standing alone in the woods and then stop, feeling foolish. Clinging to the trunk of one of the old dead elms that Logbook Man intends turning into firewood are eye-catching fans of white, a bit like skate wings, arranged in clusters up and down the trunk. Oyster mushrooms? I think so. They're "edible and popular" according to the mushroom book, and sold for a bundle at a fancy organic greengrocers in Toronto. Yet Logbook Man would probably be as aghast at the suggestion of cooking them as he was with the *Agaricus campestris*, so I leave them where they are.

And then Ann springs a surprise. She's been out for a walk along the road with daughter Elizabeth, who's still at the age when she doesn't object to exploring the outdoors under parental supervision. One afternoon they both appear at the back door, so excited they can hardly speak.

"Did you know that you have morels on your land?" Ann says breathlessly. "It's amazing. You actually have morels! They're so rare around here."

"Yes," Elizabeth, aged five, pipes up in a squeaky voice. "You better not tell anybody."

In North America, the morel mushroom, *Morchella esculenta*, is certainly the crème de la crème of wild mushrooms. It's also scarcer than hen's teeth. Once, back in Toronto, I joined a bunch of hearty mushroom hunting types on a mini-van jaunt to woods north of the city. It was a cold, wet, miserable day. On the orders of a bossy guy called Helmut, we scrabbled around in leaves and forest duff till it got dark. Helmut found one pathetic morel, shrivelled up, black and mouldy. All I got was a stinking cold—courtesy of Helmut, who wouldn't stop wiping his phlegmy nose on the sleeve of his jacket. I declined to go again.

Yet now, these fantastic fungi, these marvellous morels, the ones that Helmut and the hunting party searched for in vain, have shown up only metres from my back door. Ann, hawk-eyed microbiologist that she is, spotted their peculiar shapes poking up from some fallen ash leaves near the road. They are disappointing at first glance—like crunched up balls of brownish paper, or a deflated balloon that's been sitting around for a long time and developed dozens of wrinkles. Not at all appetizing-looking. Yet they smell good—very mushroomy. And they have no worms, the morels on our land, because they are so fresh. So I'm eager to try them.

Ann and Elizabeth get invited to an impromptu mushroom-tasting in a few hours. Then I hurry down to the trim white bungalow because with this delicacy from our own woods, rare and precious as truffles, some fluffy omelettes would be perfect.

Bark lets me in. He is unusually subdued. Most days when I come visiting, there's a friendly smile by way of greeting, whether it happens to Bark, Bob or Bill opening the door, followed by some discussion of the kind of weather we're having. But not today. Bark simply says "Hi, come in" in a voice that's as low as a child's whisper. His round face is grave, creased with worry behind his glasses. I hover on the door mat as he disappears into the kitchen for the eggs.

His brothers don't seem to be home. But there is a short woman of about twenty-five standing in the living room, examining the TV guide in a disinterested way. She looks up. She has olive skin and lovely thick shiny black hair looped up untidily on top of her head, held in place with two raspberry pink barrettes. Her body is chunky and rather masculine, with broad shoulders and narrow hips—and her features are flat, as if someone's grabbed her under the chin and pushed her face inwards with a fist. Bright red acne spots are blossoming on her cheeks under deep, dark-set eyes. For an instant, I wonder if the Beattie Boys have hired themselves a cleaning woman who is about to start tidying up the living room, even though it's not necessary. Bark keeps the place spotless.

Then I notice the fuzz on the woman's upper lip. Of course. The Filipino bride.

She looks tired, this newlywed back from her honeymoon in the land of heart-shaped bathtubs. The smile directed at me is thin and without warmth. Moving over to the sofa, she picks up a Harlequin paperback that's lying open on the sofa's arm. When Bark comes out of the kitchen with the eggs, he shoots a furtive glance at her as if he's not sure what to say.

"This here is um, Araceli," he stumbles over the name, making it sound like Arry-Silly. "She's my brother Bert's wife."

"Well, how nice to meet you, Araceli," I say warmly, going over to the sofa and putting out my hand. "Welcome to Canada. I hear you went to Niagara Falls. What do you think of our big waterfall? Impressive, eh?"

Araceli's handshake is limp. She doesn't smile and mumbles something about Canada and Canadians being very nice and then plunks herself down on the sofa. She's wearing a pink polyester track suit and running shoes and has sparkly diamond studs in her ears. She starts pointedly reading the book. It's clear that she doesn't want to make conversation or to answer any more of my gushy questions.

Bark's voice remains muted as he opens the front door for me to go. He doesn't seem eager to chat about anything today. In fact, he is remarkably anxious that I leave.

"There's been a ... uh ... a problem," he says, coming out on the step, looking back furtively at Araceli. Strain shows in his face now. His voice is croaky, so low-pitched, I can hardly hear it. "It's my brother, you see. Bert has passed away."

Passed away? Right after he got spliced? Surely not. I'm instantly full of curiosity. With the excuse that I want Dan and his girlfriend Caterina to try the morels, I drop by their place. They live among spruce and pines a long way off the road, in an A-frame house that Dan mostly built himself. And the timing is great—he's just back from Beijing. His navy blue pilot hat with the gold trim hangs on a hook by the front door. He's sitting in the kitchen sipping coffee and looking his usual roguish self in a slim-fitting white bathrobe that clearly has nothing underneath it.

Caterina, who is pretty and dark and younger than Dan, offers me a cappuccino. I give them a portion of the sautéed morels. I've saved them from the supper I had last night with Ann and Elizabeth. I assure Caterina and Dan that they're delicious—which they are—explaining that they've been sautéed with garlic. It's been surprising to discover that morels are even more flavourful than my much-loved meadow mushrooms. Eating them was like savouring a wonderful wine. Dan, who consumes enough garlic to keep ten vampires at bay, says great, they'll have the morels for supper and we exchange pleasantries about how wet the spring has been. I ask about Beijing.

"Good," Dan says. "A good place to shop for deals."

Dan loves deals. He talks on and on about his latest purchases—a new digital camera for him and a parka he picked up for Caterina. They are a quarter the price in China that they are in Canada, he says, shaking his head. It's the same with everything, he adds. I glance furtively at my watch. I'm impatient to move on from this discussion about shopping. I hate shopping. Unable to contain my curiosity any longer about our mutual neighbours, I blurt out the question that I've been dying to have answered ever since my visit yesterday to the trim white bungalow.

"Um, what's the story on Bert, Dan?" I ask. "I met the Filipino bride yesterday and Bark said that Bert has DIED. It sounds so weird. Is it true?"

Dan looks serious for a moment, then his expression changes. It's as if he's trying to suppress a chuckle.

"It's true," he says. "I heard about it this morning from Bark. He called me. They've asked if I can help with the arrangements and I said I would. Poor old guys, they seem a bit lost."

He sips his cappuccino.

"Well, what happened?" I ask eagerly.

"It seems that it hit him shortly after they checked into the hotel in Niagara Falls. Bert had a heart attack."

"Oh no."

"Oh yeah. A massive one."

"What a shame, on his honeymoon and everything."

"Yeah. Killed him on the spot."

Dan permits himself a short bark of laughter. But he cuts it off abruptly and looks at me in a hesitant way, clearly wondering if I might think he's being callous.

"Yeah. I think that when it happened ..." He pauses, clamping his lips down on a chuckle that is trying to get out. "I think that they were—you know—doing it."

Seventeen

With the arrival of spring, visitors start showing up. The most welcome is Stoob. He drops by early one morning unannounced. No longer muffled up in his Michelin Man parka, he reveals himself to be more muscular than I remember, with meaty thighs and shoulders topped by a thick boxer's neck. He has navy blue coveralls on and a toolbelt around his waist, with a hammer dangling from one side. He looks like a repairman come to tune up the furnace.

Stoob is en route to another renovation project on a nearby concession road. He and his "guys," as he calls them, are building a new log house for a couple who have also moved out from the city and bought thirty acres of mostly woods like ours. But soon it seems—very soon—it will be our turn.

"I'd like you to clean everything out of the old part of the house in the next week. And I mean everything. No chairs. No clothes in the closets. Nothing," he says with the air of a drill sergeant, pursing the rosebud lips between each crisply-voiced request. "I don't want anything left in here. And hang up some old sheets in the entrance to the living room so we can keep the dust down in there. We'll be coming in with a dumpster and totally gutting the place. . . ." he casts his eyes quickly around ". . . and it must be absolutely empty."

Yes, sir. It's almost tempting to click my heels and salute. Our renovator is still careful to make no mention of timing, yet Stoob does seem to be methodical, prepared, business-like. It surely means that the job will be done well, and on time. No dilly-dallying, as is so often the case with renovations. And in any case the edict to move all the household stuff, some still packed in cardboard boxes, dumped in our Victorian lady's interior and gradually forgotten over the winter, is the push we need to get better organized ourselves. The decrepit part of our home has been ignored for too long. We don't like going in there now. It was too cold and smelly in winter, the holes in the walls a constant reminder of the folly of buying a place without getting it inspected. Yet once some Mennonite magic is worked within the thick beams that hold the old structure up, it will change everything.

Stoob's next edict is less welcome. He needs a cheque for a mindboggling amount of money up front, if we don't mind, please. Yikes. We do—a little. Over a third of the cost of the total reno to be handed over already? Yet after the initial shock sinks in, this demand is acceded to with equanimity because we can do it. Thank heavens. At the bank in Fernfield we've encountered—to our everlasting relief—a friendly loans lady, who's the total opposite of leather-skirted Ms. Cruella Kowalchuk in Toronto. Our new banker is tall with clipped black hair and very high heels. She towers over us as we're ushered into her cubicle. She wears a navy blue suit with a red scarf tied at the neck and thickly applied lipstick to match. Skipping the standard homilies about how happy the bank is to have us as customers, she introduces herself as Sharon Rooney and reveals that she's renovated two old houses in the county herself. "One with my husband, one after our divorce," she adds, with a cryptic smile. And then we sign on the dotted line for a hefty line of credit to cover the cost of our own project.

"I know how the costs keep adding up. All those little extras," she says comfortably, glancing at figures flashing by on her computer screen. "It can be very stressful renovating old houses. You're going to want a pool of cash to dip into whenever the need arises. And it'll need to be substantial."

Right, I think nervously.

The spring warmth is as welcome as a Hudson's Bay blanket was in February. The sun shines almost every day. Peeper frogs start their high-pitched singing down at the pond. Fat, salmon-pink buds open on the oaks beside the driveway. I fling windows wide for the first time since winter began and hear crickets. They are suddenly everywhere, making that unmistakable sound that's like a thousand scissors cutting through silk.

Prompted by the weather, people in the city start calling. Like suburbanites with a new swimming pool in their backyard, we find ourselves being contacted by friends that we didn't know we had.

"Martin and I thought we'd drop by for a light lunch on Saturday. We'd like to check out property in the area," says a woman called Melanie who has a wispy Jackie Kennedy-ish voice. I vaguely remember her at a barbecue on Tim and Caron's deck years ago. Blonde, pretty, childlike. And so thin, Logbook Man thought she was going to fall through the cracks in the deck.

"We could make it there by about noon," she whispers. "Would that be okay?"

Well no, Melanie, sorry. I'm out of lettuce leaves and skinless chicken breasts. I don't think you'd exactly fit in with pickups and deer hunters anyway. Another couple announces that they've sold their cottage because they no longer need one. They plan on spending their weekends with us instead.

"We can help, you know," they say. "We're very willing. We'll stop at Home Depot on the way if you like and get some paint. What's your colour scheme?"

A balding elderly man appears in the driveway one Saturday morning and hoists two flats of tiny tree seedlings out of his station wagon.

"I started these this past winter in my basement," he says, looking inordinately pleased with himself and clearly expecting a heap of praise from me too. "Don't have the space for them in my garden in Toronto. It's way too small. Thought right away of you, dear. I know you won't want to waste them."

"Er, yes," I say. "I mean, no."

Baldy wanders around the property exclaiming at the view and taking photographs with an ancient Pentax. I count the seedlings. There are a hundred and twenty in each flat, each no bigger than a little finger. After his vehicle has rumbled away down the road to the lake, I haul the flats over to the compost heap and dump the contents in.

Mum wants to come up. So do arty acquaintances of Logbook Man. And eager gardening buddies. It's tempting to tell everyone to please go away until the reno's done, because it won't be possible to cook anything or wash one sheet until that's over. But losing touch with genuine friends is not a smart idea, not in middle age. So I clean a dead bat caught by one of the cats off on the lawn, check that there are no beheaded squirrels lying around either and organize a get-together. Several friends we've known for years, including thick-or-thin girlfriend Lorraine come up. So does Mum, bringing her left-over Wonder Bread and an apple pie. It's a tight fit—the living room looks like a hostel with everyone sleeping on mattresses—but we spend the week-end eating too much and revelling in the joy of barbecuing without having to worry about smoking out the neighbours. The spring nights stay mild, stippled with bright stars. Much wine gets quaffed on the deck as our visi-tors compete to see who can pick out Cassiopeia's chair and the seven stars which constitute the Pleiades first. Mum wins. Everyone marvels at how clear the sky is after being in Toronto. Then Sunday night rolls around, we kiss the guests goodbye and Logbook Man and I stay up till the small hours, cleaning up, moving furniture and washing dishes in case Stoob arrives with his troops Monday morning.

He doesn't. Not yet. Our Mennonite renovator clearly believes a little suspense is good for the soul.

Instead, I have an intimidating visitor. Her name is Deirdre Pettingsley-Richards.

Deirdre is a hoity hort. It's what I call a certain type of gardener who knows absolutely everything, and who insists on making everyone else aware of the fact.

I write a lot about gardening and thus encounters with hoity horts come with the territory. Yet whatever the occasion, it's always a humbling experience, because these folks are more formidable than the Encyclopedia Britannica. A hoity hort would make even the likes of Linnaeus and Pliny the Elder feel hopelessly inadequate. Their tactics are invariably the same. When someone brings a mystery plant to garden club meetings, the hoity hort can always identify it—instantly. If you're discussing Campanulas and waxing enthusiastic about a variety called *punctata*, she (hoity horts are usually, but not always, female) will invariably chip in with: "Ah yes, but you really should try the *garganica*. I discovered it on a hiking trip in the Caucasus mountains last spring and it's far, far superior to *punctata*." And in the minefield of botanical terminology, even some horror like *Scrophulariaceae* doesn't faze her. Plant names flow as smoothly and effortlessly from a hoity hort's lips as maple syrup poured on to pancakes.

The matter of plant pronunciation triggers an anxiety attack the moment Deirdre announces her imminent arrival from the city. We've become acquainted a few times through a gardening group. She sends an email (hoity horts don't wait for invitations) in which there's a promise to bring along a *Daphne cneorum* for "your undoubtedly delightful new garden." This is in fact welcome news, because I love daphnes—such elegant shrubs, with a perfume to match—and with forty-eight acres to care for, I need all the freebies I can get. But then, yikes, there's that word "*cneorum.*" How is this peculiar combination of letters pronounced? Like a sneeze? Or is it supposed to sound like a joint problem affecting middle-aged gardeners? I have no idea. And what if I say "*cneorum*" wrong? Will Deirdre smirk and dismiss me as an utter rube? For sure, yes. That's what hoity horts love to do.

I call Lorraine in a tizzy. In spite of her English first name, Lorraine is Greek (or at least her parents are) and *cneorum*, I'm sure, is a word with Greek origins.

Lorraine laughs her head off.

"You gardeners," she says. "The first letter is probably silent. Say knee-orum. But then again, translated into English, I'm not really sure.…"

And she laughs again and says she has to go into a meeting.

Deirdre, who is on the plump side, arrives in a beige windbreaker pulled tight over her middle. She's wearing brown corduroy trousers, a battered Tilley hat with pins from horticultural events stuck all over it and old hiking boots which have mismatched laces—standard gear for hoity horts, who seldom, if ever, are interested in appearances. Of humans, that is. Their obsession is plants, anything to do with plants, and of course, letting everyone else know just how knowledgeable this obsession has made them. The promised shrub is proffered in a plastic pot. It's a small offshoot from the daphne growing in her own Toronto garden, Deirdre explains in an upper-class accent as clipped as a privet hedge. I listen with the manners of a well-behaved schoolgirl, my ears on high alert, hoping to hear the magic word "*cneorum*" uttered, so that at long last the secret to its correct pronunciation will be revealed.

But the dratted woman doesn't deliver. She simply calls it a daphne.

There are sandwiches and salad on the kitchen counter. I've prepared them especially for this visit, yet Deirdre barely takes a bite. She's agitated, eager to get outside and air her knowledge about the plant world. The desire to put me in my place is on the tip of her tongue, that's obvious from the way she keeps peering out of the living room windows—and the fact that she doesn't even remove her hat with the horticultural pins. I can hear the likes of *Phalaris arundinacea* var. *picta* and *Sanguisorba bakusanensis* var. *obtusa* spilling out of her mouth already, all pronounced perfectly. As we amble around outside, the sun high in the sky, my visitor examines emerging bits of greenery like some fat female Sherlock Holmes searching for clues with which to trap the unwary. And I feel like Watson trailing in her wake, about to get reprimanded for my botanical shortcomings at every opportunity.

"The daphne should go right here" she decrees, pointing a stubby finger at an area of the flowerbed where closely spaced clumps of green raspy leaves are emerging.

"Ah yes," I say anxiously, peering at the clumps, clasping and unclasping my hands. "I have way too many purple coneflowers growing there, don't I?"

"My dear, if I'm not mistaken," Deirdre says, tearing off a leaf and peering at it, triumph registering behind her big round spectacles. "these plants are *Rudbeckia*, not *Echinacea*, aren't they?"

If you say so, Deirdre. A clump of *Euphorbia polychroma* gets admired in a half-hearted way, yet I'm informed that a burgundy-leafed *Euphorbia griffithii* would look much, much prettier in the garden. And Deirdre thinks I've planted Ann's gift of a peony too high. It won't bloom. Definitely not. The bud union must be precisely five centimetres below the surface of the soil. While she nods approvingly at the lasagna beds where the bigger flowerbeds will be, she waves off my plans for a vegetable garden on the other side of the split rail fence. Yet I'm not surprised. Not in the least. Hoity horts are seldom interested in anything edible. Growing vegetables is for rubes. And non-edibles—shrubs, flowers, trees—offer many more opportunities for showing off dexterity with plant pronunciation. As a parting shot, she is outright dismissive of the Jacob's ladder, which is just starting to emerge from the soil in the flowerbed.

"There's a delightfully different Jacob's ladder called 'Brise d'Anjou,' which has stripy leaves," she says. "Quite honestly, I'm surprised that a keen gardener like you hasn't heard of it."

"And quite honestly, Deirdre," I shoot back, "I'm surprised that I haven't clobbered you with a garden fork."

Well, not really. But it's fun to fantasize.

Eighteen

Stoob has arrived. Things are finally starting to happen. A big blue dumpster with a dent in one side appeared yesterday afternoon in front of the house, dropped off by a man driving a flatbed truck with a crane on the back. It was raining hard. The driver leapt out. He looked briefly up at the grey sky, said, "Fucking weather," by way of greeting, then made his delivery and sped off without saying another word. The high-sided container is standing in the goutweed that's galloping all along the edge of the road. Then at seven this morning, three pickups with muddy wheels arrived in a slow procession down the driveway. They parked neatly, side by side. Five men in work clothes, one of them Stoob, got out. He opened the cab of the first truck, produced yellow hard hats plus a huge oblong toolbox. Now this quintet is inside the Victorian lady, ripping her guts apart.

The gutting involves a lot of banging and the sound of heavy things being hauled across the floor. The old lady groans in protest now and then. Broken-up chunks of particleboard keep being pushed through the sash windows out into the dumpster along with styrofoam sheeting stained with squirrel excrement. Brownish wads of stuff that smells foul are tossed out too. It looks like some kind of insulation installed a century ago. Dust floats in the air, because luckily it's stopped raining. The dust is settling on the grey clapboard and shrubs in front of the house, coating them in a grubby bridal veil.

Stoob's workers are a surprise. All so contemporary. None resembles the earnest black-garbed males with suspenders that came to mind when Big Brenda mentioned that Stoob was a Mennonite. Stoob made brief introductions: Toby, Mick, Dennis, and Werner. They all nodded politely, then disappeared inside the old part of the house with the toolbox. Toby is no more than eighteen. He has the disconnected vague air of a dope smoker, long matted brown hair pulled off his face in a ponytail. He was suppressing a yawn when they arrived. A real stoner. And his arms and legs are like sticks. He doesn't look capable of lifting anything heavier than a roach clip. The one called Dennis is middle-aged with grey, curly hair and glasses. A college professor comes to mind when I look at him. He seems so contemplative and serious. Mick and Werner, and Stoob himself, are the only ones who come across as guys capable of doing construction work. They have meaty callused hands and the physiques of men accustomed to hard physical labour.

Different as they are, Stoob's guys seems to work well together. There's laughing and joshing amid the hammering and heaving. Sometimes an expletive gets uttered, but not often.

At midmorning, I peer in through one of the sash windows and ask "Anyone want coffee?" They shake their heads. All of them, that is, but Toby. With a white mask over his face, he's halfway up a ladder, ponytail coated in plaster dust, trying to pry a piece of crumbling drywall off the ceiling. He indicates a yes with his head and climbs down eagerly, reaching for the cigarette packet tucked into his coveralls. But Stoob barks something at him, so he goes back up the ladder again.

Stoob barks at me too. He doesn't want anyone hanging around outside the windows until the interior demolition is finished. It's too dangerous, he says. With an apologetic smile and shake of the black curls, he banishes me to the garden.

The lawn is covered with a million dandelions. At least, it looks like a million, but it could be two or even three. There's no way of knowing for sure. Whatever the number, the sight is extraordinary on this bright May morning, after all the rain. It's like some exotic fabric chosen by a decorator who's into wild colour schemes. Vivid green stippled all over with chrome yellow spots. So bright, it hurts my eyes.

Logbook Man is hopping mad about the dandelions. He says trust the French to get it right, giving them the name pissenlits. They are pissy plants. *Extrêmement pissee.* This morning before leaving for the city he stomped about on the sea of yellow, trowel in one hand, piece of toast smeared with his habitual peanut butter and jam in the other. And he kept squatting down and digging out the largest dandelions, complaining about every one as he went. He says they ruin lawns with their big taproots, crowding out the grass, and that they're the most devious inventions of Mother Nature on the planet, designed for the specific purpose of driving guys like him crazy.

"Ever notice how, when you cut a lawn, the dandelions bow down so you can't cut their heads off?" he fumed. "Then when you've finished, they pop up again."

Even with the new lasagna beds taking up a lot of space, he finds this huge lawn of ours overwhelming. He's worried that he won't be able to go gliding anymore because he'll be cutting the grass instead. As for doing the logbooks, that will be out of the question now. Yet saying no to the guys at the club, who depend on volunteers, is going to make him feel bad, he says. Very bad. He grimaces at me as if it's all my fault. What's even worse, his beloved motorbike may have to go, auctioned off at some place in Fernfield, so he can buy a massive power mower instead. He'll put the blade of this new machine on the lowest setting possible, then keep shearing at the dandelions until they give up. At least, that's the plan. The current old mower isn't up to the task.

One of the cats showed up as Logbook Man was stabbing the trowel into the dandelions. Fat old tabby Patrick nipped smartly over to a patch of catnip that's popped up at the edge of the lawn. Our feline foursome has quickly discovered that catnip grows wild on the property. Now they all trip out for a fix at least once a day.

The way Patrick purposefully picked his way across the lawn, craving written his over his face, fired Logbook Man's imagination.

"Look at him. So eager to get stoned," he said. "Why doesn't some clever plant breeder cross catnip with dandelions? Then we could get ourselves a herd of cats to nibble the dandelions down to the ground, like sheep. And we could rent the cats out and make a ton of money."

The prospect of a dandelion-devouring feline got him so excited, he dropped his toast. It landed face side down, right on top of a dandelion.

"Fuck," he said. "Fuck, just look at that." He picked a few of the golden dandelion threads off the jam, then gave up and tossed the toast into the compost heap. "I told you those bloody plants were troublemakers. I'm going into the city. There's less of them there."

After he left, I noticed some yellow species tulips with spiky petals in the flowerbed. A small clump, perhaps half a dozen or so, just bursting through. A welcome burst of colour in the dark spring earth. They're called *Tulipa acuminata*. They are the first cultivated tulip, the one planted in walled gardens by the Turks back in the sixteenth century. All the thousands of tulip varieties we grow descend from these wild tulips—which are now bred by Dutch growers—and I've been eager to see what they look like. I planted them along with the Apeldoorns last fall. Your first contributions to a garden, new or old, are always the most memorable plants you'll ever grow. Yet pleasure at seeing the *acuminata* is tempered by the realization that their colour is exactly the same as the dandelion flowers. And the petals as they emerge from the soil have the same shape as the pissenlits too.

By what accident of fate does one plant become so loved, yet the other so despised? These two grow centimetres apart in my garden. They have exactly the same hue and other characteristics in common. Yet adoration is heaped on the first, while the second faces beheading every time it dares to show its face.

Why do we find it necessary to indulge in this ethnic cleansing of the dandelion?

Dandelions aren't the only problem in the garden. Although we didn't see Bambi and his buddies much over the winter, they were busy. Devastatingly busy. They must have visited at night, after we'd gone to bed. The garden centre lady was bang on the mark back in the fall. She said deer would chomp the new euonymus and cut-leaf sumacs down to the ground. They have. Inspecting the flowerbeds and the pasture leading down to the pond, I discover that there's virtually nothing left of either. Just a few shredded bits and pieces hanging on, sticking forlornly out of the ground.

More destruction is revealed on closer inspection. Two small weigelas have suffered a similar fate. As have all the daylilies, an elderberry bush, three spireas, the tops of the Jacob's ladder and the leaves of three new heartnut trees. All gone, chewed off. Demolished by those darling Disney deer with the goofy faces. In fact, the only things they seem to have left alone are the *Euphorbia polychroma*, lady's mantle and purple coneflowers, probably because they all have raspy leaves. As deer don't have upper teeth, they can't get a grip on them. It's a relief that much of this chomping seems to have occurred recently, after Deirdre Pettingsley-Richards came up. She'd have had something to say about the devastation, and whatever her conclusion was, I would certainly have been to blame.

Skunks or raccoons have been hard at work too. Overnight, one or the other has dug up Ann's peony and a shrub rose I bought on impulse and shoved into the ground in late fall. Both are lying on the surface of the soil now, baking to death, roots exposed to the bright sun. There's some smelly black poop beside the rose. It's covered in flies. The state of the garden is not promising. What's going to happen to my precious seedlings? They're all currently waiting in pots up by the house, being hardened off, getting ready to go out there and face the world. Yet with all this four-legged competition, it's going to be tough for any of them to gain a foothold.

A plan to outwit critters is needed. Urgently. And the activity up at the house has stopped, because the renovation guys have deserted the Victorian lady and driven off into Fernfield for lunch. Indoors, I work out an action plan over a cheese sandwich. It's blissfully peaceful in the kitchen, with the workmen gone. Yet the phone, which always interrupts everything, interrupts this dreaming and scheming too.

It's another gardener acquaintance in the city called Elinor. A tiresome eco-evangelist as I recall, always nattering on about the evils of lawns.

"I'd like to come up and see your garden," she says in a commanding tone. "It would be useful to find out what you're doing there to protect the natural environment. You see, I've started this gardening group for kids at my school"—Elinor is a grade-school teacher—"and I could pick up some ideas. They're really interested in growing vegetables. All organically, of course."

I think for a moment.

"Okay, come up," I say dreading the visit but agreeing nonetheless because Elinor is one of those people who will make me feel Guilty As All Hell if I say no. Especially to her precious kids.

"I'm filled with curiosity," she says. "I presume you're going organic?"

"Well, yes, I think so. But my style is er...." I ponder the designs I drew out over lunch "...well, it's what you'd call critterus interruptus."

"Sorry? Critter what?"

"Critterus interruptus. It's a new trend. Especially in the country."

I chuckle.

There's a puzzled silence.

"Sorry, but I've never heard of anything like that." Elinor hesitates clearly wondering if she should express ignorance about this trend I've mentioned, for fear of looking out of touch.

"It doesn't," she harrumphs, "sound like anything that has been endorsed by the green movement."

"Well, it is green, I guess," I reply with a brittle laugh. "Critterus interruptus is certainly a green approach."

"Well, I'm very glad to hear it."

I wish Elinor wasn't coming. She's annoying and preachy. Yet the world falls basically into two types of personalities, PIOS and GIOS. The first are Put It Off people, the procrastinators. The second just sigh and Get It Over. I'm a GIO, so we make a date for the following weekend.

Back outside, more critters are running amok. Squirrels. They're living in the black walnut now and have bitten the tops off most of the Apeldoorn tulips I planted in the fall in the big flowerbed. I didn't notice their nibbling before, absorbed as I was by the deer damage. Yet the bushy-tails' destructiveness is just as bad. The only tulips left are the acuminatas. They survived because they're up by the house.

A scream erupts in the garden as I make this discovery. It's me.

Over in the barn, there's a ton of promising material with which to institute my critterus interruptus garden. A bunch of old wire baskets that used to belong in a cupboard in the city will be perfect. So will some wooden boxes with slatted sides found on garbage night outside a greengrocer's. There are milk crates in red and blue. And plastic pots. And an old bike basket. And a bonanza for the vegetable garden: two fat packages of black plastic netting hidden under a tarp. Logbook Man bought the netting at big expense in the fall, then forgot what he wanted to do with it—a fairly regular occurrence.

My pace is feverish, setting up these examples of garden installation art. The milk crates go over the spireas, weigelas and other shrubs. The wire ones protect the few perennials that the interlopers haven't touched. Tomato, lettuce and celeriac seedlings which I've planted behind the split rail fence are swathed in the netting, along with redcurrant bushes and flowerpots up on the deck. With their bottoms cut out, plastic pots are slid in place over any other plant that's looking vulnerable to attack. And the bike basket provides a cage around a baby buddleia.

The garden looks like the aftermath of a garage sale when I'm finished. But hey, new trends in art always take a while to catch on. It will be fine. I crack open a beer to celebrate.

Stoob and company have almost completely gutted the Victorian lady. Her innards now lie in the dumpster, smashed to pieces. The basement behemoth has gone too, hauled up and heaved out through a hole in the wall with much cursing and sweating by the beefy pair Mike and Werner. Toby was nowhere in sight when this heavy lifting went on today. He's always sneaking off to the bench by the pond. I think he's smoking joints down there when Stoob's back is turned. A skunky smell keeps wafting up the hill. Dennis doesn't concern himself with the dirty work either. He is, Stoob announced rather proudly, a master carpenter who's won awards for his craftsmanship. So Dennis is always running around measuring things, with a pencil tucked behind his ear and he's destined to build the new staircase and the wooden mouldings. Stoob disappears every afternoon too, driving off in his pickup to the log cabin that the couple from the city are building two concession roads away. It seems he's juggling both of us at the same time.

Still, it's progressing. The furnace is now tipped over on its side, next to the dumpster. It looks like a rusting hulk at some abandoned shipyard in Scotland. Logbook Man clambered on top of it yesterday and did a victory jig in the afternoon sun. Werner watched, wiping the sweat off his forehead, laughing and smoking a cigarette. He's a big, solid German with tattoos down his arms and stained teeth. He keeps saying "Ya, ya."

The big metal drum of the furnace made a clanging noise under Logbook Man's feet, empty of oil, its life drained away. Yet we felt no sadness, only relief to be rid of all that rumbling. Stoob is planning to install a high-efficiency propane furnace, which he promises will be cheaper, cleaner and quieter.

The Victorian lady is another matter, though. The unceremonious way she's been ripped apart has been on my mind. The walls and beams constructed inside her have remained intact for over a hundred years. Will she be resentful of the radical changes that we're subjecting her to? Old houses develop a definite soul. Although the physical decline of ours—the stale smells, the holes, the general decrepitness—has become repugnant, I want to keep her soul alive.

The evening after the furnace goes, Logbook Man and I are alone for the first time since the renovation started. The men aren't scheduled to return till next week. The weather is warm. A cloud of gnats hovers in the air but they're not the biting kind. There's not a sound along the road. The cats have come out, curious to check out what's been going on. We're curious too. We climb carefully through a window opening into the gutted part of the house. It's completely stripped from rafters to basement. Nothing remains. Just a shell of rough-hewn old timbers with a couple of heavy crossbeams left in place to stop the structure from collapsing. Hovering on a beam, I feel like a gymnast at the Olympics, except that at any moment I'm likely to plummet into the basement a long way below and break my neck. Yet how thrilling it is to be inside. I look around. Feel reassured. There is a spiritual calm to the place now. With the sun beaming in through the holes where the old windows were, it's like being inside a church.

Our Victorian lady clearly approves. She doesn't mind being moved into the twenty-first century.

Summer

"One year's seed, seven years' weed"
—Old saying

Nineteen

Now that the soil has warmed up, a frightening truth has been revealed. I am turning into an old BAG—a Bindweed Afflicted Gardener.

And it's not just me. The greatest threat to human survival in the twenty-first century is not the polar ice caps melting or sky-high terrorists wearing exploding shoes. It's something far more insidious: a plant called bindweed, or to use its correct name, *Convolvulus arvensis.*

If this moniker sounds like something that's tangled up, it's appropriate. Convolvulus IS a tangle, a horrible tangle, but not in the benign manner of a ball of wool dropped on the floor and kicked about by some cute kitten. One day in the not too distant future, Convolvulus intends wrapping itself tightly around the world, over and over again, like those odd skeins encircling a cantaloupe melon, and as a consequence, everything living thing, including all of us, will be trapped, suffocated, wiped out.

I know this for a fact because the dratted plant is already a tenth of the way towards its goal in my garden.

It's only the end of May and the confounded bindweed is coming up everywhere. I am disillusioned and fed up. No sooner did I get the wildlife problem licked (the critterus interruptus installations are working pretty well. Only one has been pushed aside by a skunk) than this Boston Strangler of plants launched its attack. The twining tentacles have already suffocated a clematis, some bellflowers, the Jacob's ladder and the shrub rose. Now it's streaking up the fledgling coneflowers and rudbeckias and Logbook Man is fretting that there's a ton of its arrow-shaped leaves coming up in the lawn. And why on earth was I worried about deer invading the vegetable beds? There's hardly anything left for those Johnny-come-latelys. The bindweed has succeeding in smothering some of the tomato seedlings underneath the black plastic netting before they're even a few centimetres high.

Bindweed is one of the common names given to *Convolvulus arvensis*, but there are other, more colourful ones. The best by far is "devil's guts." That's what folks in the north of England called this demonic creation of Mother Nature centuries ago, and they weren't just a bunch of superstitious ninnies who needed to smarten up. There is an undeniable whiff of Satan attached to a plant whose spaghetti-like roots extend thirty metres into the ground, which bindweed's roots do. And some kind of dark deviousness has to be at work down there because it is virtually impossible to completely remove these Australia-deep underpinnings. Dig, dig and dig and you'll never get every bit of bindweed out. The roots snap off, branch out, twist themselves in knots, go sideways, do anything they can to keep going. Then at every possible opportunity they streak towards the soil's surface, sending out stringy tentacles tough as Teflon, whose sole purpose in life seems to be to squeeze anything in their reach to death.

It gets worse. The plant comes in more varieties than Heinz—there's field bindweed, hedge bindweed, bracted bindweed, black bindweed, ivy bindweed, knot bindweed and—a small ray of hope—lesser bindweed. And each plant produced by these horrors is capable of producing over five hundred seeds a season, which stay viable in the soil for up to half a century. What chance does human kind have against bindweed? No chance at all, when you think about it.

Much has been penned about the incredible tenacity of this plant. Outside the concrete confines of cities, it's a major problem in countries all over the world, and some folks even get a kick out of fighting it. The British gardening writer Margery Fish, who was around in the 1950s, described the war as "more exciting than golf or fishing." Fish said the reward for scrabbling around in the soil trying to thwart bindweed's progress through her garden was "...a barrowload of obscene, twisting white roots and the joy of burning them."

Well, perhaps Ms. Fish didn't get out much. Either that or, being a Brit, she was a masochist. In fact, I picture this eminent gardener as one of those hardy tweedy types who fling windows open in the middle of winter. But I'm North American by adoption. And soft. I can think of a hundred things I'd rather be doing than loading up the garden cart with bindweed roots and making a bonfire. So I lean towards getting out the heavy artillery. No more hand-to-hand combat with this warrior. The battle has become boring already. Playing nice environmentally friendly lady, asking this plant to please behave itself and live in harmony with the rest of us is becoming tiresome. Because bindweed won't behave. It doesn't care. It's indifferent to the plight of everything it meets. It's like a bunch of Hell's Angels hogging the highway on a Sunday afternoon. It won't get out of the way for anything or anybody. We can all go to hell as far as bindweed is concerned.

So it's payback time. I want to do what farmers do. Kill it.

Visiting Ann, I bitch about the bindweed. She laughs, looks rueful, says it's the same in her garden. I ask her what a farmer like Don does. After all, his fields surround Ann's place. And there are no more than fifty metres separating these fields from my own property across the road, so those devious white bindweed roots could surely snake their way underground out of Anne's garden and mine and into where Don grows his soybeans and corn.

Ann pushes her rimless glasses up her nose and looks tentative. She's lived in this area most of her life, but hasn't exactly led a sheltered existence. Microbiology research has taken her to Australia, the Netherlands and France. And she knows about the great divide between city and country when it comes to the matter of pesticides. Her expression indicates that she wonders if it's a good idea to take up the touchy topic with me now.

"I know that um, people like you aren't too keen on using any chemicals ..."

she says and stops. The rest of the sentence is left hanging in the air, like a cloud of crop dust.

We're standing outside her house. The acreage that Don farms almost encircles us, stretching as far as the eye can see to the north, then down a gentle hill to the west and butting up to the lake road on the eastern side. This year, he's growing corn in the field next to Ann's. Last year it was soybeans. Like all the local farmers, Don practises crop rotation to keep his soil healthy. The corn is starting to come up now in wavy lines, like pale green stripes on a brown sweater. And there's not a hint of a weed anywhere among those stripes. I'm envious of this neatness. I want my garden to look like that. Unnatural and chemically induced it may be, but I'm eager for an end to the bloody bindweed snaking everywhere.

"Well," I say, "I have to confess that I'm changing my mind about a lot of things since moving out here. I realize now that it would be very difficult for farmers like Don to grow stuff like corn without the help of chemicals, because so many crops would be choked out by weeds."

"Yes, and bindweed's not the only problem," Ann says. She laughs. "Don't get him started on milkweed, will you? That's a big nuisance plant. He'll go on and on about it. City people love milkweed because of monarch butterflies, but if soybeans are polluted with so much as one milkweed plant, you can't sell them."

There's a hint of I-told-you-so in Ann's voice now—and it's becoming familiar. Harlan sounded the same way when I told him about the muskrats in the pond. Now this. I am learning how it feels to go against the grain of contemporary thinking.

"Okay," Ann says, getting serious now. "Don would use Roundup on something like bindweed. That's the trade name. But it's really called glyphosate and you know…" she pauses, staring at the field "…people lump chemicals altogether but glyphosate is not that bad. Of all the things you can use to kill weeds, it's the least harmful because it doesn't stick around long in the soil."

Glyphosate is a post-emergent herbicide, she explains. That means it must be applied to weeds after they've leafed out. My best bet will be to paint the stuff full strength on to the bindweed leaves in the garden, leave them for a week, then repeat the process.

"Okay, I'm going to give it a try," I say, realizing that I've metamorphosed from dedicated organic gardener into chemical-toting killer in less than three minutes.

"It's expensive," she warns. "You'll pay a fortune for it at a garden centre."

"I don't care," I say.

"I'll tell you what," says Ann. "Don gets Roundup at a reduced rate from the Co-Op. I'll ask him to pick up a container for you, if you like."

"Great," I say. "Thanks."

My days as an old BAG are numbered.

It's a good-to-be-alive kind of morning when Elinor comes up from the city. The sky is clear, the air scented with spring. Two old apple trees in the pasture resemble bridal gowns, covered all over in white blossom. Their perfume wafts up the hill. The poplars behind the pond are clouds of lime green. In front of the house where we picked the morels, quill pens of ferns are erupting into seas of foamy emerald. Clumps of violets have opened too, in both purple and white. Close up, the white ones look like the little wrinkled faces of old men. And a big bleeding heart is starting to show itself in the flowerbed.

The property looks pretty, idyllic almost, at this time of year. In spite of the critterus interruptus contraptions and the burgeoning bindweed, there's a lot to show off to an eco-freak like Elinor. With all this natural beauty surrounding her, she's bound to be impressed.

She arrives mid-morning and I make coffee. I've been careful to buy a bag of the free-trade kind from the health food store in Fernfield, because I know Elinor will refuse to drink anything else. She is a short, mousy woman with a big bum and salt-and-pepper hair frizzing out around her moon face. She wears no makeup. And she looks so earnest. It's easy to picture Elinor bossing her grade-schoolers around, hammering words like "environment" "green" and "sustainability" into their heads a hundred times a day. She's dressed in a shapeless calf-length jumper of beige fabric that's certainly made from organic hemp, with a pale blue cotton T-shirt underneath it. This is Elinor's standard uniform. Indeed, I have never seen her wear any other outfit. Today, there's a stain of what looks like tomato sauce on the front of the jumper—and that is undoubtedly organic too, like everything about Elinor. Well, almost everything. I think she might have slipped up with her feet. She's wearing flat black cotton Chinese slippers—the kind of slippers that make every Western woman who puts them on look like a peasant working in the rice fields—and the materials that have gone into making the ugliest footwear on the planet surely aren't green, if China's environmental record is anything to go by.

Elinor has a small hatchback car with a green and white sticker on the back fender which says: "Your lawn is a drug addict." She frowns at a grey truck parked at the end of the driveway. This pickup doesn't belong to Stoob or any of his workers. They're taking a couple of days off again, having just poured the new concrete basement floor in the Victorian lady. Now it has to harden before they can continue. The truck, I confess a bit sheepishly to Elinor, is ours. We splurged on it in February when the snowdrifts got too high for me to battle out of the driveway in my decrepit old car. And we love our gas guzzler, although I don't say so. It's a 4x4, a modest one, an ordinary grey, with big high wheels. Now that spring has arrived, zooming around the gravel roads in this pickup, going up to Don's place to collect straw to use as mulch in the vegetable garden, makes me feel I belong here, because everyone else in the country drives pickups too. And it was certainly a lifesaver in winter.

Yet Elinor disapproves. Deeply. That's obvious from the way her forehead wrinkles up. The frown becomes more pronounced as her unorganic Chinese slippers negotiate the soccer field of a lawn.

"What a huge waste of time," she says, gesturing belligerently at the grass. "So unenvironmentally friendly. You'll be getting rid of it, won't you? You'll put in shrubs instead?"

"Yes, I'm in the process of making the flowerbeds bigger," I tell her, pointing out the lasagna beds. The layers of organic material have rotted down nicely over the winter and these big curving areas are empty of plants now, apart from a few inevitable strands of bindweed and some thistles. All that's left is to plant them up with my flower seedlings. I'm planning on big swath of *Nicotiana sylvestris* in one of them.

"But you'll have such a lot of lawn left," she objects, looking around her, still frowning. "There's SO much grass here."

"Yes, but we're not getting rid of the rest of it," I say, as we stand together on the lawn, which is still stippled with dandelion heads like a Klimt landscape. "We've discovered that we like having some cut grass up here."

She raises her eyebrows.

"You get a lot less bugs for one thing, and for another, it's less work than big flowerbeds, which all need so much weeding." I add rather defensively. "But you do need a big mower. So we plan on buying one when we can afford it."

Elinor is appalled by this little speech. Her jaw drops open at the mention of the mower. It's as if I've just admitted to being a child molester or selling porn on the Internet.

"But we don't dump any chemicals on the lawn, you'll be glad to know," I add even more defensively, because she looks so horrified. "It's just grass and lots of dandelions, as you can see." I bend down, pull feebly at a dandelion and laugh. "If you know a remedy for dandelions, let me know."

Elinor doesn't laugh.

"Dandelions are delightful flowers," she says primly. "And you can make wine with them."

I want to tell her that I'd rather drink wine made from grapes. And that I have no desire to frig around with dandelions making my own wine, because there's too much else to do on the property. But I don't.

"Well..." she continues in her disapproving tone, drawing a deep breath and exhaling, "lawns are the most environmentally unfriendly thing you can have. I'm kind of shocked at your attitude."

"Elinor, what do you propose we do out here?" I reply, my voice rising. "Let the whole place turn into an overgrown jungle? Get eaten alive by mosquitoes every time we go outside?"

"Yes," she declares, looking around her with the smugness of one who presumes to know everything. "We must live in harmony with the land, not fight it."

At that moment, Logbook Man staggers into view, up the hill from the pond. He looks sweaty and exhausted. He's been pulling out milkweed plants. There are hundreds and hundreds of them coming up around the pond and in the pasture. And although they are ethereally beautiful in the fall with their silky seedheads, we've come to the conclusion that they need to be thinned out. If the milkweed is allowed to run rampant, it will crowd out all the other wild flowers we'd like to encourage. Added to that, Don isn't exactly ecstatic about all our milkweed seeds blowing over into his fields.

"Got rid of exactly seven-hundred and twenty-one this morning," Logbook Man says with a satisfied grin, pulling off his work gloves. "I counted as I pulled them up, so it would make the job go by quicker."

He asks if there's any coffee left, smiles at Elinor and says hi. She doesn't smile back.

"Did you know that monarch butterflies lay their eggs on milkweed?" she calls out after him in the school teacher tone that she undoubtedly employs with her young charges. "And that you are destroying their habitat by pulling those plants out?"

"Oh listen, there's plenty of milkweed left down there for the monarchs. Go take a look," Logbook Man calls back sharply, looking around. He shoots a why-on-earth-did-you-invite-this-fucking-woman-up-here look in my direction and escapes into the house.

Elinor and I tour the critterus interruptus contraptions in the flowerbeds. She nods approvingly for the first time. But her expression changes when she spots my home-made plant markers in the vegetable garden.

"Not a good idea," she says, shaking her head vigorously. "Definitely not. You shouldn't recycle those old venetian blinds as markers. They're full of lead that will get into your soil. And you probably aren't aware of this," she surveys a line of carrot seedlings that are just starting to pop up, "but ecologists, people who KNOW about these things, they're all saying that you shouldn't plant vegetables in rows as you have. We need biodiversity in our gardens, not monoculture."

"In fact, I am aware of that, Elinor," I say, gritting my teeth. "But the truth is, I like the look of neat vegetables in rows. It's, um… visually appealing. And I can't see what harm a few little rows like mine are going to do. I also …" I bend down and yank out a thistle "…I don't want to mix everything up for practical reasons. When you do that, it's easy to mistake the veggie seedlings for weeds and pull them out."

"We must live in harmony with the land," she repeats, ignoring my statement in the way a politician does, looking around her with the plump complacency of a cat that's swallowed all the cream.

Where, oh where, is the garden fork? Coping with Elinor on this lovely spring morning is even worse than the Jehovah's Witnesses or Deirdre Pettingsley-Richards.

Mercy materializes in the shape of a meeting. She looks at her watch and says she had better get going. She's chairing a get-together of the Ontario Alliance for the Protection of Monarch Habitats in Toronto in the afternoon. I debate giving her one of Logbook Man's yanked-out milkweed plants to take along to the meeting, and decide no. Not a good idea. It might encourage a whole army of Elinors to head up here, lecturing us about our wrongheaded ways. As we say goodbye by her car, Ann appears at the top of the driveway. She hurries down towards us holding out a big plastic bag.

"Got it," she shouts, grinning. "Don picked it up for you this morning."

Ann opens the bag. It's the Roundup. A big white plastic bottle of the stuff with a blue and white label. There's a pump attached to one side and a skull and crossbones on the front.

Elinor backs away as if Ann is holding a hand grenade. Her mousy face turns almost as white as the plastic bag. I wonder if she's about to pass out. I pray that won't it happen.

If this eco-evangelist isn't gone from here within thirty seconds, I AM going to get out the garden fork.

Twenty

A car—a very elegant car—is purring along the road towards me. I watch, mildly curious. I'm standing at the front of the house, holding the loppers. The gloriously scented purple lilacs have finished blooming and big brown seedpods are taking over, so an attack of the GGs has clicked in. It's the acronym I used to describe gardening guilt, a malady which winds up afflicting everyone who grows things. I'll feel guilty if the darn lilacs aren't deadheaded. And as Stoob doesn't want anyone getting in the way of his guys hammering inside the house, it's a good opportunity to get the tiresome task over.

The car is a Mercedes. A classic one. Immaculate, steel grey, lovingly cared for. It's the kind of car Logbook Man would drool over, then launch into a mournful recitation of his my-life-is-a-failure speech, because he can't afford such a car himself. And the sight of it is surprising in these parts, where pickups—plus the odd Mennonite buggy, black and creaking, pulled by a tired horse—are the norm. Automobile fanciers don't normally bring their prized possessions down dusty gravel roads like ours. It wrecks the suspension and tires.

What's more surprising is the little figure crouched inside. I spot Bob Beattie. The top of his bald head is sticking up over the steering wheel. He waves shyly, then with a flash of polished grey leather upholstery and shiny walnut interior the car disappears over the hill, presumably down to the trim white bungalow.

This is astonishing. An old farmer like Bob has a fancy Mercedes? I've only ever noticed two vehicles in the big garage next to the bungalow. On the rare occasions when the garage doors have been left open, there's an old John Deere tractor, yellow and rusting with much of the paint peeled off. Parked beside it—or occasionally outside now that the winter's over—is an ordinary American sedan, cream-coloured, with a dent in the driver's door. No automobile that could be described as "upscale" is evident. Indeed, there's not a hint of that overworked word anywhere around their place.

It's been several weeks since I went down to the bungalow for eggs. Bark looked so grave the last time, it didn't seem a good idea to intrude on their grief about Bert. Far better to let the boys adjust on their own. Yet now, with one of the brothers bopping around at the wheel of this very expensive car, the mourning period has clearly come to an end. And I need an excuse to get away from the lilacs. My muscles are protesting at all this energetic pruning and Bark's eggs are the best around, half the price of the less-than-fresh free-range ones I've been buying at the health food store in Fernfield. So the loppers go away in the barn, the lilac branches get piled up in readiness for a bonfire near the pond and I trudge down the hill.

The Mercedes is nowhere to be seen. The garage doors are firmly closed. But Bark is back to his usual self, flashing a shy little smile at the front door. He says "Come in" in a welcoming way and asks if I'd like a couple of dozen eggs, not one. The hens are laying good now, he explains. He's inundated. We go around to the back of the house so he can show me the chicken coop. It's basically a big recycled shipping container, with a homemade door and chicken wire windows to let the light in. His brown and white hens, which all look fat and prosperous, are picking at a pile of old lettuce leaves.

When we go back into the bungalow, Bob is stretched out in his usual spot on the La-Z-Boy doing his ever-present crossword puzzle. Bill sits on the old sofa, one thin leg hung over the other, toes pointed down in the posture of old men everywhere. The local newspaper, the Fernfield Advertiser, is spread out across his bony knees. There is no sign of the Filipino bride. The only evidence of her recent presence in the bungalow is the Harlequin paperback called *Passion in Purple* which sits beside the TV, on top of a cribbage board.

Even so, I mumble, "Sorry about your brother," to the two guys because it seems appropriate in the circumstances. They both shrug in response, making no mention of Bert or his young wife and Bark switches in a deliberate way to talking about the weather. The forecasters are predicting a hot dry summer, he says. He thinks that'll mean watering our vegetable gardens a lot and asks if I've ever thought about installing a solar pump so we can get water up from the pond. They aren't very expensive, he adds. Bark, like all farmers, is intensely frugal. It's a trait I've come to admire since moving to the country. That's what makes the Mercedes so puzzling.

The other two don't say anything at all. They've become comfortable enough to just nod and smile when I visit. Conversation seems unnecessary. None of these guys is a big talker at the best of times but it's clearly not a case of grief keeping their lips buttoned now. They don't seem to be burdened by any thoughts about Bert—or if they are, they're keeping such sentiments to themselves. The strained atmosphere I felt in the house the last time has completely evaporated.

I grumble to Bark about the ever-present wildlife.

"I don't even know if it's worth trying to grow any veggies at my place," I say gloomily. "The deer have wrecked everything over the winter. And I guess they're going to stick around all summer too."

"Yep, there's a lot more of 'em here now than there used to be," chimes in Bill Beattie, looking up. He reads out a story from the paper. It reiterates the information reported in the magazine article that Dan brought along during the fall. The population of white-tailed deer is exploding everywhere. There are now so many, backyards and parks in Fernfield are under attack, with shrubs and perennials like mine routinely munched down to the ground as soon as they're planted.

"There's some animal rights type here wanting to give 'em all vasectomies," Bill says with a grunt, rubbing his bald head. "Well, I don't know about that, I'm sure."

Bark giggles at the mention of vasectomies. Bob chuckles, without looking up from his crossword. Then Bark blushes and looks away, as if this allusion to male anatomy in front of a female visitor has embarrassed him.

There is something clipped out of the newspaper sitting on the TV table next to the Filipino bride's paperback. It's a small oblong piece of newsprint with a black border surrounding the type. In the corner, I spot an oval photograph of a man. It's clearly the funeral announcement for Bert Beattie. While Bark is away in the kitchen getting the eggs, I sneak a look.

The man in the photo looks somewhat like his brothers, although he's shown at a much younger age than they are now. His hair is thick, his face unlined and he's smiling in the guarded way of someone who doesn't like having his photograph taken. There are details about surviving members of the family—they clearly have a lot of cousins—and the location of the funeral. The service took place two weeks before at the Presbyterian Church, where Gordie sang on Christmas Eve. But there is no mention of Bert Beattie having a wife except one brief line at the bottom. It reads:

"Condolences also to Araceli Beattie and her family in the Philippines."

Where, I wonder, is Araceli now? And what's with this Mercedes? I have a hunch the two are connected.

"Well, the altar in the sky sure didn't provide a very comfortable resting place for old Bert."

"Oh, so you know what Araceli means?"

"Course I do, babes. Don't forget, Caterina is from Argentina. But aren't you the clever one, knowing Spanish?"

Dan grins. He's sitting on the deck, sipping his second beer and sort of flirting with me. And I'm flirting back. But it doesn't mean anything. When you're over fifty, the fruit is better left on the tree. Pick it and it's likely to be rotten inside. Or leave a bitter aftertaste. We're discussing the demise of the one Beattie brother who was brave enough to pluck the fruit, but at far too advanced an age for the act to be wise. Dan is of the opinion that the Filipino bride conned him.

It's a hot day. The weather is turning out just as Bark predicted. The clouds are high and puffy, the sky cerulean. The sun feels forceful on my skin, yet there's a cooling breeze. I've been swimming in the pond this morning. And now spread out behind the shimmering surface of the water is a palette of greens, some tinted yellow, some blue, some streaked with raw sienna because now everything's in full luscious life. The poplars and maples have leafed out fully and bright green grass is shooting up in the pasture. Summer comes with such swiftness in Canada, the transformation often catches us by surprise. One minute we're battling winter, the next there's this almost tropical lushness that doesn't seem quite believable. Perennial poppies planted by the previous owners are unfolding in one of the flowerbeds, shucking off their odd little fuzzy grey-green caps. They are flamboyant and red, with huge crepe paper petals. Their black twirly centres look like pubic hair. Such sexy flowers, they make me think of gypsy petticoats worn by Bizet's Carmen. Yet Dan isn't remotely interested in eighteenth-century French composers, nor in my poppies. Not at all. He's not a gardener. He leaves that to Caterina. The renovation is what has brought him over here. He wanted to see the progress, so we've just taken a tour of the Victorian lady. And Dan thinks we're nuts to be paying Stoob a ton of money to refit her. He keeps saying that we could have supervised the job ourselves, hiring carpenters and drywallers as he did when he built his house. That's how Dan is, a wheeler dealer, a do-it-yourselfer, the kind of guy you encounter a lot in the country. He doesn't believe in paying cash for anything. He's always horse-trading with folks in Fernfield, swapping something he has for something he wants. He got a big plastic water storage tank this spring in exchange for some maple syrup he made. He's using it at his camp up north. And soon he'll be broaching the subject again of hunting on our land, along with chopping down the dead elms for firewood. I know that. But not yet. Right now, on this gorgeous day, the drama unfolding at the Beattie boys' place is far more fun to talk about. We sip our beers and ponder the situation.

The name Araceli means "altar in the sky" in Spanish—and it's popular in both Latin America and the Philippines. I know because Logbook Man and I once lived in Costa Rica, where we learned the language. Dan, who has picked up some Spanish courtesy of Caterina, does as well. But he also knows something about Araceli that's quite disturbing. It could seriously affect the old boys. Thanks to their eldest brother's rash marriage, they may have to sell up their home and move.

After their parents died, Dan explains, the four bachelor brothers pulled down the old red brick farmhouse that was located on the next concession road and built the bungalow to retire in. But they kept the hundred acres surrounding the house and some cousins now farm it, paying a nominal rent. The inheritance of this property was divided equally between the four boys; therein lies the problem. Because Araceli Beattie is Bert's widow and as such his rightful heir, she's entitled to a quarter share. Now she's demanding that they hand it over.

"What a cunning little operator," fumes Dan, shaking his head. "She fucks this old guy a couple of times at most and gets a big chunk of cash to set herself up in Canada in return. That's a pretty good deal, if you ask me."

He takes an indignant sip of beer.

"Oh come on, she wasn't to know he was going to die right away, was she?" I say, feeling duty bound to defend a member of my sex, even if I suspect that what Dan says is true.

"No, but she must have had a pretty good idea it was going to happen soon," Dan says, still fuming. "He'd apparently had heart trouble for years."

"Perhaps he misrepresented himself, though. People do on the Internet, you know."

"Yeah, I guess."

"When they were swapping emails, he might have told her that he was some sexy young Adonis," I say, grinning. "Like you."

Dan beams. He loves this sort of talk. How men do lap up compliments from women. His cheeks go a bit pink.

"True," he says.

"What's true, that you're an Adonis or that Bert misrepresented himself?"

"Both." He beams again and almost bats his eyelashes.

"But seriously, I still don't understand," I say, moving on from the sexual bantering. "Why do the boys have to sell the place? Can't they just pay this Araceli off?"

"No, that's the thing. They don't have the money to do that. All they have is their government pensions. They never made much money, you know. Small farmers like them don't. They're land rich, cash poor."

Dan shakes his head again.

"Poor old guys," he says. He stares into his beer. "They're going to have to leave the place where they've lived in all their lives and go somewhere smaller just so this little bitch with the moustache can have her share. Makes me mad."

Since he's adamant that Araceli's motives in marrying Bert were less than honourable, I stop trying to defend her.

"When's this going to happen?" I ask.

"Soon, I guess."

"Are you sure? I went by yesterday for eggs. They didn't mention anything about moving when I was there."

"Well, they wouldn't to you. You're a woman. You don't count." Dan thinks this is very funny. He snorts with laughter and practically chokes on his beer. Recovering, he says: "What I mean is, they'd be too shy to say anything to you. Bark told me all about it."

I reflect on the possibility of the Beattie Boys moving while staring at the poppies. How sad it must be for them to be faced with saying goodbye to their home out here among the cornfields. It's so serene and beautiful, I'm growing to love it too.

"But isn't there a way out?" I ask. "Can't they see a lawyer?"

"They have, in Fernfield. I sent them to mine. He says they don't have any choice. She has to get a quarter share of the value of the farm because Bert made a will leaving his assets to her."

"Couldn't they ... well, just give her a quarter of the land then?"

Dan snorts.

"To do what?"

"I don't know. Maybe build a house on it."

"Would you want Miss Moustache living next door to you? And in any case, you can't divide farm property up here without a huge hassle."

"No, I guess not."

We sip in meditative silence for a few minutes. It's so quiet. There's no one around but us today, and because it's Saturday, I can hear no noise of farm machinery moving down the lake road. The only sound comes from bumble bees. They're buzzing around the spotted throats of some pink and cream foxgloves, springtime flowers that seem to act like a magnet to all insects. Stoob's guys are off for the weekend and Logbook Man has gone over to the club. To go soaring, he said. But I suspect he's being roped into doing those damn logbooks.

"But there might be a way out," Dan says at length.

"For the boys, you mean?"

"Yeah. See, they won a chunk of money with a lottery ticket a while ago and they bought an old Mercedes with it. A real beauty." He purses his lips and almost salivates.

"Yes, I saw it," I say excitedly.

"You did?" Dan is surprised. "When?"

"Two days ago. Bob Beattie drove by and I couldn't believe what a beautiful car it was. But why on earth would the boys buy something like that?"

Dan shrugs, laughs again.

"Who knows? Perhaps they were bored with the sheltered lives they've led and they wanted to break out. I think Bert was probably the instigator. I'll bet he suggested buying the ticket. Bark is too practical to be interested in expensive cars or lotteries for that matter. Anyway, they bought this Mercedes, then they put it at the back of the garage with a tarp over it and never drove it anywhere. It's in mint condition, you know."

"Yes, it did look sort of untouched," I say. Not that cars are a consuming interest of mine.

"Well, if they've taken it out on the road," Dan rubs his chin thoughtfully, "I guess that means they're planning to do what my lawyer suggested."

"Which is?"

"He said they should go and get the car evaluated. And then they could offer this little bi—this wife of Bert's—a deal."

"What kind of deal?"

Dan takes a big swallow of beer.

"The bitch gets the Mercedes…" His angry tone indicates that he'd rather murder the Filipino bride than hand over such a beautiful vehicle himself.

"And the boys," he says slowly, looking into his beer sadly, "well, they get to keep their land."

It happens. Exactly as Dan says. At least I presume that's what happens, but being a no-account female, I'm not made privy to the full details. The Mercedes disappears. The only time I got to admire it was the day I pruned the lilacs.

And Araceli, the altar in the sky, disappears too. She's gone, vanished, swallowed up by the clouds. I never meet her again.

The paperback she left behind is still in the Beattie Boys' house though. It's been moved to a shelf, the lone Harlequin romance among a row of condensed Readers' Digest books. It really stands out against their rust red spines. And every time I see the lurid cover of *Passion in Purple*, I think of this plain woman with the lovely name who flew all the way from the Philippines to become Bert's wife for such a brief time. Was she as grasping as Dan claims, or simply a victim of circumstances? Is she driving around now in the Beattie boys' beautiful old automobile? Has she hooked up with another unsuspecting old geezer? Or has she—as I hope—sold the Mercedes and used the money to get training for a decent job in this country, so she won't have to go around marrying men old enough to be her grandfather?

I'll probably never know. Dan is keeping mum. Perhaps they've asked him not to talk about it. Whatever the real story is, I'm glad the Beattie Boys didn't sell up and move. I like dropping by the trim white bungalow for eggs. We're friends now.

Life is back to normal on our quiet gravel road out in the boonies.

Almost, that is. In mid-July, a new drama unfolds.

Twenty-one

"Useless. Utterly useless." Stoob, normally mild-mannered and businesslike, is furious. He looks like he wants to attack somebody with the hammer hanging from his belt.

We're standing outside the Victorian lady. The day is already clammy and airless, although it's only just after nine a.m. Good old Ontario humidity has started to kick in. The wet dishrag atmosphere that's always prevalent in mid-summer in this part of Canada has returned with the depressing predictability of gridlock in Toronto on Monday mornings. Droplets of sweat are standing out on Stoob's creased forehead. The black curls poke damply out from under a worn black baseball cap that says "Feed the World" in gold letters on the front. Stoob's had enough—of this enervating weather, work, everything, that's obvious from his expression. But what's really bugging him is that he's having a hassle with one of his guys.

It's Toby. The stoner with the pony tail and skinny limbs hasn't shown up for work. Today of all days, when our lady is about to get her new windows on the world. The renovation has so far been going like gangbusters. Dennis, aided by Werner, has roughed in a magnificent master bedroom and bathroom in the old attic, with a dormer on the south side that looks out on to the pond. The old downstairs room which had the horrid holes in the walls has been split into two rooms and the pink sixties bathroom in the corner has given way to an updated design, with an outside window. There's nothing like the thrill of seeing a renovation start to come together. The new sash windows were supposed to be fitted in today, with Toby acting as gofer and doing some of the heavy lifting. Yet the youngest member of Team Stoob is nowhere to be found. He's disappeared.

"Kids," says Stoob sighing deeply. "You have kids?"

I shake my head. Kids weren't in the cards for me, due to a serious illness in my thirties. And I never had any great urge to hear the pitter-patter of little feet anyway. Stoob, who has two grown-up daughters and a teenage son, tells me ruefully that I'm lucky. He speaks with the resignation of a father who sometimes wonders what parenthood is all about.

"Toby's the son of a friend of mine at church," he explains. "I agreed to give him a job this summer to help my friend and his wife out because they're tearing their hair out over this kid. But all Toby wants to do," Stoob looks exasperated and kicks at a stone "…is hang out with his girlfriend and smoke pot."

Ah yes, pot. Toby's not alone. There's an awful lot of pot circulating in and around Fernfield. Take a deep breath and you can even sometimes smell it along the concession roads. The tell-tale skunky odour lurks in the air, mixed in with the more powerful stink of pig manure that wafts over the cleared fields during spring and fall. Southwestern Ontario doesn't yet rival British Columbia—out there, every savvy soul with a piece of land larger than a postage stamp is contributing to the nation's biggest cash crop—but we're on our way. Folks in Fernfield don't talk about it much, not in this more conservative, law-abiding part of the land. Rural Ontarians haven't an awful lot in common with wacky west-coasters. Pot is still a hush-hush sort of subject in these parts, whispered about over the styrofoam plates of roast beef and corn served at community suppers in church halls. Yet it's around, even if it's not discussed openly.

By adults, that is. Kids have a different attitude, Stoob acknowledges. They buy marijuana openly on the main street in Fernfield. From the way his mouth is turned down at the corners, he doesn't approve.

"They can't handle it," he says. "Toby smokes the stuff all the time, his dad says. And it just makes him apathetic and lazy. He's a bright kid and they were hoping he'd go to university. But now..."

He shakes his head. He tears open one of huge cardboard boxes containing the windows. They were delivered yesterday on a flatbed truck and are propped up against the house. He inspects a window, then seems to have second thoughts about unpacking it. Carefully patting the cardboard flap back in place, he says he'd better call Mike and Werner and tell them not to come today, because they can't really get started without Toby's help.

"But don't worry," he calls out, heading towards his pickup, cellphone in hand, keys jangling in his jeans pocket. "If I can't find Toby, I'll get someone else. I'll be back soon. You won't have to wait long."

He drives away in a hurry, the baseball cap shielding his worried frown from the sun.

After Stoob's gone, Logbook Man comes up to the house. He's sweating too and breathing hard. He wonders if it's time for coffee. He was up early raking weeds and dead leaves out the pond. Our mini-lake, cool and green, is proving to be a great spot for swimming, with the muskrats banished and hot weather now in full swing. I love being down there, swimming to and fro or dangling bare feet over the edge of the old jetty. It's blissful in the evening too with a glass of wine, listening to the bullfrogs go *ruhk ruhk*. That feeling of rapture a year ago sitting on the bench with Gordie wasn't an aberration. The pond is still my most treasured place on the property. Yet keeping its clear green water free of detritus that will precipitate algae bloom is—like everything else on these forty-eight acres—a ton of work. One of us is always cleaning the pond with a rake and net.

"The guys not working today?" Logbook Man asks, disappointed. He's as anxious to get the renovation finished as I am. We're camping in the living room on a mattress, unable to use most of the house.

I tell him about Toby.

"Yeah?" he laughs and shakes his head. "Right after they started the reno, he asked me if he could grow some dope here."

"HERE?" I am as annoyed as Stoob. "What a ... what a nervy kid. Where did he want to grow it?"

"Down there." He nods towards the western half of our land, which adjoins the Beattie Boys' property. It's a jungle of vegetation, mostly overgrown dogwoods, scrubby willows and basswood, low lying and swampy. There's no trail through yet and we won't even try to make one this summer. We'd get eaten alive by mosquitoes.

"He thought it would be a good place. You know, well hidden. No one could see it from the road."

"Well," I say crossly. "I hope you didn't say yes."

Logbook Man laughs again.

The Fernfield *Advertiser* is suddenly brimming with news stories about pot. Every week there are reports of farmers calling the Ontario Provincial Police to report that they've found marijuana growing among their cornstalks. Either that, or they've discovered entire fields of the big weedy plants in their woods or tucked away in bush bordering quiet sideroads.

People who do the growing keep getting busted too. There's now a regular list of offenders printed in the weekly paper, which sometimes takes up half a column. Mostly what happens is that these amateur farmers get stopped by the cops when they're moving their haul of Mary Jane elsewhere in the middle of the night. In one instance, the *Advertiser* reports, a police cruiser "…apprehended a pickup at 2.35 a.m. on Sideroad 25 in Fernfield and OPP Constable Mike Farrow ascertained that a quantity of marijuana plants with a street value of $1 million were being transported in the back of the vehicle."

Phew. That's an awesome amount of dope to squeeze into one pickup. And there seems to be more and more being found every day. So much marijuana is apparently cultivated in the county, the Ontario Provincial Police have taken the step of issuing an "advisory notice," telling homeowners how to be alert for signs that it's growing on their land. This advisory is stapled to telephone poles around town. When I go to the convenience store in Fernfield to buy milk, I spot one and read it with curiosity.

"Every year, during the summer, people involved in growing marijuana head into rural areas to tend crops of marijuana, in some cases very large ones," says the advisory sententiously. It details in small, hard to read type a list of tell-tale signs.

The advisory describes the marijuana plant as being "bright green in colour, with leaves that have seven jagged fingers and growing between three and five feet tall." Property owners are warned to be on the look-out for people walking in remote areas for no apparent reason. It also notes that one of the most obvious signs of a secret marijuana field is an empty truck or minivan parked at the side of a concession road. There may also be empty bags of fertilizers and planting trays lying around. The report concludes that "growers especially like to use swamps, cornfields and wooded areas along rivers and streams."

In other words, our overgrown land would be a perfect place to cultivate marijuana in secret. Just as Toby said.

The redcurrants on the bush in the garden are ripening. They glisten in the sunshine like clusters of red pearls—a thrilling sight as I kneel beside the bush filling up a colander. They stain my fingers so that they look like they're bleeding and although it is tedious and time-consuming to pick this bountiful crop, I feel excited to be harvesting my first produce from the land—food that is organically grown and left to ripen naturally until it is ready to eat. The redcurrants are particularly precious because the way things are going, they might be the only edible things I harvest this summer. My efforts to grow lettuce, tomato, basil and Swiss chard are being thwarted at every turn. It's not the damn deer—or the bindweed—that's the problem now. The deer seemed to vanish into the woods with the advent of summer, so I removed the critterus interruptus installations—and some plants are actually managing to weather on in spite of the advances of the Boston Strangler. Yet now groundhogs and rabbits are sneaking up from the pasture, running amok in the vegetable patch under the cover of night. They're such cunning little critters, nibbling everything. And slugs are sliming their way all over the lettuce and Swiss chard, creating a Swiss cheese of holes in every leaf. To top it off, there's something making holes in the beets, but I'm not sure what it is, dammit.

I would be tearing my hair out if it weren't for the indestructible redcurrants. They grow like weeds, so prolific, so pretty. And nothing seems to bother them, apart from a few goldfinches sneaking under the split rail fence and pecking away, out of sight. More little pearls keep ripening every day so

I've been playing thrifty farmer's wife, making pots of jam. Now there's a cake in the offing. The recipe is called "Ravishing Redcurrant Cake" and I've devised it myself, modifying one I found in an old cookbook that used blue-berries instead of currants.

And I need eggs for this cake. So I head down to the trim white bungalow.

It's a hot and sweaty walk in summer. There hasn't been much rain since the humid weather started, the road is dry as a bone. A truck laden with massive spools of hay goes by and kicks up a cloud of dust even though the driver helpfully switches to the other side of the road. The dust gets into my mouth and clings to my bare arms. By the time I reach the bungalow, I'm dying for a drink of water. Bark's face is grave as he opens the door. It's puzzling because there's no little welcoming smile this time and I quickly wonder what's wrong. He has the same kind of tense expression as when the Filipino bride was in residence. Has Araceli come back? There's no sign of the Mercedes outside. He ushers me inside quickly, as if he can't wait to spill the beans about something.

Before I can even ask him to get some water, he comes out with it.

"Did you know," he asks in a tone of mild indignation, "that someone has been growing marijuana on your land?"

I stare at him. I don't know what to say.

Because I realize immediately that this is Toby's doing. It has to be. Damn stupid stoned-out-of-his mind Toby. And it's all the fault of Logbook Man. He's so easygoing and unthinking—at least where the matter of marijuana is concerned. Logbook Man has a benign attitude towards the matter of smoking dope. Like at least half of Canadians, he thinks it should be legalized, that it's no more harmful than alcohol or cigarettes—although I fall into the category of the "undecideds." And he laughed when I told him what Stoob said about Toby. So he's certainly given the silly stoner permission to go out into our woods and grow his own cache, and then conveniently neglected to tell me about it.

"Where is the marijuana planted?" I ask after an awkward pause. My heart's going pitter-pat. I'm inwardly fuming at Logbook Man but I try to look calm.

Bark goes to a window in his living room, pulls back the net curtain and points with a grave expression over to the swampy area that's on the western edge of our property. It butts right up to a field he owns with Bob and Bill. It is exactly where Toby wanted to grow the dope. Bark explains that Bill (who, like his brother, doesn't seem to be home right now) discovered the plants while he was helping their cousin Caleb take off the winter wheat. It was hot working in the field, so Bill ventured in among the dogwoods to take a rest and cool down. He'd intended to go over to our stream and wash his face. And there they were: at least a dozen marijuana plants as far as he could tell. He counted them. They'd been planted in an area where someone had carefully cleared out all the vegetation.

I nod, feeling worried now, because Bark is giving me a funny look. A very funny look. His eyebrows are raised in a quizzical way behind the rimless glasses. He clearly thinks we've grown this stuff ourselves. And in the next breath he says he wants to call the police.

Yikes. The cops coming here? I don't want to get Toby into trouble with the law. He's a stupid kid for sure, but he doesn't deserve to be saddled with a police record that will cause him grief for the rest of his life. Yet even more alarming is what might happen to Logbook Man. He's likely to be implicated too, because Toby will undoubtedly admit under questioning that he was given permission to grow the marijuana on our land.

I laugh nervously, joke that I've read in the paper that marijuana is growing all over Fernfield, in among the corn stalks and everything, and that perhaps some farmers are getting rich out of it and wouldn't that be great? And Bark's lips do curl up into a sort of smile at the mention of the word "rich." He doesn't pursue the matter of calling the cops.

Going out to the kitchen sink, he brings me a glass of water and my customary carton of eggs. I drink the water in a few quick gulps and say I'd better be going because I've picked a bunch of redcurrants and I want to make my cake before the fruit gets too soft and squashy. He continues to smile. Yet it's a strange sort of smile, rather questioning and doubtful. He clearly thinks he knows who planted the marijuana. He thinks it was us.

Logbook Man is away in the city working at the art studio. I call him in a rage the moment I get into the house.

"How could you let Toby do this!"

"Do what?"

"How could you? Now Bark wants to call the police. And I've put him off so I could talk to you first but...."

Logbook Man is stunned. He doesn't understand what I'm talking about. But when I'm halfway through explaining what happened, he explodes with anger himself. His voice is so loud, I have to hold the phone away from my ear.

"You think I said yes to the kid? I told him no," he yells. "What do you think I am, a fucking idiot? I wouldn't dream of letting anybody grow dope on our land."

"Well, who did it then?"

"I don't know," he says grimly, quieter now. "But it isn't Toby. Really, it isn't. And you'd better let Bark call the cops, so he doesn't think we did it."

The Ontario Provincial Police are duly summoned. The next morning, a big young lug of a guy shows up in front of the house, driving one of their black and white cruisers. He has sandy hair and looks a bit wet behind the ears. And he's not exactly up to snuff about secret marijuana growing operations—that's clear—because when I tell him about the one on our land, he starts marching across the lawn towards the vegetable patch.

"It's not planted up here," I protest. And why on earth would it be, you dummy? I want to say. But I restrain myself. "It's down there, somewhere among those dogwoods."

"The what?"

"The dogwoods. Those shrubby things over there."

I point westwards down the hill in the direction of the Beattie Boys' house, nearly a kilometre away. Their house isn't visible from where we are standing, because of the rampant dogwoods, scrubby willows and shoulder-high weeds. They form a thick mass that starts just beyond our barn. The cop stares down at this tangle of vegetation, pulling a face.

"It looks kinda swampy down there," he says dubiously. "And I don't have boots."

"Do you want to borrow some then?"

"Sure."

We return to the house and I get out Logbook Man's knee-high waders, which he uses for cleaning the pond. I also pick up our old machete. Since this young green cop seems so ill equipped for the task of hacking his way through bush seeking out the hidden marijuana field, it's clearly going to be my job.

"I have to call in," he says, galumphing over to the cruiser in the big olive green boots. "If I go more than fifty yards away from the car, they have to know where I'm going. There could be um...people down there with guns."

Guns! I grip the machete nervously. Is this august member of the OPP up to the task of protecting us? I somehow doubt it.

"Yeah," he says. "Motorbike gangs. They're the ones cultivating this stuff now. And they have guns with them. So be careful. Don't ever approach them."

Right.

It's muddy down among the dogwoods. Our boots squelch as we sink in, and I wish too late that we'd approached this overgrown area via the Beattie Boys' field, instead of going down through our own rampant jungle. The cop complains as one of his boots gets sucked off by the thick black mud. He leans against a poplar tree straightening his sock, putting the boot back on again with a sigh. He mops his brow. From his expression, he looks as if he wishes he was a million miles away. He clearly doesn't like floundering around in swamps in the heat, searching for evidence of dope growers. I don't like it either. I haven't even ventured into this area since we bought the place. Nor has Logbook Man. It's a northern jungle, airless, damp, incredibly hot. It reminds me of the Florida Everglades. It's almost as impenetrable as the Everglades too, and full of bugs. All that's missing are the alligators. You've surely got to be determined to make a few bucks, or totally nuts, to try and grow marijuana out here. I tread warily through the mud, expecting a leather-jacketed Hell's Angel to materialize and blast my head off with a shotgun at any moment, but all we keep running into are mosquitoes. Swarms of them. They besiege us mercilessly, biting at any exposed bit of flesh they can find. A cloud going *nyee, nyee,* nyee encircles the cop's head as he ducks under a dogwood branch in front of me. The branches he pulls to the side whip back into my face, slashing at my cheeks. Ouch, what an idiot this guy is. Why couldn't he wait for me to cut a path through with the machete? I want to give up and go around the other way through the Beattie Boys' land. It would certainly be easier. I debate asking him to stop but he's forging ahead, impatient to get this over, grumbling as he goes that he's never seen bush as thick as this and that someone should clear it away. His bum keeps sticking out in front of me as he crawls under the dogwoods and I get the urge to poke the black uniformed buttocks with the machete. He seems like such a witless oaf.

Then suddenly there it is. We stumble into the marijuana field. It's been cunningly concealed behind some thick mounds of tall grass growing near the stream that runs through the back of our property. Whoever did this has hacked down several clumps of dogwoods, willows and a couple of basswood trees, clearing a space about thirty square feet to squeeze the plants in.

And I am relieved. I heave a tremendous sigh of relief. So much relief engulfs me, I wonder if the cop will notice.

Because these aren't new plants. They're old ones, obviously grown last year. A dozen or so, just as Bill Beattie said. All that's left of them now are dried-up stalks, turned a greyish colour over the winter, each about the thickness of a man's thumb. They stick up from the cleared muddy ground encircled by pieces of fine-gauge wire netting, presumably put in place because the dope growers had as many hassles with munching critters as I am experiencing in the garden. There's an empty plastic fertilizer bag lying in the mud, just as the advisory in Fernfield said. It looks as if the bag has been there for a long time. Something has nibbled the edge of the plastic, probably raccoons or mice. And leaning against a small basswood tree is a long spade. The shaft and bowl have accumulated an overcoat of orange rust, undoubtedly from being covered by snowdrifts for months.

Behind other mounds of grass we discover more stalks, dib-dobbed here and there. I count at least twenty-two other plants. They're all encircled with lengths of chicken wire, and like the first plants, they've been cut off about six inches from the ground, probably last fall. I pull at one. The roots are rotten, so the stalk comes out of the ground easily.

So Toby couldn't possibly have done this. And Logbook Man clearly didn't tell him he could. Phew. This was the work of mystery trespassers. They clambered over the barbed wire fence by the road then tramped through the undergrowth to get here before we even moved into the house.

And although they've long gone, there's a sinister feeling in this place. It's so hot, so still. Nothing moving. I don't like being out here. I sense a malevolent presence. A twig cracks suddenly and I jump. So does the cop. Could bikers with guns be cultivating another marijuana field further into our woods? Anything is possible now that there's such a huge demand for this illegal crop. We are both relieved to trudge out of the jungle, back to the house. I don't even care that the mosquitoes are biting. In the dining room, my OPP protector collapses on a chair, pulls off Logbook Man's boots and scratches with a peeved expression at his bites. He is very red in the face and seems exhausted. Putting his shoes back on, he straightens out his uniform and makes a few scribblings in the notebook kept in his breast pocket. There's a big welt developing on his forehead and two smaller ones on his cheek. His sandy hair is standing on end, revealing a bald patch that's been bitten too. And his big pink hands with ginger tufts on the backs are covered in red marks and scratches. He smells of sweat. Recovering, back in OPP officer mode, he refuses an offer of coffee. He tells me to call them again if we ever notice anything suspicious like a van or truck parked down the hill, close to the swampy area. Then the moment this little recitation is over, he heads for the front door, clearly glad to be getting out of the boonies and back to civilization.

I smile at him and nod. I'm glad he's going too. Opening the front door, I practically push him out, hoping that I don't ever have to encounter a cop—or a marijuana plant—again.

I'm not keen on seeing Toby again either. And fortunately, I don't have to. Stoob, Dennis and Werner return the following day accompanied by a new recruit called Markus. He is young and beefy with an olive green T-shirt that has a Heineken logo on the front. His thighs and forearms are twice the thickness of Toby's. He seems to be a relative of Werner's, handsome and blond, and apparently fresh from Germany, because he doesn't speak English very well.

"Toby's gone," Stoob explains, out of earshot of the trio. "I found him at his girlfriend's place and I fired him."

"Good."

I offer all the guys a hefty slice of redcurrant cake each and Markus's eyes light up.

"Oooo, rote Johannisbeere," he says happily. "Vee haff zees in Chermany. My muzzer, she mek jam wiz zem."

They wolf their slices down and get to work.

Twenty-two

The renovations progress. So does the summer. Hot sunny days glide by like a canoe on a fast-flowing river. Canadian summers are blissful and far warmer than people in other countries imagine. Yet they are also alarmingly short. No sooner does the frozen north unfreeze itself than—whoops—cold nights return and it's time to stash the shorts and flip-flops away again.

Not yet, though. It's mid-August. Everyone's still in shirt sleeves. The crickets rasp as we take long lazy swims in the pond. The bullfrogs grunt, and red slider turtles, annoyed by our trespassing on their turf, plop back into the water from a rock where they've been basking unbothered in the sun. Indolence is everywhere.

Yet up at the house Stoob is still hard at work, methodically ticking off each step of the renovation like a tour director counting bus passengers. He banishes us when the electrician comes to install new wiring. Then the plumber arrives to put in two new bathrooms and modify the kitchen, and we have to vacate the place again. After that, it's the turn of the drywallers.

"You don't want to be around when drywallers come," he says, laughing ruefully. "They're a law unto themselves. They show up when they feel like it, do exactly what they want and if you don't like it, they'll just pick up and leave. Those guys are in such demand"—he purses the rosebud lips and gives a soft whistle—"they make a fortune."

Stoob's not kidding. Four tough-looking young men in cutoff T-shirts with tattoos all down their brawny arms show up in a big white pickup, embellished with lettering that says "Dave's Drywall Services." They unload six cases of beer and a ghetto blaster along with their tools. The radio goes on immediately and rock music reverberates throughout the house. The cats look shocked and stalk off to the barn. We go into the city and return three days later to empty beer bottles piled in a heap outside the back door. Yet Dave and the gang do deliver. Our new smooth walls and ceilings look perfect and are now ready for painting, which we'll do ourselves.

Dennis gets busy now. Showing the prowess that Stoob boasted about, our gentle master carpenter, pencil permanently behind his ear, builds a maple staircase into the attic. He hums hymns like "Rock of Ages" while he works and tops the job off with a beautiful, smooth banister railing.

Heating guys in blue overalls show up with the new high-efficiency propane furnace. This masterpiece of modern mechanical wizardry is a quarter the size of the old basement behemoth. I examine it with the reverence of a praying nun. Although the weather still feels too warm to try the furnace out, we're assured it will be quiet and well behaved.

Building inspectors from Fernfield drop by, clipboards under their arms. There's a lot of murmuring about "code." Everything must be done to code, Stoob explains, looking resigned and rejecting my dream of a door on to the deck from the kitchen. "The door wouldn't be tall enough. It's not to code," he says, gesturing at the south-facing wall of the living room, where the ceiling slopes down to a height of no more than six feet. I shrug, disappointed. Yet Stoob is in a happy mood now with Toby gone. And so am I, in spite of the not-to-be-installed door, because everything is taking shape at last. So cleanly. So efficiently. Our transformed Victorian lady will be no glamour queen, but she's going to be blissfully functional and warm when winter comes.

Unable to work on writing assignments indoors, I spend hours outside weeding, gratified that at least a few plantings have survived my ham-fisted efforts and the depredations of visiting wildlife. The Nicotiana started in flats over the winter is skyscraper high. It fills the lasagna beds, scenting the entire garden, exactly as I planned, with a perfume so powerful that I am transported back to sensual jasmine-filled nights in the Caribbean. Four surviving tomato plants have—thrillingly—started to set fruit and there are butternut squash vines galloping all over the veggie patch. Rabbits and groundhogs seem to steer clear of squash, not liking their raspy leaves, and beneath this foliage a treasure trove waits: half a dozen squashes, buff-coloured and curvaceous as little submarines, swelling every day. One will be perfect for the Thanksgiving dinner that's coming soon.

Uninterested in growing things himself, Logbook Man limits his involvement to cutting the lawn, and extravagant praise of my gardening efforts. He goes off on his motorbike to the flying club and soars in a glider over the house, taking pictures. I stand on the lawn, waving madly at the shiny metal dragonfly that whooshes through the sky far above my head. He comes home excitedly a couple of hours later, grinning from ear to ear, saying that the place looked fantastic from the air and that I must go up too. But I'm not keen. I hate flying.

And when we're not writing cheques for frightening amounts of money to Stoob, we make forays into and around Fernfield. The time has come, we've decided, to get to know this distinctly rural world that has become our new home.

One discovery is Marjie's. Stoob urges us to go.

"It's the kind of place you never find unless someone else tells you about it," he says with a grin. "Their breakfasts are amazing."

We head off during the week, as he warns about lineups at weekends. And it's a revelation right from the start, this unpretentious restaurant run by Mennonites, located in a hamlet twenty kilometres outside Fernfield. Surrounding the hamlet are vast farms, their fields full of soybean foliage the colour of digestive biscuits in the late summer sunshine. The village itself, quiet and empty, is no more than a traffic light, a convenience store, a brick church and a handful of white clapboard houses clustered at the crossroads. The only sign of life is a big black dog. It's lying near the traffic lights as we approach and I think with horror that it's been killed by a car. But the animal heaves itself up, stiff-legged, and starts jumping around, barking excitedly as if we've made his day. We drive right through the village past the dog and reach the other side in thirty seconds flat. Yet where is Marjie's?

She doesn't look too promising when we backtrack and finally find her. Marjie's occupies an ugly boxy building set back from the road. The sign hanging outside has faded. Once bright red, it's a sickly orange now, all its white lettering fallen off, so there's nothing to indicate a restaurant within. The entrance is a simple screen door, frayed on one side. Green paint has peeled off around the door frame. It looks like the kind of run-down place where you stop in desperation during a long car journey because you're just too tired to drive any further. Yet if we need any proof that Marjie's is worth visiting, there's the parking lot. It's practically full. Although the hour is only just after eight in the morning, pickup trucks and minivans are squeezed into almost every available space.

Inside the building a blast of hot air hits us, and it's as noisy and crowded as a New York deli. The reason becomes obvious right away. It's the food, baby. Just the food. The smells are marvellous. At Marjie's, appearances don't matter. Here I finally get to find out what Mennonite cooking—REAL Mennonite cooking—is all about. Sliding on to bench seats at a wooden table, we tuck into mountains of local sausage, scrambled eggs, home fries and thick, homemade toast, lavishly buttered, with real strawberry jam that's served in a little dish, not foil-covered packets. As we eat, perspiring Mennonite women are visible in the kitchen at the back, lacy white caps holding coils of hair out of harm's way. They mop pale foreheads with big practical hands and keep scooping gargantuan portions onto a procession of white plates. The patrons are mostly men, plaid jackets hung on hooks beside the tables, baseball caps still on their heads. And how these burly guys do eat, smacking their lips with pleasure and laughing among themselves, as they mop great hunks of toast around the plates, savouring every morsel.

Our server, plump, lace-capped and wearing a white apron, looks perplexed when we shake our heads and say no more toast, thanks. With a motherly smile, she suggests a slice of elderberry pie instead. It's freshly made, she adds, because the berries are in season. And I say sure, why not? The overly-sweet layer of pastry underlaid with deep purple berries gets washed down with another mug of coffee, on top of the biggest breakfast I've had in years. The check, when it comes, is for a surprisingly small amount.

Driving home, waistband tight across my belly, I feel a kinship developing with the fatties of Fernfield. Yet there's contentment too. It's fun eating out here, where no one ever mentions the words "low fat."

Towards the end of August, we make another discovery. Fernfield is tarting itself up in tartan. Big time. Our nearest town was settled by the Scots back in the eighteenth century and most residents are still mighty proud of those underpinnings. Even now, some local fans of all things Scottish persist in pronouncing the name with a Gaelic inflection, although they've probably been Canadian for several generations. They get a kick out of saying FAIRN-field, not FERN-field.

And while kilts and bagpipes are dismissed as hokey tourist claptrap by many Scots back home, not so in Fairnfield. Tartan starts appearing everywhere. As the summer days shorten, red-and-green-checked bunting swings from lampposts on the main street and is draped on the bridge over the river. Virtually every store in town puts displays of Scottish memorabilia in its windows. The bakery, called Murray's, does a roaring business in shortbread and meat pies. There's a general air of excitement in the streets.

The hubbub is a run-up to the Fernfield Highland Games. One of the largest festivals of its type in North America, it's set to start next week, bringing in crowds of tourists. And the biggest hint of what's coming are the bagpipes.

Eeek—those bagpipes. What an extraordinary sound they make, audible all over town. Heading out of the library downtown one hot afternoon I hear a loud wheezing noise, as if an enormously fat man has ten men sitting on his chest, squeezing all the breath out of him. I walk around the corner and there they are—the local bagpipe band. Or at least a few of its members. Nine men and women of all ages are practising in the park by the river, wearing jeans and T-shirts, not their customary kilts. They're all sweating, pinched lips pursed around the pipes. A small crowd has gathered to watch. As they blow strenuously, squeezing the curious black sacks—called drones— at the same time, it's clearly an effort to produce the required bagpipe sound. When they've finished, the pipers droop like wilted hothouse flowers. One middle-aged woman with thin, grey hair takes deep breaths as if she's been running a marathon. Her face is ashen.

And all this arduous blowing and squeezing is taking place out the open air, I surmise, because making the racket that bagpipes make indoors would probably get them ejected from every building in town.

But I love hearing them play. It seems so right, so appropriate, bagpipes wailing in this little Scottish town of stone buildings bordering the river. I want to see the band perform.

"Let's go to the tattoo," I say to Logbook Man that night. He shudders. Like many Canadians, he loathes bagpipes.

We go anyway. And what a magical sight it is, this tattoo, even though Logbook Man grimaces and puts his hands over his ears. As it gets dark, bands of bagpipers in colourful matching kilts and black velvet jackets march under rising moonlight on to a playing field on the edge of Fernfield. They look like ghosts, enveloped in a swirl of dry ice. I think of Banquo, and Scottish castles with turrets. Then as the pumped-in mist lifts, the bagpipes start their peculiar mewling sound. They get louder and louder. A roar goes up in the crowd. Everyone cheers and claps and stamps their feet. The pipes, the pipes are calling—and the folks in Fernfield sure do love to hear them approaching.

The whole town seems to have turned out for the show. Young couples sit up in the bleachers, bouncing awed toddlers on their laps. Down below, grandparents are ensconced comfortably in lawn chairs. Onlookers of all ages wander around in kilts, bending down frequently to pull up the long wool knee socks that always seem to fall down. Even the guys dispensing Tylenol in the first aid tent are garbed *à l'écossaise*. And there are lots of blankets draped over legs and shoulders, because it's an unusually cold night for late August. Many people light candles as the night progresses and warm their hands around the flames. They chat and pass bags of chips and candy bars to each other between the performances, animated faces lit up by the flickering light. Tattoos are military in origin—the word comes from the medieval Dutch *Doe den tap toe* (turn off the taps) a cry voiced at inns in the Low Countries during the seventeenth century (and earlier) to get soldiers to return to their regiments—yet there is the atmosphere of a family outing to this night of piped pageantry in the Canadian countryside.

"First time?" asks a man sitting beside me with a young boy. They are both in blue and green kilts, with windbreakers on top.

I nod. "Yes. First time."

He smiles and says they come every year. And that he wants his son to be proud of his ancestry because so many people in Canada aren't.

The next day, I learn the truth. What Scotsmen truly wear under their kilts is revealed. One casually disrobes in front of me. He's standing in the competitors' tent and I am, like a handful of other curious onlookers, watching from the bleacher seats next door. He undoes the buckle on the thick wool wraparound skirt. It drops to the floor in a heap. And it's all a huge anti-climax.

Because underneath are shiny black bicycle pants.

"But he's not really a Scot," objects Logbook Man, who claims some Scottish forebears. "He's an American, see. It says here in the program. Real Scots don't wear anything underneath."

The disrobing giant is a black man, and his home is a very different kind of highlands from those of Scotland. Harrison Bailey has travelled to Fernfield from the mountains of Pennsylvania. He's one of the best in the world at tossing the caber, and it's an entertaining sight, this African American cradling a telephone pole three metres long in the lap of a red tartan kilt, then heaving it in the air, across the vast field where the tattoo took place last night.

Women also compete in these tough-guy spectacles, which are called "heavy" events. And heavy they are, involving mostly tossing around huge rocks and lead weights that I couldn't even raise a few inches from the ground. Yet while the males are invariably big and brawny, with thighs and biceps like great slabs of ham, their female counterparts tend to be surprisingly diminutive. One stands no more than five feet tall. She has bleached blonde hair in a ponytail and wears Doc Martens. She looks at a distance like a cheerleader at a football match. Yet this young woman is no sissy, that's clear from the unusually broad shoulders and her face, which has a take-no-prisoners look as she gets closer to the bleachers. To encouraging cheers from the crowd, she hoists her kilt up above her knees, plunks one hand on a muscular thigh, then twists around and around before flinging a big lead ball with the other hand. Yet her throw falls short. The cheers evaporate. Everyone in the bleachers lapses into silence, disappointed. Another competitor, also blonde, short and young, has beaten this Canadian star by a yard or so.

The two female competitors laugh, shrug, embrace one another in the manner of old friends and head into the competitors' tent. And like Harrison Bailey, they immediately peel off their kilts oblivious to the audience watching. It's as if they can't bear being wrapped up in all that hot prickly wool a moment longer than the competition requires. Underneath their kilts, the women are wearing bicycle pants.

In the white tents surrounding the field, there are items for sale that would make a thrifty Scotsman gasp. A Bonnie Prince Charlie velvet vest is going for $450. If browsers want to try their hand at playing traditional Scottish music themselves, some cheapie bagpipes will set them back a thousand dollars, while a more upscale version goes for $2500. Yikes. There are brooches and plaques and frilly white blouses for little girls to do Highland dancing in, and everything is pricey. Yet these Scottish-themed souvenirs are not, it seems, in high demand. The salespeople look gloomy and bored, chatting among themselves, their tents mostly empty. The action is at the snack bars dishing up french fries and hamburgers, and at the beer tent down one end of the field, where the music blaring out is distinctly un-Scottish and sounds more like hard rock. A smell of cooking fat hangs in the air. The food looks greasy and unappetizing. But outside one tent, sitting quietly at picnic tables, a huddle of people are scarfing down some promising-looking pies.

I've heard about these meat pies. They're baked every year especially for the games by squads of ladies at Fernfield's United Church. Wielding baking tins and pastry cutters in the church's basement must be a thankless task for the volunteers, yet they do it cheerfully—another reminder of the community spirit that does indeed prevail in small towns. And even though I'm not fond of any kind of meat pie, these little individual offerings served with the peculiar British dish called mushy peas are lip-smackingly good—on a par with the Mennonite fare dished up at Marjie's.

My waistband gets even tighter. Heading home, I wonder if perhaps the time has come to embrace the monastic confines of skimmed milk and low-fat everything. But I change into a pair of looser jeans instead.

The first day of fall is closing in. Stoob continues to tick off jobs that are still on the list. He looks weary now, the Feed the World cap askew on his head, but he says we're "getting there." And we're tired of the renovation too. The constant comings and goings have meant people being around from 7 a.m. until dusk for months. We're continuing to camp on a mattress in the living room. It's hard to get writing assignments done. The line of credit granted by Sharon Rooney has ballooned, exactly as she predicted, to alarming proportions. I need to start working again, earning some money to pay for all this costly remodelling. But the end is in sight. The last big step in the project is Varathaning Dennis's new staircase and maple floors—and Stoob doesn't want any cats nosing around while it's going on.

"Nothing can walk on the floors for twenty-four hours," he says firmly, adding with a grin, "you don't want cat hairs stuck permanently to every-thing, do you?"

No indeed. The local feline walk-ins get shut out of the house with a bowl of water and dried food and we put the two protesting tabby sissies into cages and head into the city for a couple of days. And how odd it feels to be back in Toronto. The streets seem uncomfortably crowded. I can't get used to the noise. We go out for a meal at Pasta Magnifica, but find the place pretentious and absurdly overpriced. It's a relief to head home, the cats squalling in the back seat, to inspect our shiny new floors. Sliding around on them in socks, I whoop with delight. They are fantastic. Indeed, everything is fantastic. Our Mennonite renovator has done it. He's pulled the tired old Victorian lady up by her bootstraps into the twenty-first century, and she's looking rejuvenated and ready for a brand new life.

Stoob smiles. He looks pleased too. He says softly that he knows we're dying for him to leave, and while there are bits and pieces that need finish-ing, he's going to let us get our lives back for a while. So we write the last cheque with a gulp, wave goodbye and celebrate with tea and my "ravishing" redcurrant cake on the deck.

"Perhaps we should think about giving the place a name now," I say happily to Logbook Man.

"You think so?" he says.

"Yes. What about Golden Hill, because of all the goldenrod?" I wave a hand down towards the pasture, which is lit up with brilliant bronzy yellow.

"Nah," he says dismissively, taking a bite of cake. "Sounds too Martha Stewartish."

"Osier Hill then?" Willows are running rampant behind the pond, and "osier" is one Latin name for these weedy trees.

He shakes his head.

"Dogwood Acres?" he proposes, grinning.

"Idiot. We aren't hillbillies in the Ozarks," I say crossly.

So he insists on "Greenwood." A family with the name of Green lived here once, we've discovered. Logbook Man thinks it's the only name that's appropriate.

But now it's my turn to shake my head. No, sorry. Too ordinary, too well-used. We're not going for "Greenwood" and that's that. More possibilities get tossed about, but we can't seem to agree on any of them.

So in the end, our new home stays anonymous. Which is surely the way it should be anyway. Out here in the boonies, it's only the newcomers who give names to their houses. The locals don't bother. They stick to practicalities. Affixed to the mailboxes along our concession roads, the labels say simply: "Bert and Vera McWhinnie" "Fred Vermer" and "The Weaver Family." There are no elegant wooden plaques hanging outside, ornamented with gold letters which read "Shady Cedars" or "Harmony Hill."

And I'm a local now. Or at least I aspire to be. I like being a country person, out here on my quiet dirt road in the boonies.

Logbook Man likes it too. A lot. And although we continue to bicker about silly things, we do at least agree on one thing.

Moving to the country in middle age is a great way to avoid the dreaded expecteds.

Seven years later

"The world is a raucous radio held to one's ear. Silence is now the most expensive commodity on earth."

—Graham Greene

Twenty-three

There is a lot of blood. Thick and ruby red, it spreads in a pool over the chopping block. Blobs drip off onto the kitchen counter as I slice the firmly textured flesh into chunks.

Yet the sight doesn't make me queasy anymore. This is deer meat, freshly killed. Dan brought it over yesterday. And I saw the animal it came from, a big buck. It was hanging upside down in his woodshed before Dan cut it up. He and Caterina are doing their own butchering now. I felt sadness looking at this animal, its stomach slit wide open, head slumped, eyes glazed, majestic antlers no longer pointing up towards the sky. It was one of the deer that roamed on my land before Dan went out there with his gun. I perhaps even saw this particular buck down in the woods. But I'm no longer sentimental about such things. I've grown accustomed to them. Living in the country changes you that way. I like the taste of deer meat. And I'm fast coming to the conclusion that it's the only kind of meat I want to eat anyway.

In the years since Logbook Man and I moved up here, the world has changed too. Mad cow disease, avian flu, E. coli and listeria outbreaks, melamine contamination of food and other disasters have kept hitting the headlines. They've made many people start to think about where our food comes from, and, in the case of animals, how they are raised. And as the movement towards "organic" keeps growing by leaps and bounds, I can't help wondering why one issue—hunting—has been left out of the equation. Those who like to hunt for food are still vilified, still regarded with the kind of scorn in the media that I admittedly once heaped on Harlan and Dan. In a recent magazine article, a New Brunswick hunter noted ruefully: "When I was a kid, having a Dad who was a hunter made you a hero at school. Now it's the kind of thing you keep under your hat."

Yet what could be more "organic" than my wild deer meat? I have become one of those hicks who sees nothing wrong with hunting. I've even started to wonder if one day I might summon the courage to pull the trigger myself. Because the deer that's going into the stew I'll be serving tonight had a life before Dan ended it, quickly and probably painlessly. That buck roamed free, in the open air. It wandered in the woods, as I do. It saw the sun rise. It wasn't crammed into a cage inside a locked building, pumped full of antibiotics, kept under lights twenty-four hours a day, like so many of the animals we eat unthinkingly, simply because they're served up in styrofoam packages at the supermarket. It wasn't even raised on a so-called "organic" farm. It ran free as the wind and did exactly what it wanted. And that buck probably mated with a doe, who produced more deer to replace it. White-tailed deer are everywhere now, multiplying rapidly due to an absence of predators and—perhaps—the consequences of climate change. Their numbers do need to be thinned out, just as Dan says. So I feel no guilt about eating this one. Just pleasure and a sense of gratitude that it gave up its life so I could prepare this meal.

I've invited a bunch of people to a fall feast of food from our land. We'll be quite a crowd. Dan and Caterina are coming. Ann, too. Plus old friends from the city and new ones from Fernfield—I would have asked the Beattie Boys, except that I think they'd be too shy to attend.

It's November. The week that constitutes the hunting season in our part of Ontario has just ended. Four cats are ensconced once more in their box seats around the woodstove, savouring the warmth, yet they have changed too. The tabbies, Patrick and Tilly, are still with us, along with feisty Sparky. But Blackie got killed by a car two years ago and another newcomer, a female, also black, took his place. She showed up under the deck on a cold night before Christmas, in much the same manner as Blackie. I suspect she's one of his relatives. Like deer and hunters, abandoned starving cats are occurrences you get accustomed to coping with in the country. We had a fifth feline arrive recently, but found a warm home for him in a friend's barn. And although Bark Beattie still raises his eyebrows, I remain a softie in that respect. I let the foundlings come indoors.

Another change is in the way we heat the house. The new propane furnace Stoob installed was a disappointment, although everything else about the renovation has worked out just fine. We're glad we spent all that money, fixing the place up. The house functions well, yet the furnace is costly to run and not very warm, although we do use it as a back-up. The grey enamel woodstove is no longer making a contribution either. It's gone. We bought firewood from Roman and his missus for several years, then he finally decided he was getting too old for cotting voot and something broke in the stove's firebox and no one around here sold the spare parts to make repairs. So now we depend on our big new wood pellet stove. Stacks of shiny white sacks containing tiny ground up sausages of wood sit under the eaves where we used to keep the logs. I miss the look of the old stove, and the sense of tranquillity it bestowed. I also miss the yearly encounters with randy old Roman, and being able to throw another length of maple into the glowing firebox. Yet the new stove—a brilliant design, by an inventor in Pennsylvania—is vastly easier to handle, very warm and less polluting. And I have to acknowledge that with the passing of the years I'm on the way to getting old myself now, with limited energy for tasks like lugging firewood.

The dead elms are still there, down in the woods. Some are rotting. Others have crashed to the ground in winter storms, for which I'm now much better prepared. We never have found the time to cut the elms, although Logbook Man keeps saying he plans to one day, and that he'll burn them in a little woodstove in his workshop. But unlike the elms, the black walnut in the garden has disappeared. Ed, our local tree pruner, removed it in less than an hour, wielding a big chain saw. Trees take so long to grow, and are gone so fast. It was a sad day. Yet we had to take this difficult decision about the walnut because the squirrels came back, somehow finding new ways to get inside the Victorian lady, and the only sensible solution was to get rid of the green tennis balls that drew the critters here in the first place. And it's helped, for sure. We don't miss the black walnut. Most of the squirrels disappeared once the nuts were gone. Even so, there'll always be a few bushytails nosing around looking for a cosy berth at this time of year, just as there will also be a whole parade of other interlopers—deer, chipmunks, raccoons, skunks, rabbits, groundhogs and the odd opossum rummaging in the compost heap. And of course, the muskrats. They come back to the pond sometimes—they always will—necessitating visits from Harlan to trap them. It's how country life is. Full of difficult decisions.

Perhaps the biggest change that has taken place over the years, however, is in the garden. Every summer, there are big glorious swaths of annual flowers adorning my lasagna beds now, just as I wanted. But shrubs are mostly absent; the deer eat them in wintertime no matter how hard I try to stop this happening. They chomped down Deirdre Pettingsley-Richards's daphne and some new weigelas. So I've finally taken the advice of the garden centre lady and planted a few prickly specimens like potentillas and barberry. That's another thing you learn in the country—to listen to the locals. And there's lots of *Euphorbia polychroma* encircling perennials that need protecting— a tip I learned at the garden centre as well. This plant, which is related to poinsettias, contains a stinging white sap that deer don't like. Deirdre turned her hoity-hort nose up at *E. polychroma*, but I don't, because it's practical— and it pays to be practical out here.

Elinor would be glad to know that I am back to being an organic gardener. The Roundup was a failure with the bindweed. Its Boston Stranger tentacles simply shrank in disgust a couple of weeks after I applied the stuff, then bounced back with a kind of "Ouch, that hurt, but listen up, lady, you don't get rid of us that easily" gesture. I've concluded that there are some nuisances you simply learn to live with in the country. For me, bindweed is one of them.

And as lovely as my ornamental plantings look now, out of the living room window, I've had a change of heart about those, too. I'm much more interested now in what's happening on the other side of the split rail fence, where the vegetables are. That area is no longer simply a "patch" relegated to the garden sidelines. Instead, it keeps getting bigger and bigger, because in the past few years, I've become passionate about growing my own food. What prompted this, I suspect, is one of the biggest issues that's come along since I moved away from the city: the trend towards "eating local." The publication of books like *The Hundred Mile Diet* has started everyone questioning the wisdom of food that's shipped thousands of miles from where it's grown—and as a consequence, I now see my own garden in a radically different light. I want it to be productive, not merely aesthetically pleasing. So along with the *Nicotiana* and zinnias started under lights in the basement every winter, there are seedlings of celeriac, Swiss chard, tomatoes, herbs and any other edibles that pique my interest. This year it was artichokes, ground cherries and yard-long purple beans from Asia. Then directly into the garden every spring, I plant a plethora of tried-and-true standbys—butternut squash, potatoes, carrots, onions—the kind of vegetables the pioneers liked, because they store well. And in the fall, it's the turn of garlic. I bring my haul into a cold room, formerly a front porch, that we've created on the north side of the house. There's a black curtain hanging at its small window, so the potatoes, carrots and garlic don't go green. And my foodstuffs are all organically grown, unsullied by anything questionable throughout their growing life. It's the most satisfying thing I've ever done in a garden. In uncertain economic times it's reassuring, too, to have a larderful of satisfying fare like potatoes and onions to fall back on. I tell Logbook Man that we can always live on soup, if things get really bad. I'm toying with the idea of my own chickens next, except that they would mean no more regular visits to the Beattie Boys—and friendship like theirs is so comforting in the country.

And the critters still come. Installing my critterus-interruptus contraptions over the vegetable beds every spring is a must, because rabbits breed like, er, rabbits. Groundhogs do as well. So it's a constant battle, but with my increasing presence out there, weeding and digging and puttering about, the four-legged invasions do seem to be declining.

Logbook Man has had a change of heart too. He no longer goes gliding. He hasn't sat in that little room at the club updating the club's logbooks for three summers. He's unlikely to go at all now. He's regretful—what pilot ever wants to leave the sky?—but there's too much to do around here on our forty-eight acres, he says. In fact, a better name for him now would be Brush-mower Man. A few summers ago, we sold his motorbike and bought a big, beautiful red and black machine that manages to handle three tasks associated with country living very effectively. It clears trails through our woods, it cuts the lawn and it transforms itself into a snowblower in winter. Along with the bread machine, which still chunters along, thrilling us on cold mornings, our brush mower is the most useful thing we have acquired. And usefulness is what counts to us now.

Rustic wood furniture is Logbook Man's new passion. He's making tables and chairs out of the old black walnut, and from cedars, pines, and willows and any other workable wood that he can find on the land. Gardening interests him too, for the first time. He's taken charge of bringing our old apple trees back to life and planted pear and nut trees. And he's out so often in the woods, perhaps that's why the marijuana growers have never come back. We're relieved about them, but sorry that another surprise visitor has chosen to stay away. The delicious morel mushrooms appeared only once, then vanished.

Yet some things—and people—don't change. They remain as they always are. As I'm preparing the food for tonight, the phone rings. It's Tim and Caron. I haven't spoken to them in years, although news came via the grapevine that their condo development in Collingwood was a spectacular success. Tim wasn't just being cocky. Since then they've moved on to construct more of the same type of buildings described as "adult lifestyle" in the weekend newspapers. They're in various locales and the details are hazy because Tim gave up long ago trying to get us interested. He's twigged that the adult lifestyle, whatever that is, isn't the kind of life we want anyway.

Yet now he announces—unsurprisingly—that they are just back from Tuscany.

"We've bought a big old farm property there," he says with breathless excitement. "It's awesome. Thick stone walls, olive trees, a terrace overlooking the hills. And we're turning it into a time share. You guys interested? Fractional properties are the way to go now and…"

"Yes," Caron chips in. "It's near Cortona. And the food is fantastic." She sighs rapturously. "You'd have such a ball, you know. There's nothing like the food over there. It's REAL."

I look around my own kitchen as they babble away into the phone, interrupting each other as they always do, enumerating the charms of *la bella Italia*. As I listen, reddish French fingerlings from the garden, soil still clinging to their sides, are sitting in a basket on the counter. These yummy little potatoes, roasted, will be part of the feast tonight. A big rooty celeriac is in the sink waiting to be washed. I'll cut that in fat slices, then dip the pieces in oil and roast them in the oven too. A redcurrant cake, baked at this time of year from frozen berries, is cooling on a rack, along with a mile-high apple pie that Logbook Man has made with the surprisingly good apples from trees he has resurrected on the land. There's local goat and sheep cheese, plus red pepper jelly sitting in the fridge, ready to be used as an appetizer, along with organic butter and the best vanilla ice-cream I've ever tasted, produced at a farm that's opened a few concession roads away. I even have a few heirloom tomatoes left, carefully saved from the garden in late September, wrapped in newspapers in the cold room and kept especially for this occasion. They're called Costoluto, an Italian variety with ridged sides. I'll slice and serve them as another appetizer, on a platter drizzled with a pesto concoction made with my own fat cloves of garlic and fresh basil leaves. In a few minutes, the bread machine will get to work producing a big crusty loaf. It will be served warm when my guests come. And in the meantime, the venison stew is in the oven, simmering and sending out divine smells that fill the kitchen.

If that isn't real food, I don't know what is. So I want to interrupt Tim and Caron and start babbling myself, about carbon footprints and the joy of eating local food and of staying put to experience the kind of pleasures that they're talking about. I'd love to tell them that it isn't necessary to fly half way across the world. That these pleasures are all available here—at home.

But I don't of course. When they've slowed down, expectantly waiting for my response to the offer of a hideously expensive two-week share in their little piece of paradise, I simply murmur: "Well, *tutti i gusti soni i gusti...*"

A puzzled silence follows.

"What?" Tim says.

I explain that it's an expression Italians use. It roughly means "to each his own."

"And what do you mean by that?" Caron says, rather indignantly.

"What I say."

"C'mon, you're saying that you don't like Italy?" asks Tim.

"Sure I like it. I lived there once," I say quietly, and they seem astonished by this news. "But the truth is, I think Canada is better."

And in many ways, it is. There are undeniable drawbacks to this great northern land of ours. The winter, for one thing. That inevitable express train is getting ready to leave the station as I sit at my computer, writing this. The nights are getting shorter. The leaves are starting to fall off the silver maple. The morning sun slides over the poplars behind the pond very late now, so that when I stumble out of bed to make the tea, it's still dark. The air is crisp. Soon there will be snow. It will pile up around the house, as it always does. I will have to don crampons when I walk down the icy road in February to buy eggs at the trim white bungalow. Digging out will be continually tiresome, and I will lose at least one mitt somewhere in a drift by the car, which I won't find until spring. Because, like it or not, ours is a predominantly cold country. We'll never rival Italy in the matter of climate.

Yet Italy is overcrowded. Tuscany, particularly. There are too many Tims and Carons moving in. They've pushed the prices of properties so sky high, the poor beleaguered locals can't afford homes of their own anymore. And Italy, for all its glorious antiquities, tall dark green cypress trees, delicious Mediterranean diet and a Disneyland that's called Florence, is noisy. Horribly noisy to someone my age. Every Italian has a cellphone and uses it non-stop. Just try travelling by train in Italy and you'll see what I mean. Yet Canada—cold, unglamorous Canada—is one of the few relatively empty countries left on our jam-packed planet. It's still possible, in our rural areas, to discover the peace and utter serenity that comes from not being surrounded by thousands of other people all the time. I love that peace. It's what enticed me out here in the first place and what keeps me grounded here now, living quietly among my maple and spruce trees, more or less detached from an increasingly angry and chaotic world.

So I raise a glass of wine—Ontario wine, naturally—when the friends arrive, and we drink a toast to the end of the growing season in this great country of ours where the wide open spaces seem to go on forever. And as we sit down to tuck into the fall feast I've prepared, I recall how the old Victorian lady called to me that humid day in July eight years ago.

And I feel glad—so very glad—that I listened.

Recipes

Great Venison Stew

The success of this dish lies in cooking it for a long time in a slow oven. In my experience, even the supposedly tender cuts of deer meat can be tough if they are insufficiently cooked.

Ingredients

Three pounds of deer meat (approximately) cut in 2-inch (3 cm) pieces. Any cut—fresh or frozen—will do. The tougher the meat, the longer the cooking time. If using frozen meat, thaw it a little before sautéing.
Vegetable oil (preferably canola or some other oil with no flavour)
4 tbsp. flour
A couple of large onions, chopped
A stalk of celery (optional)
Several carrots

3 cloves of garlic

2 tbsp. tomato paste

2 cups dry, red wine

2–3 cups beef stock (Or use a tablespoon of Marmite, a British concoction. Mixed into hot water, it makes excellent stock).

2 tsp. juniper berries

Lots of black pepper, ground

3 whole cloves of garlic

2 bay leaves

2 tsp. rosemary, fresh or dried

2 tsp. thyme, fresh or dried

1 cup dried cranberries or currants. (In a pinch you can use raisins.)

Heat the vegetable oil in a heavy frying pan. Roll the deer meat pieces in the flour, then sauté them until they're a bit brown. Do this in batches. Set the meat aside in a glass or earthenware dish which has a lid. Keep scraping up the bits that accumulate on the bottom of the pan and throw them on top of the meat. (They add flavour.)

Add the onions, celery and carrots to the frying pan and sauté until the onion looks see-through, then add the chopped up garlic and sauté a bit longer. Spoon in the tomato paste, mix it in, cook for a few more minutes, then add the wine and stock. Simmer till everything is mixed together.

Pour the liquid in the frying pan over the meat, so that it's covered. (If there's insufficient liquid, add a bit more water, wine or stock.) Add the herbs. Mix them in. Don't leave them lying on the top.

Cook the casserole in a slow oven (around 325 deg.) for at least two hours. Add stock if it gets dry. Check if the meat is tender by pulling apart a piece with a fork. If it still looks tough and doesn't separate easily, cook longer. Sometimes, if the meat comes from an old animal, it will take up to eight hours to become tender. A crockpot is useful for this.

Serve with potatoes—roasted or mashed—and other winter vegetables like butternut squash and turnips.

Roasted French Fingerling Potatoes

Fingerlings are sausage-shaped, with red skins and a reddish streaking in their flesh. They have a nuttier taste than other potatoes. If you grow your own, don't wait too long to harvest them. They are best cooked small.

Ingredients

Quantity of fingerlings
1/2 cup olive oil (or canola)
2 garlic cloves, cut into slivers
1 tsp. chopped rosemary (preferably fresh, but dried is fine)
Salt and pepper.

Wash potatoes well, but don't peel them. Pat dry with a tea towel. If they're small, leave whole. Otherwise cut them in wedges. Mix the oil and garlic together, then toss the potatoes in this mixture. Place in a single layer in a roasting tin. Cook at about 400 degrees F (200 Celsius) for about half an hour until they look crisp on top.

Sprinkle the rosemary on top halfway through the cooking time.

Note: Some people hate the taste of rosemary. In that case, use chopped parsley instead, but add it right before serving.

Bahamian Pumpkin Soup

This is one of my favourite soups, rich, creamy and fragrant. It was given to me years ago by my mother and it's very easy to make. In the Bahamas, a kind of pumpkin not grown in Canada is used. I substitute butternut squash here, which works just fine.

A large butternut squash (about 3 pounds) or two small ones
3 peeled carrots
3 potatoes, peeled
4 onions
Chopped thyme
1 tsp. of pepper sauce like Rebel Fire No. 3 (made with Jamaican scotch bonnet peppers) or two small chili peppers, chopped

Butter
Milk or cream (Or use tinned evaporated milk which is a standard ingredient
in the Bahamas)
A bit of unflavoured cooking oil
Salt and pepper

Slash the squash in half, paint the cut surfaces with oil and place face down on
a cookie sheet. Cook in the oven for an hour at 350 F. Let cool, remove the skin
and seeds, chop the soft squash in chunks.

Note: This is by far the best way to prepare butternut squash, which is a chore
to peel when raw.

Sauté the sliced onions in butter in a big saucepan until soft. Add all the ingredients except the thyme and milk or cream and only just cover with water.
(Don't add too much water.) Boil until very soft, usually about an hour. Throw
the chopped thyme in about three-quarters of the way through the cooking
time. Bahamians love this herb and add great quantities to anything they cook.
Canadian palates are more accustomed to a less powerful taste.

Mash the mixture with a potato masher or whir in the blender. Then add milk
or cream to thin. But be careful not to boil the soup now, as too much heat will
destroy the creamy texture.

Ravishing Redcurrant Cake

Everyone who tastes this cake does indeed rave about it.

4 cups fresh redcurrants (approximately)
Zest of an orange (optional)
4 tbsp. unsalted butter, softened
1/4 cup canola oil
1 1/2 cups sugar
3 large eggs
1 Tbsp. baking powder
3 1/2 cups cake flour
1 cup milk

Cream butter and sugar together. Mix in the oil, then beat the eggs together in a mixing jug and add them to the bowl. Sieve the flour and baking powder together in a separate bowl. Mix the flour into the wet ingredients gradually, adding a bit of milk as you go. Finally fold in the redcurrants and orange zest.

Bake at 350 degrees F for an hour or longer. Test if the cake is ready by inserting a dry knife in the centre. If it comes out clean, it's done. If there's wet dough on the fork, bake longer. Sometimes this cake takes an hour and a half to bake, depending on how soft the berries are.

Note: If using frozen berries, don't thaw them before folding them into the batter and add at least half an hour to the baking time. For special occasions, a butter icing makes the cake even more delicious.

Logbook Man's Mile High Apple Pie

Ingredients

A pie pastry shell (or make your own pastry)
About 6 cups sliced apples
1/2 cup white sugar (more if the apples are tart)
3 Tbsp. flour
Pinch cinnamon
Dash salt
2 Tbsp. cold butter

Put the apple slices in a bowl and mix together with sugar, flour, cinnamon and salt, so that the slices are well coated. Layer the slices in the pastry shell. Make the pile higher in the middle than the sides. Chop up the cold butter and drop the chunks on top.

Bake at 375 degrees F for about 25 minutes, then turn the oven down to 325 degrees F for another 20 minutes or so.

Note: The apple slices are inclined to fall off. Adding a lattice of pastry strips on top will keep them anchored in the pastry shell.

Author's note

This is a true story. However, I have changed some names, personalities and the circumstances in which certain incidents happened, in the interests of creating a readable and entertaining account. The town of Fernfield also exists, but under another name. Like Stephen Leacock, I felt compelled to give it a different identity in case some sensitive souls take offence at what I have written.

Acknowledgements

I owe a debt of gratitude to Carolyn Forde of Westwood Creative Artists and Michael Mouland of Key Porter Books who both liked the idea of this book right from the start—and who gave me the confidence to continue writing it.

I'm also grateful to writer Marjorie Harris for her practical efforts on my behalf and her unflagging insistence that "you just have to get that memoir of yours published."

Kudos to designer Alison Carr who worked so hard on the cover. Heartfelt thanks to all those other hardworking souls in the book publishing and selling business who devote so many hours to helping authors like me find an audience.

Writers aren't the easiest people to live with. So a big kiss to my spouse

Barrie Murdock who kept some great pizzas coming when I was too busy writing to concentrate on anything else.

The quotes on page 51 and page 305 come from Greene on Capri—a Memoir, by Shirley Hazzard. (Virago Press, 2001.) I appreciate the help of Susan Day of Paris, France and Luigi Durante of Torino, Italy in clarifying Italian expressions. Also, Carol Cowan of Toronto, whose wizardry with Word was enlightening, to say the least.

But most of all, I want to say a big thank you to all the colourful characters who inhabit a certain part of Ontario that I now call home. Without you, this book would not have been written.